For Akiko and Malika,
and for the sacred laughter we share

Studies in Continental Thought

John Sallis, general editor

Contents

Acknowledgments

The first and abiding event in my philosophical development occurred when I lied to my mother at age sixteen.

She was overprotective, forbidding me from playing varsity football and permitting me to play basketball only because she thought the game involved no contact. I was not allowed to take summer jobs in neighborhoods that could be conceivably considered unsafe. If she knew that I wasn't really taking a bus and subway from Yonkers to New York City in order to go to the Metropolitan Museum of Art (or to another high school with my teammates to play basketball) but to Harlem's Apollo Theatre, she would have keeled over at once from apoplexy. However, she proved prophetic in one respect. She told one and all that I was so absent-minded I could only become a professor.

So the seeds for this book were planted in my well-spent youth when I would sneak off with friends to the Apollo Theatre in Harlem in the 1960s, and my first acknowledgement goes to those African-American comedians who taught me both how joyous and how profound comedy could be. The first such artist I ever witnessed was the great ventriloquist Willie Tyler (who still works), who provided the opening act on a James Brown show. I was also fortunate enough to be present for performances by Moms Mabley, Pigmeat Markham, Redd Foxx, Godfrey Cambridge, and Dick Gregory (who also came to my high school). These comedians often addressed themselves to political subjects with great insight and creativity. Sadly, while much comedy in this vein is time-bound and grows obsolete, many of the same social ills pertaining to race that these comedians addressed still persist. I hope that they heal. However, even after a most thorough healing, the work of these comedians will remain fresh. For their work addresses the fundamental concerns of our human condition.

Human wisdom, human folly, truth, lie, reason, custom, education, justice, beauty, age, gender, marriage, friendship, hatred, war, peace, good speech, rhetoric, demagoguery, statesmanship, sex—and love and death that impel them all—these are the subjects that I found informing their comedy, and their treatment lingered continuously in my thought. Then in college, I met their worthy ancestor, the artist-thinker whose work inspires this book: Aristophanes. If there were no Moms Mabley, Pigmeat Markham, Redd Foxx, Godfrey Cambridge, and Dick Gregory, I could never have found my way to the depth and the joy that belongs to Aristophanic comedy.

More immediately, I owe a great deal to my department at Slippery Rock University for their philosophical acumen and friendship. Richard Findler, Bradley Wilson, Katherine Cooklin, and Andrew Colvin could not be better colleagues. Herman Boler could not be a more dedicated and efficient secretary. Conversations with them on a regular basis are among my greatest gifts. I am in their debt also for their patience with my sense of humor, which is occasionally indecorous and which is an acquired taste that some (many?) never acquire.

I also owe a great deal of gratitude to Michael Rudar, who patiently proofread this manuscript and who raised many useful points upon it. He is currently completing his graduate studies at Duquesne University, and is certain to be a first-rate professor, a fine teacher and friend to his students, and an excellent scholar as well.

The superb staff of Bailey Library at my home institution always made sure I received all necessary materials promptly. Kathleen Manning, Rita McClelland, and Christine Agostino have my abiding appreciation for this, and for being such delightful people with whom to work.

Conversations with friends such as Claudia Baracchi, Sara Brill, Walter Brogan, Daniel Dahlstrom, Zeynep Direk, Francisco Gonzalez, Elizabeth Hoppe, Drew Hyland, Robert Metcalf, Michael Naas, Gregory Recco, James Risser, David Roochnik, John Rose, John Russon, John and Jerry Sallis, Eric Sanday, Dennis Schmidt, Susan Schoenbaum, Gary Scott, P. Christopher Smith, Sonja Tanner, Peter Warnek, and Jason Wirth have provided both help and pleasure.

My new colleagues at Koç University in Istanbul have provided both a warm welcome and an encouraging atmosphere for the completion of this book. I thank President Attila Aşkar, Provost Yaman Arkun, Dean Ersin Yurtsever, Associate Dean Sami Gülgöz, Philosophy colleagues Patrick Roney and Hülya Durudoğan, our assistant Denis Durmuş, and our heroic College of Arts and Sciences secretary Filiz Koca.

I also gladly acknowledge the aid of the supremely talented Dee Mortensen, Sponsoring Editor of Indiana University Press. It is an honor to have this book appear under its imprint. I also thank her fine assistant Laura MacLeod. The two anonymous readers provided both valuable suggestions and encouragement, and I happily credit them for improving this book.

My Indiana University Press copyeditor extraordinaire, David Dusenbury, handled the text with care and insight.

Finally, to my wife Akiko Kotani, "circumspect, blameless, shining among women," endless gratefulness, and to my splendid daughter Malika who has brought me so much pride and joy, endless gratefulness as well.

Philosophy & Comedy

Introduction

On the Underlying Sense of Aristophanic Comedy

While the Aristophanes literature stands as a worthy testament to the comic poet's greatness in many respects and to his significance in the classical world, there is no book to my knowledge that presents a systematic *philosophical* treatment of his comedies. It is my firm belief that Aristophanes stands with history's finest inspired artists, and that his poems are truth-disclosing works that speak to us thoughtfully as well as dramatically across the centuries. His comedies deserve an elucidation that reveals their philosophical depth. In this volume, I propose to provide such an exposition of four of them.

The seed for this book was first planted by a talk given by John Sallis on philosophy and comedy at Duquesne University in the mid-1970s. It was then fertilized by my study of his seminal *Being and Logos: Reading the Platonic Dialogues,* in which he shows how comedy is an essential element of the philosophical enterprise.

While I did not think that the nurturing process would take quite so long, its completion comes at a fortuitous time. Not long ago, Dennis Schmidt wrote: "In the end, the full treatment of the relation of tragedy and philosophy . . . needs to address the place of comedy in that relation."[1] While this book stands on its own, I hope it contributes toward the meeting of that need, as it directly treats the relation of comedy and philosophy.

The methodology of this book is driven by a single focus, namely philosophical insight revealed through the Aristophanic text. All other matters, such as historical matters, matters that might pertain to performance and production, prosodic matters, and cultural matters will be considered insofar as they contribute to a close and rigorous interpretation of the written work. First and foremost, this book is a direct and sequential textual exegesis written for philosophers, classicists, literary scholars, and readers who both enjoy and take a deep interest in comedy of the finest caliber.

At *Republic* 378d7–e1, in his controversial discourse that seems to censor the poets, Socrates obliquely acknowledges that poetry can have an "underlying sense" (*huponoia*). This view is borne out later. The first poetic passage expunged from the education of the guardians is quoted at 386c 5–7, at the beginning of book 3. It presents Achilles' apparent lament over his death, a lament that would endanger the inculcation of courage in the guardians: "I would rather be on the soil, a serf to another, / to a man without lot whose means of life are not great, / than to rule over all the dead who have perished" (*Odyssey* 11, 489–91). But this same "expunged" passage is the first one the man who has been liberated from the cave will hear at 516d5–7, toward the beginning of book 7. In that context, the passage connotes something altogether different: its *huponoia.* The free human being would rather endure a wretched fate on the earth, seeing its truth-shining light, than to rule among those who are bound to shadows, i.e., to the opinions of the city. In this book I will attempt to bring the *huponoia* of several of Aristophanes' poetic plays before the reader in a way that will make both the insight and the joyfulness in them more accessible.

Plato turned his attention primarily to Homer and the tragic poets. Since then, philosophy has found tragedy a much richer subject than comedy, although there have been occasional works addressing comedy philosophically. (I have contributed some scattered reflections of my own.) Many of them have focused, and in a way quite properly, upon the Dionysian origin and nature of comedy, and upon its place at the Dionysiad. To be sure, the Old Comedy to which the work of Aristophanes belongs[2] evolved from the original celebrations of the Dionysian cult consisting of "dances, disguises, lyrical trances, and jocular turmoil"[3] following a phallus-pole procession. As the revelers grew more and more inebriated, the lewd jokes and gestures grew more aggressive, culminating in an evening orgy. The more refined activities of the cult eventually found their musical outlet in the dithyramb, the material for tragedy, while the more earthy ones found theirs in the *kōmos,* the basis for comedy. *Kōmos* means song of revelry, and also refers to the revelers themselves. Gradually Dorian mime, a practice ridiculing someone present, was added to the *kōmos.* If we were to capture the skeletal structure of much Old Comedy in a single and simple equation, it might be: *Kōmos* + Dorian mime = Old Comedy.

However, the quality of Aristophanes' art far exceeds both its category and its origin. Perhaps surprisingly, Hegel was and remains the philosopher best able to take Aristophanes' measure. In Aristophanes' work, Hegel discerns a profound presentation of essential human joy and human freedom: "If you have not read him, you can scarcely realize how thoroughly jolly men can be."[4] He brought to the stage "a freedom we would not dream of were it not historically authenticated."[5] Hegel regards his comedy as "in itself as real a part of the Athenian people, and Aristophanes as essential a figure, as were the sublime Pericles, the happy Alcibiades, the divine Sophocles and the moral Socrates."[6] Thus, he regards comedy to be equal in spiritual significance to statesmanship, philosophy, and tragedy. Aristophanic comedy is called essential because the matters it addresses, e.g., the state, philosophy, war and peace, gender, and the general relation of gods to humans, are truly substantial and so transcend mere amusement and entertainment. In his *Phenomenology of Spirit,* Aristophanic comedy occurs shortly before the end of Spirit's journey, serving as the penultimate shape of representational thinking in "Revealed Religion," the chapter that immediately precedes "Absolute Knowing," its finale.

Hegel very much admired his contemporary Schiller, both for Schiller's poetry and for his contributions to philosophy.[7] If there is a philosopher who prized the disclosive power of comedy to a higher degree than Hegel, it is Schiller. The tragic poet must "make a leap," the comic poet must already "be at home." For comedy, "all the dimensions are already contained, flowing unconstrainedly and effortlessly . . . and it is, according to its capacity, an infinitude at every point in its path."[8] While tragic poetry is "only intermittently and with effort free," the comic poet "is free with facility and always."[9] While tragedy's point is more significant, "comedy proceeds to a more significant purpose and it would, were it to attain it, render tragedy superfluous and impossible."[10]

Somewhat ironically, the poet Schiller, who in his philosophical writings located a fundamental play-impulse (*Spieltrieb*) in human beings, does not endorse Aristophanic comedy, while the "grey on grey" philosopher Hegel gives Aristophanes the wreath, calling him "the genuine comedian."[11] Schiller criticizes Aristophanes on account of his excesses in provoking coarse laughter at the expense of the lower class: "Many scenes of Aristophanes are of this kind, which step over the boundaries now and again and are absolutely reprehensible (*schlechterdings verwerflich*)."[12] Schiller prefers parodies in which roles are reversed, and all are "treated with dignity and respect." On the other hand, the word for the "jolly" humanity that Aristophanes brings to human beings as does no other and that Hegel so enjoyed, is *sauwohl* in German. *Eine Sau* is "a hog." Unlike Schiller, Hegel could vicariously take pleasure in the baseness to which we are all given over by virtue of our humanity.

My reading of Aristophanes, while very different from either Hegel's or Schiller's (or anyone else's, to the best of my knowledge), owes a great deal to their insights. From Hegel, I have learned to treat Aristophanes' written word with the utmost respect, a respect that honors both its humorous and its serious side simultaneously.[13] From Schiller I have learned to focus upon comedy's higher purpose.

The book will be divided into two major sections. The first will concern Aristophanes' treatment of *logos* (human speech) and its perversions. I will present chapters on *Clouds* and *Wasps* that attempt to bring the Clouds and the Wasps near, i.e., to show how the poet discloses those limits within which a human being properly lives in terms of *logos.* The second will concern Aristophanes' treatment of *erōs* (love). I will present readings of *Assemblywomen* (*Ecclesiazusae*) and *Lysistrata* that attempt to show how the poet discloses those limits within which a human being's erotic nature can best belong to her or his life. In the course of each chapter, I will incorporate material from the Platonic dialogues that serve to illuminate what I call the "ridiculous thoughtfulness" of Aristophanes. Both positive views and celebrations of human *logos* and *erōs* emerge from this comic thoughtfulness.

To present an overview, the ridicule in *Clouds* and *Wasps* concerns the manipulation of *logos* in terms of law and in terms of its use in seeking advantage. My reading of *Clouds* will be at least somewhat original (and hopefully not merely idiosyncratic), since it will not address the much-discussed matter of Aristophanes' intention in his representation of Socrates. Rather, I will interpret the Aristophanic Socrates precisely as he occurs in the text and will do the same for Strepsiades, who has been maligned so much and so unfairly in the literature. The comedy culminates in the disclosure of the equally preposterous nature of both Weaker *Logos* and Stronger *Logos,* of their effect upon father Strepsiades and son Pheidippides, and in lines 1495–1496, the final occurrence of a *logos*-related word.

As the chastened Strepsiades begins to set fire to the roof of Socrates' "thinkery" (*phrontistērion*), a student of Socrates' "thinkery" asks: "What are you doing, man?" Strepsiades replies: "What am I doing? What else but engaging in fine discourse (*dialeptologoumai*) with the beams of your house?" This comic togetherness of *logos* and *ergon* in the destruction of the sophistical thinkery provides a counter-image suggesting their constructive bond, which I will trace out in my reading. Unlike most scholars, I interpret Strepsiades' concluding rage as the rise of the god Dionysus, in whose name the festival occasioning the play occurs. In other words, it announces a comic rejuvenation bringing those healthier impulses to which Strepsiades once ascribed.

In a similar spirit, my reading of *Wasps* will not concern itself with Aristophanes' quite obvious detestation of Cleon. Instead, the nerve points of my reading will be the "debate" between father Philocleon (Lovecleon) and son Bdelocleon (Hatecleon), Philocleon's jury service in the trial of a dog who brings another dog to "court" for not sharing a hunk of Sicilian cheese, and the "use" of *logos* by both father and son at the feast they attend as the play nears its end. As is Aristophanes' creative practice, both father and son (and everyone else) deserve ridicule in some fundamental sense. Just as surely, beneath the ridicule lives much that is worth seeking and discussing. Even the changing posture of the Chorus, which evolves from a resentful and ludicrous cohort of old men to an apparently thoughtful and rational group of sages, is not without its comic side—and so not without genuine philosophical significance as well. Another depth-disclosing phenomenon is the dance of the rejuvenated Philocleon at the comedy's end.

In *Assemblywomen,* the role of the chorus is both considerably smaller and considerably different. It behaves much like a minor character, echoing the wishes of Praxagora, the comic heroine, and directing the advance of the women upon the assembly that they will come to rule. Here, we find a marked divergence in nature from the male comic heroes in *Clouds* and *Wasps,* and their female counterparts in *Assemblywomen* and *Lysistrata.* The women display shrewd and steady intelligence, coolness under fire, and qualities of leadership that are entirely out of the men's range. Where both Strepsiades and Philocleon spent almost all of the time in their respective plays flailing about helplessly, both Praxagora and Lysistrata are purposeful and sure-footed. The women are *comic* not because of any character weakness, but because they enjoin their charges to extend human behavior so that it exceeds its limits. Their proposals treat human beings as if there were no constraints upon the constitution of their embodiment and upon the desires intimately connected with it. Their apparently feeble and often blathering male counterparts, however, are far from merely laughable. Through Aristophanes' marvelous art they display a most worthy side of humanity, when thoughtfully considered, that complements the virtues of the women.

The political and the erotic converge in Praxagora's vision. There will be no more private property in Athens, instead all will draw equally and sufficiently from a common store. As a result of this equality, no one owns anything and there is enough for all. Consequently, all strife between human beings over these matters will come to an end. With one "slight" adjustment, everyone's erotic needs will also be met. The men will continue to have access to their young and beautiful girlfriends—but only after first "servicing" an old and ugly woman. The same law holds for young women, who must first give their favors to old and ugly men. This produces some raucous difficulty for several Athenian men, but her initially addled husband Blepyrus comes to make interesting adjustments to this new regime. *Assemblywomen* also ends with a scene dominated by the theme of rejuvenation, the philosophical sense of which will be treated at its conclusion and in the chapter that concludes this book.

The frequently performed *Lysistrata* begins with Lysistrata's famous plot to bring peace across all of Greece by having the women from all its states withhold sexual favors from their husbands until a treaty is signed and put into practice.[14] The backdrop is the Peloponnesian War, and war is presented as the result of male irrationality, just as male incompetence was presented as the root of Athens' mismanagement in *Assemblywomen.* But *Lysistrata* differs from *Assemblywomen* in three important ways: Athens is at war, while there was a respite at the time of *Assemblywomen;* the plan here encompasses all of Greece, and not just Athens; and the command here is not for sexual congress to be granted, but rather for it to be denied. What can be said about this plot? Understood properly, I suggest, this is not merely a far-fetched comic concoction, but a paean to marital *erōs.* The laughter-provoking sexual ache for their husbands that the women display is of a piece with their desire to have them home alive. For their part, the husbands, having sublimated their *erōs* into *polemos* (war) that may bring them before *thanatos* (death), discover—by means of the acute priapism that they develop when apart from their wives—that such sublimation must ultimately fail. They ache even more acutely than the women. They, too, miss their spouses and long for home.

A sharp conflict between a Chorus of Old Men and a Chorus of Young Women reflects this mutual longing. Initially, it seems as if the men are totally humiliated. But the conflict in *Lysistrata* between men and woman, although it culminates in one of the most ludicrous scenes in the history of drama, transforms into reconciliation by means of one of drama's loveliest gestures. Here, the vulnerability of the warriors who risk their lives and the power of the women's gentleness and generosity shine together. This thoughtful incorporation of gesture into *logos* comprises one of its subtler philosophical dimensions.

The comic subjection of *erōs* to conscious human purposes unites both plays and, in Aristophanes' unique way, discloses the release of erotic rejoicing within the appropriately human limits.

In all four plays, Aristophanes' inimitable and spectacular vulgarity is on full display.[15] But as Hegel observed, Aristophanes is no idle joker but a serious thinker.[16] Accordingly, I will treat those crude passages that contribute significantly to philosophical reflections as carefully as I will the less earthy candidates.

A final chapter will collect the prior reflections into a coherent whole that will demonstrate Aristophanes' unique contribution to *thought,* and will also suggest the considerable philosophical yield of the four comedies when read as interacting with the germane portions of the dialogues of Plato. The texts of the comedies, like the epics of Homer for Plato, have a *huponoia* that belies the apparent excesses discernible on its surface. If one wanted to ban laughter from the education of the guardians, as Socrates says he does at *Republic* 388e5–389b1, one would certainly wish to ban most if not all of Aristophanes. However, a person who is free of the constraints of the city's educational requirements might need to hear Aristophanes just as such a person so willingly heard the Homeric "Achilles in Hades" passage after the release from the cave. Kinesias' declaration of his true love for his Myrrhine even after she has made a laughingstock of him before her women colleagues in *Lysistrata* might reveal the truth about genuine *erōs,* just as the light of the sun celebrated in the Homeric words reveals the truth about nature. The Aristophanic contribution, then, will consist not only of the exhibition of a life of pleasure within measure, but of the joyfulness of life even in the face of the greatest human folly. My primary goal includes two components corresponding to Hegel's twofold observation, namely to join together the serious insight and the experience of ultimate human joy provided by the reading of Aristophanes.

This kind of reading is best served by translations that are as literal as possible. (Accordingly, I have transliterated the Greek exactly as it appears, except for the twenty-second letter, which I will render as "*kh.*") Thus, while I will avail myself of existing translations, almost always using Henderson's,[17] I will revise them accordingly when needed. I will almost always leave *logos* untranslated, both because it surfaces as the principal matter at issue in this study and because it properly allows a wide range of meaning. Most broadly, *logos* intends "speech," but in the contexts of some of the comedies, especially *Clouds* and *Wasps,* "argument" is its narrower intention, and at other times "reason" serves better. All translations are, of course, entirely my responsibility. However, I will gratefully acknowledge whatever help I receive from other translators and from the secondary literature. I will discuss much of this literature in my endnotes.

I hope that my interpretation will bring at least a fraction of the pleasure and benefit that I received from reading Aristophanes.

Part I

Logos and Human Limits

One

Clouds and the Measuring of *Logos*

Inspired comedies provoke laughter. However, the laughter such comedies provoke draws upon a seriousness that is absent from merely contrived comedies. The same distinction can be made between inspired tragedies and melodramas. The "horror and pity" provoked by inspired tragedies differs not only in degree but in kind from the only apparently kindred kinds of emotional responses experienced upon viewing works that merely manipulate these feelings. Inspired comedies and inspired tragedies both engage the spectators in their own deepest humanity. They address those matters that lie closest to us. While there are historical explanations for the evolution of both, this is the ultimate reason why, in the classical age of Greece, both comedies and tragedies were performed at the Dionysian festivals.

We can understand Aristophanes' employment of Socrates as a dramatic character in *Clouds* as a function of Dorian mime (although this quite external function can easily prove misleading). Similarly, in the context of comedy's origin we can understand the coarseness of Aristophanes' language. This language, which can fall so disturbingly upon a sensibility informed by the Judeo-Christian heritage and often reaches outrageous proportions even for the most liberated among us,[1] is a *sacred* vulgarity in its own context. (As the interpretation of the text[2] of *Clouds* proceeds, more on this topic will emerge.)

hai kharites temenos ti labein hoper oukhi peseitai
zēlousai, psukhēn Aristophanous

"The Graces, seeking an imperishable sanctuary,
found the soul of Aristophanes."

Plato, frag. 14

This fragment, of some disputed authenticity, is as good a place as any to begin this interpretation of *Clouds.* There may be no way to guarantee its provenance historically, but it is my conviction that it can be strongly supported *interpretively.* No advance proof exists as to Aristophanes' intentions. But as I will attempt to show by means of close attention to the text of *Clouds,* Plato's admiration for Aristophanes was genuine, and he had an acute sense for Aristophanes' depiction of Socrates, the principal interlocutor of so many of the Platonic dialogues. For purposes of this reading, the phrase "the genuine Socrates" refers to Plato's Socrates, the philosopher who is always seeking the best *logos* for the sake of the best life.[3]

For his part, Aristophanes shows himself in *Clouds* to have a profound understanding of genuine Socratic activity.[4] He demonstrates this through the stunning precision of his mockery. Virtually every sophistical move made by his comic Socrates is the precise opposite of Socratic activity as presented in Platonic dialogues of Socrates that appeared some years later.[5] Of course, no mere assertion can establish the truth of this claim. I believe that the interpretation that follows can provide strong justification for it.

I have broken the reading into sections of varying length, based only upon what seems to be the most natural textual transitions in subject matter, rather than upon Aristophanes' incorporation of the formula for Greek comedy.

LINES 1–125

While Strepsiades may well contend for the honor of being the most entertaining comic character in the history of drama, his uproarious declamations in these lines have a crucial dramatic function. While they surely reveal much about his suffering and about his moral shortcomings, they also present much significant information about his son. Their relationship, as well as the relationship to Socrates and his school the *phrontistērion* ("thinkery"), constitutes not only the heart of the comedy, but also the location of its philosophical material. Pheidippides, as we shall see, can hardly be called "comic," despite his opening and amusing "sounds." Together, they illuminate the matter of *logos* and proper measure.

First, let us consider Strepsiades. Surely, Strepsiades' painful condition is manifold. Financially, he faces ruin. Psychologically, he is in great distress over his mounting debts and over the carelessness of his son. He responds to his psychological pain with moral turpitude: he tries to persuade his son to enroll in the *phrontistērion,* in order to learn sophistical techniques in *logos* so that these debts can be erased by means of cleverness in court. Sexually, his aristocratic wife is so demanding that his marital bed promises no pleasure, but rather brings fear that he will be worn out entirely.

Eminent readers of Aristophanes who have considered the "comic hero" in his work have found many useful markers. To Aristotle, the comic hero was "worse than the average" with respect to "the Ridiculous as a species of the Ugly."[6] In C. H. Whitman's landmark study, he ascribed great individualism, wickedness,[7] and a balance of *eirōn* and *alazōn.* "Calculated fraudulence" might be as good a rendering as any (a mixture of dissembling and being an impostor). While some have argued that Strepsiades is too straightforward and too foolish for such calculated fraudulence and thus does not meet these standards for one of Whitman's comic heroes, I think that both Whitman and his critics have underestimated the complexity of Aristophanes' creation, both in terms of character and in terms of disclosive function.[8]

The details Strepsiades discloses about his life make him more rather than less sympathetic, and the moral turpitude he displays reveals as much the desperation of a man at the end of his rope as it does the cupidity of a scoundrel. He cannot sleep on account of his many worries. His son, whose profligacy has caused his despair, sleeps comfortably as he dreams of horses and "farts away (*perdetai*) under five woolen coverlets"[9] (9–10). His slaves also sleep well; he cannot beat them for fear they'll desert. His marriage to a "high-class wife"[10] (*gunaiki tagathē*) (61) is a shambles, due not only to their divergent sexual capacities but also due to their son's taking on the traits of his mother almost exclusively. Strepsiades' dream that Pheidippides would take after his father and choose the pleasant, rural life of a goatherd has disappeared into "the galloping trots" (*hipperon*) (74). Further, he has no control over Pheidippides, who grows his hair long, rides horses, and enters chariot races, i.e., engages in activities common to the wealthy, but unknown and not respected by a rural man like Strepsiades. Soon, we will learn that Strepsiades cannot enforce his paternal authority because a rich uncle on his wife's side, named Megacles,[11] will provide for Pheidippides (although this uncle will not take on the responsibility for the debts incurred by his nephew). Strepsiades faces ruin, and sees no honorable way out.

Any blanket condemnation of Strepsiades' character is unjustified. If there is a *prōtos pseudēs* (first false move) here, it might be located in the match that brought him together with his wife, who became dominant in the marriage and whose name he can no longer bear to speak. In his presentation, he declares that his own virtues of simplicity, straightforwardness, and hard work are no match for the luxuries offered by his wife and her side of the family for influence over the soul of Pheidippides. This assessment is borne out by the latter's attitude and action. To be sure, Strepsiades' plan to defraud his debtors of their rightful payments is unjust, and so deserves reproach. But as David Hume astutely observed, there is no need for justice either in the *poetical* fiction of unlimited plenty, or in the *philosophical* fiction of unlimited scarcity.[12] At least in his individual condition, Strepsiades' situation approaches the latter. Today, we call this a "mitigating circumstance." To gather all of this together in a fair manner that does not exceed "the facts" as they are presented in the text, we can say that Strepsiades is a fully human character whose behavior spectators can surely understand, even as they realize its flaws. However, as we will see, Strepsiades is blind to the consequences of his conscious choice of injustice. These consequences unfold ever so subtly in this so apparently unsubtle work, which also has the merit of being a close study of injustice. As *logos* becomes gradually more and more unmoored from justice and truth, Strepsiades suffers greater and greater comic pain.

The break between father and son had its roots as far back as childhood, taking place according to Strepsiades in the following crucial way: *all' ouk epeitheto tois emois ouden* ***logois:*** "But he wouldn't listen to anything I ***said***" (73, emphasis mine). An alternate, more literal reading might be: "But he was never persuaded by any of my arguments." The insufficiency of what might be called ordinary *logoi,* with their ordinary give and take, their compromises, and the ongoing exchanges, marks the break between father and son. Given the natural respect owed by a son to his father, Strepsiades certainly has reason for his lament. To assess Strepsiades' character accurately, one must note that it is only here, at the latter's breaking point, that his "devilishly marvelous" (*daimoniōs huperphua*) (76) plan to have his son master other kinds of *logoi* occurs to him. One must also note that the Greek words *daimoniōs* and *huperphua* suggest *excess.* There is a sense in Strepsiades, even through his despair, that what he proposes is inappropriate for a human being, even though these concerns are outweighed by his desire to relieve his distress.

Looking away briefly from Strepsiades' expression of disappointment at his son's rejection of a life of agriculture, as well as from Pheidippides' refusal even to entertain his father's discussion of such a life, let us consider two cases of the breaking-off of *logos* presented in the Platonic dialogues.

1. *Protagoras* 334c7–338e5 is outrageously labeled *Interlude* in the often-assigned Ostwald/Jowett edition. Far from being a mere interruption, this

exchange constitutes the heart of the dialogue. It finds the interlocutors wrestling with the issue of how the exchange in *logos* between Socrates and Protagoras should proceed.[13] At first, Protagoras refuses to agree to a dialogue with Socrates in the latter's preferred manner of exchanging questions and answers. "Socrates, he replied, many a battle of words (*agōna logōn*) have I fought, and if I had conducted discussions (*dialegesthai*) which my adversaries (*antilegōn*) commanded, as you want me to do, in no way would I have been better than another, and the name of Protagoras would not have appeared through all of Hellas" (335a4–8). Socrates acknowledges Protagoras' mastery in both lengthy speech and short speech (*en makrologia kai en brakhulogia*). Claiming that his weakness of memory makes him unable to follow one of Protagoras' lengthy discourses, Socrates insists that both keep their *logoi* short. Since Protagoras seems unwilling (*ouk atheleis*) to speak in short answers, Socrates rises to leave.

For genuine *logos* to take place, some common ground of agreement must be found. Clearly, if there is no such agreement even as to the nature of the *logoi* that will occur in the discussion, then it is senseless even to begin. By "genuine *logos*" here, I mean an exchange of speeches, thoughts, arguments that aim at a good solution, whether that solution concerns intellectual truth, ethical goodness, or aesthetic beauty. In the *Protagoras,* the various partisans of both Socrates and Protagoras persuade their "leaders" to a compromise allowing the dialogue to continue: Protagoras will begin questioning Socrates, and when he is through Socrates will question Protagoras—but some looseness in the length of the answers will be permitted (337d1–338d1). The dialogue thereafter takes some surprising twists and turns. The doctrinal outcome, for example, finds Socrates and Protagoras reversing their original positions on the teachability of virtue. However, this "aporetic" conclusion has a positive resonance. (The confusion issues from the mutual failure to say what *aretē* [virtue] is, before pursuing the subsequent matter of its teachability.) The common ground upon which the dialogue could take place made possible both the real and substantive confusion leading to the mutual and salutary recognition of ignorance, and to the positive outcome of keeping the "what is virtue?" question alive.

2. In the *Meno,* Socrates presents Meno with a direct account of the procedures for genuine *logos.* After a frustrated Meno raises bogus objections to Socrates' attempt to provide a paradigm for treating the "what is virtue?" question,[14] Socrates presents two legitimate dialogical options. The first is direct refutation (*elenkhein*) of an answer given by one's opponent. The second is finding a common ground, using agreed-upon terms known to the questioner (*di' ekeinōn hōn an prosomologē eidenai ho erōtōmenos*) (75d6–7).

The break in *logos* between father and son in *Clouds* echoes these Platonic concerns in a comic context. Father and son lack a common ground of agreement on both the nature of a genuine dialogue on life and on the particular matter of handling the family's debt load.[15] At the end of the *Meno* and on account of his wealth, Meno can walk away from dialogue unaffected by the healthy confusion that Socrates attempted to instill in his soul. Similarly here in *Clouds,* Pheidippides can walk away from his angry father who threatens to banish him because his rich uncle Megacles (*Megakleēs*—literally, "of great fame") will furnish him with all of the food and the horses he may desire.

It seems entirely evident to me, contrary to some accounts, that Aristophanes has written a great deal of self-reflectiveness, self-awareness, and even intellectual and moral acumen into the character of Strepsiades.[16] He recognizes both the desperation and the hilarity of his position. His lamentations include a dose of laughter at himself for his plight. His rant against the matchmaker who convinced him to marry his wife, his recollections of country life that include its being moldy (*eurōtiōn*) and unswept (*akorētos*) as well as aimless (43–44), all indicate a consciousness both of the (unspoken) reasons for his condition and of the humorous figure he cuts as a result and in which he revels through the construction and the power of his own *logoi.*

Further, his observations on the character of the *phrontistērion* bear witness to both moral and intellectual acumen. Concerning both the former and the latter, he first speaks of Socrates' school in terms of irony and ridicule. He says that it is for "wise souls" (*psukhōn sophōn*), some of whom can argue successfully that heaven is a barbecue lid surrounding us, and we're the coals. If you give them money, they can "argue victoriously whether just or unjust" (*legonta nikan kai dikaia kadika*) (98–99). Neither here nor elsewhere in this study do I wish to enter into protracted argumentation concerning either Aristophanes' intention vis-à-vis Socrates, or the latter's response,[17] a subject on which a long and learned literature already exists.[18] I want merely to note here that this is indeed clearly a caricature of Socrates as the latter is depicted in the Platonic dialogues, where Socrates refuses payment and regards with ill-disguised contempt those who teach the skill of argumentation for the sake of mere persuasion rather than the pursuit of truth and goodness. Here, Strepsiades sounds more like a demonically inspired Socrates calling attention to fraud in *logos,* than like an innocent and foolish goatherd.

Within his diatribe, he reveals the event of the naming of his son. His wife wished to add *hippos* to the boy's name, calling him Xanthippus, Khairippus, or Callipides ("Golden Horse," "Joyful Horse," and "Beautiful" or "Noble Horse," respectively), while Strepsiades wanted to call him Pheidonides ("Thrifty Son"). Their comic compromise nevertheless placed the *hippos* at the center of his name, and his mother's wish coupled with her uncle's influence shaped Pheidippides' character while pushing his father's to the margins.

Pheidippides is no doubt spoiled and disrespectful, but at first seems to have a similarly astute take on the *phrontistērion,* as does his father. The Socrates and the Chaerophon depicted in Aristophanes' creation of the *phrontistērion* are indeed wretched (*kakodaimōn*) (104), as Pheidippides claims. Unlike Socrates, who walks the agora seeking to engage his fellow Athenians in discussion and who opposes sophistry in any form, Aristophanes' *phrontistērion* teaches both the stronger (*kreitton*[*a*]) and the weaker (*hēttona*) argument (112). Strepsiades asks his son to enter and learn "this unjust argument" (*adikon touton logon*) (117) so that he will be entirely free of the debts incurred by Pheidippides.

At this point, however, the marked difference between father and son surfaces clearly. Pheidippides refuses on the ground of the wretchedness of Socrates and Chaerophon, and on the ground of the damage it would do to his reputation. Not a word about his father's plight, or his major role in producing it, is heard. One should note that Strepsiades associates the weaker argument with the unjust argument, and Pheidippides expresses no disagreement. They are both aware of the moral wrongness of arguing well in order to escape a justly incurred obligation. Given the way the characters are situated, however, the only consideration concerns the existential consequences of their respective choices. They are grave for Strepsiades, so he resorts to this stratagem. They are nonexistent for Pheidippides. For him, the issue of morality does not even arise.

This lack of a common ground that would match their *logoi* to one another in even a superficial manner is indicated by Pheidippides' first swearing by Dionysus to obey his father's request (*peisomai, nē ton Dionuson*) (90–91), and then swearing the opposite by Dionysus shortly thereafter (*ouk an ma ton Dionuson*) (108–109), when asked to study at the *phrontistērion.* We are reading a comedy and not a moral and/or intellectual treatise. However, this comedy was destined for the Dionysian festival, during which the most sacred concerns of human beings were presented and celebrated in the poetic/dramatic art. In this light, we are presented with an obviously "immoral" surface in *Clouds,* namely the attempt by Strepsiades to escape justly incurred debt by consciously devious and dishonest means. But the deeper "immorality" may be the carelessness with which Pheidippides invokes the god whose name names the festival as surety for his *logoi,* not to mention his carelessness in running up debts that can only bring misery and ruin to his father.

Perhaps strangely, their ridiculously disconnected *logoi* reveal something essential and deeply philosophical about justice and its relation to *logos.* Both agree *in principle* that however expedient it may be, it is somehow disgraceful to willfully to make the weaker *logos* appear stronger. Both also associate the weaker *logos* with injustice, affirming by implication that in *logos* justice is *in principle and in deed* stronger than injustice. In whatever way the historical argument regarding intentions and responses is played out, these "positions" on *logos* clearly accord with the positions taken by Socrates in the Platonic dialogues. The views that are presented on stage, e.g., that the stronger *logos* is on the side of justice and the weaker *logos* is on the side of injustice, are playfully concealed in the great comedian's art. They are accessible not only in spite of the laughter of the spectators, but precisely *through* this laughter. For this laughter signals the simultaneouly instinctive recognition of the absurdity of the action and the delighted surprise provoked by its unexpected and inspired artistic formulation.

I suggest here that what Plato had Socrates say in the *Ion* concerning the inspired work of the tragic poets when seized by divine madness, and in the *Apology* about poets in general, is true of this comic poet as well. Although he may not know the meaning of what he writes, the poet is a holy thing and his words unite human beings and gods by means of a kind of magnetic influence. Socrates employs the image of the stone of Herakleia, in which one set of iron filings is magnetized and so attracts and binds the others. From the Muse to the poet to the rhapsode (in this case, those connected with the play's staging to the audience), the inspired words prokove mindfulness of the gods (*Ion* 535e7–536b4). Put in non-mythical language, the comedies of Aristophanes serve to remind human beings of those matters that are most fundamental to the quality of their humanity. However, unlike the Platonic dialogues, which address these concerns through question and answer, the comedies of Aristophanes—like the works of his colleagues in the tragic art—bring these concerns to their audiences through the vicarious experiences they provide.

LINES 126–214

His son having departed into the house, Strepsiades prays to the gods and seeks to enter the *phrontistērion,* fearing that his old age, his denseness, and his forgetfulness will render him unable to gain the knowledge that he needs in order to escape his debts. Upon entering the school, Strepsiades finds himself subjected to a series of ridiculous arguments and images, and he is not at all shy about responding to them. One concerns how many of its own feet a flea can jump, the proof of which involved a pair of Persian slippers: Strepsiades calls upon Zeus to admire this "subtlety of mind" (*leptotētos tōn phrenōn*) (153). Another concerns whether gnats hum through their mouths or their anuses, and involves a hypothesis of the downward movement of the wind through the insect's gut: Strepsiades notes the "penetrating enterology" (*dientereumatos*) of this insight (166). Another has Socrates gazing heavenward, à la Thales, and having a lizard on the roof defecate into his mouth: Strepsiades remarks, "I like that!" (*hēstheēn*) (174). Yet another concerns a group of students with their eyes pressed to the ground and their rumps in the air, studying matters beyond the heavens and beneath the earth: says Strepsiades, they're "seeking onions" (189).

This unmatched satire of philosophical activity rests for it effectiveness upon two affiliated and immediate aspects of recognition: first, the tacit admission that philosophy and sophistry are indeed different. Philosophy, *philosophia,* means "love of wisdom," and seeks genuine truth and goodness for the sake of living the best life possible. The ridiculous arguments and images presented in this section provoke laughter precisely because they so obviously mischaracterize philosophy. Further, there is a tacit concession that sophistry is a lesser pursuit, as it seeks mere persuasion and concerns the acquisition of skill in argumentation alone.

The second aspect of recognition involves a truth about philosophy that is subtler and perhaps less easily admitted: to a certain degree philosophy is and must be a *comic activity.* Philosophy indeed can take the lover of wisdom on journeys of *logos* that lead into difficult and obscure regions when compared to everyday *logoi.*[19] For mere earthbound mortals, for beings subject to ongoing change, growth and decay, to attempt to contemplate principles that are eternal, unchanging, divine—or even to trace out the *empeiria* (matters of experience) faithfully—does seem to require a leap beyond what can be truly known into a region of mere speculation, requiring a language that differs markedly from the everyday. Those who condemn Aristophanes for an unjust and damaging caricature of Socrates therefore have a *prima facie* case: to an "everyday" audience that cannot distinguish satire from documentary, this apparent mockery of Socrates might indeed serve to prejudice many of them against him. But much evidence to the contrary can be drawn both from the Platonic dialogues, in which Aristophanes appears sympathetically, and also from parts of the historical record, which indicate that Socrates was present and acknowledged the play in a friendly manner.[20] In my view, however, the strongest evidence for the "innocence" of Aristophanes can be found within *Clouds* itself, where the very same practices that come in for censure in the dialogues come in for ridicule in this comedy.

Instead of examining the particular arguments, I shall focus upon the way *logos* is treated in these lines. In line 130 old Strepsiades expresses his concern, as we have seen, over his ability "to learn the hairsplitting of precise arguments": *logōn akribōn skindalamous mathēsomai.* He expects, that is, to be given a rigorous education in what we might call "applied logic" that would enable him to shine in the courts. After knocking loudly on the door and "abort[ing] a newfound discovery" (*phrontid' exēmblōkas exēurēmenēn*) by a student (137), Strepsiades learns that *logōn akribōn* are precisely *not* the subject matter treated in the *phrontistērion.* When he asks the student about the stillborn discovery, Strepsiades is told: "But it is sacrilege[21] to tell anyone but the students": *all' ou themis plēn tois mathētaisin legein* (140, emphasis mine). The measure of *logoi* in the *phrontistērion,* according to this first student, is *themis.* Henderson's rendering of this word as "sacrilege" is excellent in my view, correctly hearing the overtone of divinity in the word. This overtone is present in its meaning as "what is suitable" or "what is appropriate," especially at a festival honoring Dionysus, the god of wine and fertility. Such discoveries, Strepsiades learns, are told only to students. After declaring his intention to become a student at the *phrontistērion,* this student replies: "I'll tell you, but it is necessary to consider these matters *mysteries*": ***lexō,*** *nomisai de tauta khrē* ***mustēria*** (143, emphases mine). Thus, in the *phrontistērion, logos* and *mustēria* are inextricably bound together. Speech is sacred, the matters spoken about are held in secret between those in the inner circle. It does not seem that Strepsiades will learn what he needs in order to escape his debts.

The first impression bears this out. The curriculum of the *phrontistērion* consists primarily of a comic version of "knowledge for its own sake," rather than the kinds of skill that enable one to argue both sides of a matter with equally adept facility—in this case the "weaker" (unjust) and "stronger" (just) side, in analogy with a certain kind of law practice today. One part of the curriculum is *phrontistērion*-geometry. Strepsiades asks the student:

> "So what's that useful for?"
> "Measuring land (*gēn anametreisthai*)."[22]
> "You mean land for settlers?"
> "No, land in general (*sumpasan*)." (202–204)

This comic presentation of the uselessness of Socratic-style philosophizing in common affairs has its element of truth, namely that philosophical questioning indeed seeks insights that are not bound by everyday concerns but shed light on and encompass principles that transcend it. Neither a property owner nor a blacksmith needs to understand the science of geometry in order to do the measurements required by their craft. Nevertheless, geometry and arithmetic are the sciences that make both activities possible, and the philosopher wonders about their general nature. In this sense, while the activity of philosophy indeed both may appear to be and *be* comical to everyday people and even to the philosopher him/herself, this comic side does not exclude the seriousness of its work. Far from it: the ridiculousness of the comic presentation, the laughter it provokes, is the seal of this seriousness. The airborne Socrates introduced in the next section is its wondrously revealing image. For in my view, the inspired comedy deliberately omits this serious side precisely in order to celebrate it.[23] Philosophy does connect, often quite directly, with the affairs of human beings, even as most seem entirely unaware of this connection.

The final employment of a word related to *logos* bears witness to this concealed seriousness and consequent connection. It occurs in a brilliantly ludicrous remark resounding from the mouth of Strepsiades: "You speak elegantly (*asteion legeis*): for that sophism (*sophisma*) is demotic and useful." *Asteion* also can mean, "from the town," "refined," etc. Henderson has "sophisticated," but then has to translate *sophisma* as "device," thereby losing the overtone of a tension between philosophy and sophistry. At once Strepsiades recognizes the humbug in the *logos,* and sees how he might put *logoi* of that kind to advantage in his nefarious plan. The "knowledge for its own sake" that appeared so useless at the outset of his education has taken on an entirely new cast. He begins to sense how the "mysteries" might be used to confound his creditors, just as they confounded him on first hearing.

Gathering up the material bearing upon *logos* in these first two sets of lines, we find first of all that the assent to a common ground by both speakers is a necessary condition for genuine dialogue. Just as Strepsiades and Pheidippides can find no such ground, and their dialogue breaks off with the father's tirade and the son's retreat into his wealthy uncle's house; so Socrates rises to leave Protagoras when the latter will not agree to an exchange based on mutually agreed upon procedures, and only stays when such agreement is reached. The *Meno* adds a further dimension: one can provide direct refutation of an answer as well. This dimension will arise in future parts of *Clouds.*

Further, there is an implicit association between the stronger *logos* and justice (*dikē*), and thus between the weaker *logos* and injustice as well. Strepsiades is well aware of the injustice of his cause. He seeks to avoid ruin out of desperation—never having taken such a course in the past—acknowledging the bogus nature of the discipline he proposes to undergo and to learn, and knowing that the task of learning to argue effectively may be beyond his ability in any case.

Instead of a course in "applied logic," he finds ethereal, ludicrous, preposterous, and otherwise apparently useless *logoi* propounded by the student in the *phrontistērion.* Strepsiades ridicules such *logoi* at first, then realizes that the style of *logos* presented in *phrontistērion*-geometry might indeed be useful in bridging the gap between the comically offered erudition of philosophy and the also comically offered pragmatics of everyday life. In the next set of lines this bridge becomes personified in a remarkable way.

LINES 226–356

Socrates swings in a basket above, looking down upon both gods and mortals from his perch. When Strepsiades wants to know what Socrates is up to, the latter answers: "I tread the air and scrutinize the sun": *aerobatō kai periphronō ton hēlion* (225). When asked why he doesn't make his survey of the air, the sun, and the gods from the earth, Socrates answers that from above he can make correct discoveries about "meteorological things" (*meteōra pragmata*). Thus, Socrates inhabits the sky in order to learn about "pragmatic things" concerning the earth on which we walk. In his first answer to Strepsiades, even before he descends to meet him on the earth, he has proclaimed himself to be a bridge between erudition and common life. Socrates' speech at 228–234 identifies the *noēma* (thought) of Socrates commingling with its kindred air and "the very same thing that happens to watercress." (Strepsiades expresses surprise about the connection between the mind and watercress [231–236].)

After Socrates descends, he asks Strepsiades why he has come. "Wanting to learn to speak": *Boulomenos mathein legein* (239), is the answer. Of course, Strepsiades already knows how to speak. He declaims wonderfully and humorously. His sense of irony and sarcasm shows much development,[24] and bespeaks intelligence to go along with his coarseness. His sense of the affiliation of speech and justice also deserves praise, even as he acts against that sense. However, he knows—and he knows that he knows—that he would be helpless in a law court when trying to escape his creditors.

Although the contexts may seem dissimilar, one cannot help but think of Socrates' discussion of the man who has been liberated from the cave in book 7 of the *Republic:*

> What about what happens when someone turns from divine study to the evils of human life? Do you think it's surprising, since his sight is still dim, and he hasn't become accustomed to the darkness around him, that he behaves awkwardly and appears completely ridiculous if he's compelled, either in the courts of justice or elsewhere, about the shadows of justice or the statues of which they are the shadows and to dispute about the way these things are understood by people who have never seen justice itself?
>
> That's not surprising at all.
>
> No, it isn't . . . (517d2–e2)

In a comic sense and, I hasten to add, *only* in a comic sense, Strepsiades is the analogue of the liberated human being in the *Republic.* He has an intuitive, if limited, grasp of what justice is. He has been forcibly thrust out of the "cave" of ordinary civic and family life, if indeed only because of the behavior of his relatives. He experiences the initial pain of this unwanted displacement, employs his admittedly limited intellect to survey the new realm in which he dwells, and comes to a profound and comic Socratic discovery: he *knows that he does not know* how to proceed, and seeks help for his quandary. In the process, he will appear ridiculous by virtue of his incompetence at reading the ways of the *phrontistērion.*

Socrates, by contrast, appears not merely as a sophist, but as a grotesque caricature of one. After hearing Strepsiades ask to learn "the second of the two *logoi,* the one that repays no debts," and hearing him promise "by the gods" (*tous theous*) (244–246) to pay the *phrontistērion* in cash when he gets it, Socrates brusquely informs him that "the gods are not legal tender here" (246–247). This prefigures the denial of the existence of the Olympian gods that will occur later in the play. But first, Socrates proposes to introduce Strepsiades to the Clouds, the deities (*daimosin*) of the *phrontistērion,* with whom Strepsiades wants to enter into conversations (*suggenesthai tais Nephelaisin eis logous*) (252).

In the midst of a laughably humiliating initiation into the ranks of students, Strepsiades asks: "What's in it for me?" Socrates answers: "You will come to speak (*legein*) in an accomplished manner (*trimma*), a castanet, the finest rogue (*paipalē*)."[25] In his summons of the Clouds, who are said to traverse freely between Olympos, Okeanos, and the Nile among other places, Socrates sings their welcome. Their first Chorus sounds from afar, singing the words "deep roaring (*Baruakheos*)," "divine rivers rushing (*potamōn zatheōn keladēmata*)," "the sea crashing with deep thunder (*ponton keladonta barubromon*)," "heaven's tireless eye ablaze (*omma . . . aitheros akamaton selageitai*)," as they "survey the land with telescopic eye (*epidōmetha tēleskopō ommati gaian*)" (278–290).

Socrates asks whether Strepsiades heard "the bellowing thunder that prompts holy reverence." The terrified old student responds: "And I do revere you, most honored ones, and I wish to fart in reply to those thunderclaps: that's how much I tremble at them and fear them. And right now, whether it is sanctioned and even if it is not, I shit (*kei themis estin, nuni g' ēdē, kei mē themis esti, kheseiō*)" (293–295). Socrates then tells him "neither mock nor act like those hapless comedians (*trugodaimones*)" but keep (sacred) silence (*euphēmei*), for a great swarm of gods is on the move (297–298).

Here, one must stop and wonder about Strepsiades' response, about Socrates' reference to the comic poets, and about his subsequent warnings to keep the appropriate silence in the face of the advance of the gods (*theōn*)—given that Clouds, not the gods at all, are advancing. Here, upon close reading of the text, we find one of those locations where Aristophanes' coarse and apparently crude scatological references may be far more nuanced than first appears.

Firstly, of all human bodily responses, flatulence most resembles the thunder that Strepsiades hears and so would provide suitable mockery. Secondly, defecation is clearly in excess of this thundering. This kind of excess belongs to the very nature of the work of comic poets like Aristophanes. Hence Strepsiades indeed acts in their manner, as Socrates "correctly" notes. Finally, the still unseen Clouds are presented as having the power of *logos:* beings of nature are granted meaningful voice. Their thundering is presented as a *comprehensible* thundering, a thundering containing sense as well as sound. Taking this together, we have the ludicrous *logoi* of Socrates as he initiates Strepsiades, the Dionysian Chorus sung by advancing Clouds and, in the only appropriately measured response to these extraordinary provocations, the partly mocking, partly fearful, vulgar response of Strepsiades.

In an admittedly odd manner, can we not hear in Strepsiades' response a comic echo of certain Socratic interpolations in the Platonic dialogues, i.e., those moments when one of the interlocutors says something hubristic, excessive? Thrasymachus rages at Socrates and accuses him of being unwilling to answer the question concerning the nature of justice, using his "habitual irony" as an excuse and a dodge so that he would "do anything rather than answer if someone asked you something" (*Republic* 337d). Socrates replies: "That's because you are wise, Thrasymachus"—thereby employing this "habitual irony" in precisely the right manner, namely to attempt to bring Thrasymachus before his own ignorance and to redirect the discussion in a productive way.[26] And in *Meno,* Meno speaks in imperatives, so Socrates tells him that even if he were blind he could tell that Meno was good-looking and had many lovers. In this way, he also attempts to bring Meno before the inappropriateness of his own behavior and so redirect the discussion more productively, enabling the interlocutors to look within their own souls.

I am suggesting a noteworthy analogy between Socratic irony and wisdom and Strepsiadian coarseness and stupidity. Socratic irony is playful, but its playfulness includes the most significant seriousness. Socratic irony brings the interlocutors (including Socrates) before their own ignorance, and so attempts to open up a space wherein genuine philosophical dialogue can occur. Strepsiadian coarseness is ridiculous, but its ridiculousness calls attention to something amiss in the *logoi.* The Clouds are not goddesses, and to call them goddesses while denying the Olympians is excessive in the extreme. So too is the fear they have brought about, as is manifest in the body of Strepsiades. This "somatic response" might have, but did not, serve as a warning away from the fateful hubris of the comic Socrates. And the laughter provoked by this entire exchange provides a space wherein human beings can at once reflect upon, acknowledge, and enjoy their humanity, with its powers, its virtues, and its inevitable shortcomings.

The Clouds, it turns out, are not associated with the Olympian pantheon at all, nor do they hold sway over any other beings than the initiates at the *phrontistērion.* They are "great goddesses for idle men": *megalai theai andrasin argois* (316). In listing the skills provided to these idle men, two of the words contain uses of *logos:* the Clouds "provide us with judgment and dialectic (*dialexin*)"—also intellect (*noun*), and fantasy (*terateian*)—"and circumlocution (*perilekhin*) and verbal thrust and parry" (317–318). Thus, the deeds of the Clouds consist in obscuring key distinctions made within the very Platonic dialogues they mock. Upward-moving dialectic, for the Socrates of the Platonic dialogues, is the highest path of attaining truth. Downward-moving dialectic concerns the application of the forms (*eidē*) to their manifestations in mathematical objects. For Socrates, this intelligible activity exceeds all the others in clarity.

By allowing *dialexin* to be "clouded" together with *perilekhin,* Aristophanes clearly merits Hegel's high praise as "no mere joker," but as belonging intimately to what is highest and best in thought. Here, the comic poet demonstrated shrewd awareness of one of the key distinctions made by Socrates in the latter's practice and as revealed in the *Republic.* Strepsiades carries this "clouding" further by expressing his wish to learn to "meet argument with counterargument": *logō antilogēsai* (321). Then, he says: "I want to see them in person": *idein autas ēdē phanerōs epithumō.* This latter passage is a gem of inspired "clouding." He asks for an *idea* of the Clouds, a clear vision of a phenomenon that, by its very nature, *resists* such clear envisioning. The absurdity of Strepsiades' initial request to see the Clouds clearly is disclosed in his admission that concerning the appearance of the Clouds in the sky, "I don't know clearly" (*ouk oida saphōs*) (344).

The remainder of this textual section presents futher clouding, this time a clouding within the very notion of Clouds. On the one hand, there are the actual clouds of nature, the ones about which the dithyrambic poets compose verses (mocked by Strepsiades here). On the other hand, Strepsiades observes that these "Socratic goddesses" "have noses" (*rhinas ekhousin*) (344). However, the figures appearing before Strepsiades first look to him like "mortal women" (341). The confusion intensifies, as to who or what the Clouds are.

In the closing lines of this textual section, the confounding increases. Strepsiades is asked whether he has ever "looked upward" (*anablepsas*) and seen clouds turn into various shapes. Indeed, "they can turn into anything they want": *gignontai panth' hoti boulontai* (348). (Here, Aristophanes uses these changing shapes to mock some of his contemporaries.) Not only does

Socrates break off his talk about the Clouds with noses that look like mortal women, but also he ascribes choice to the clouds of nature!

One could hardly imagine a greater mess made of *logos* by means of the Aristophanic Socrates' effort to "cloud" every matter concerning it, both within the comedy and in contrast with genuine Socratic practice. *Logos,* comic-Socratic-style, is for the few who can afford to be idle, and a payment of money is a prerequisite for entry into the *phrontistērion.* These two claims run directly counter to what was well known about Socrates at the time of the play's production. *Noēsin* and *dianoian* (of which *dialekhis* is the action), the two clearest affections of the soul on the divided line in Plato's *Republic,* are joined together with *terateian* (marvels, fantasies) and *perilexia,* two conscious efforts to cast a fog over what is said. The "Clouds with noses" are swept aside momentarily in *logos,* for the sake of Socrates' fooling Strepsiades through reference to the shape-shifting clouds in the sky.

If we can speak of an outcome to the comedy thus far, it would have to embrace the following. (1) *Logos* is drawn into a fog—into Clouds—by Socrates, and what these clouds ultimately consist of is also murky. With this, Strepsiades also finds himself drawn into this fog of *logos,* in which genuine insight is twinned with deliberate deception both in word and in deed. (2) It is also *clear*—and I choose this word with some care—that it belongs to the nature of *logos* for such twisting-away from genuine insight, from the pursuit of truth, to occur. Everyone in the audience, and everyone who reads the comedy is aware of this possibility, and the comedy hinges upon this awareness. (I would argue further, as I indicated earlier, that it also hinges on the awareness that the Socrates of the comedy is diametrically opposite to the real Socrates who frequents the agora.) (3) This thoroughgoing awareness is eloquent testimony to the proper employment of *logos* as seeking truth and goodness for the sake of the best possible life. Otherwise, there *is* no distinction between proper and improper use. (4) Further, the spectator/reader as a human being can locate both tendencies within her/himself: the comedy of competing uses of *logos* belongs to all of us. Hence, our laughter at the doings in *Clouds* is simultaneously "informed" laughter at ourselves, disclosing our ridiculous thoughtfulness.

LINES 356–475

These lines contain one of the "stock charges" against philosophers, namely that they do not believe in the traditional gods but fashion new ones.[27] While we will certainly treat the Aristophanic-Socratic denial of the Olympian gods, once again we will focus primarily upon *logos*-related words in order to see what they further disclose to us concerning this most basic human trait.

"Hail, oldster born long ago, stalker of Muse-loving arguments": *thērata logōn philomousōn* (358). The Clouds themselves speak in ludicrously obfuscatory terms, unnecessarily repeating the aged condition of the man (for obvious and meretricious metrical and melodious reasons), and juxtaposing two words that are at odds with one another: stalking (or hunting) and Muse-loving. Also included in their dubious praise is Socrates. Here, Aristophanes juxtaposes the "comic" and the "genuine" Socrates. The comic Socrates "struts like a popinjay through the streets and casts his eyes sideward," and "wear[s] a haughty expression" (361–362); the "genuine" Socrates walks "unshod (*kanupodētos*)," "endures many woes (*kaka*)" (363), and is indeed a student of the (then-celebrated) sophist Prodicus.

What can be said about this distinction between the "comic" and what I've been calling the "genuine" Socrates? I've been suggesting that the two are indeed *one,* and that the comic Socrates created by Aristophanes consists of the "genuine" Socrates with the moral and intellectual content of the latter subtracted. If we look at the Socrates of the *Apology* as a paradigm for a philosopher, we find someone who knows his ignorance, who knows that his "wisdom is really worth nothing at all" (23a–b). He has made this discovery by means of a lifetime of argumentation with his fellow Greeks. The Aristophanic Socrates is, in that sense, a "true caricature," consisting of skill in *logos* and in unexamined ignorance pure and simple—these comic qualities are fully abstracted from the genuine playful/serious Socrates.

However, it is surely worth asking the following question: if indeed the "comic" and the "genuine" Socrates are one, what binds these two "natures" together? Plato's *Symposium* gives a strong suggestion, from the *logoi* of both Aristophanes and Socrates. In Aristophanes' account, "the name *erōs* is given for the desire for wholeness" (*Symposium* 192e10–a3). Our original four-armed, four-legged, two-faced, united nature has been severed into two parts "as people slice apples when they are going to preserve them or cut eggs with hairs" (190d8–e2). In our terms, Aristophanes' *logos* gives an earthbound, this-worldly account of *erōs*' role in the lives of human beings, one in which transcendence plays little or no role. The intervening *logos* of Agathon, while a beautiful display of virtuosity, presents *Erōs*[28] as entirely transcendent, "the most beautiful and the best and then the cause of what is best and most beautiful in others" (197c1–3), both for gods and for men.[29] (Ironically, comic poet Aristophanes presents a tragic *logos,* in which the actions of Zeus punish the original humans for their hubris, while tragic poet Agathon gives what is essentially a comic *logos* in which no account is taken of earthly desires, some of which produce that same hubris.)

In these terms at least, Socrates' *logos* can be regarded as synthesizing the strengths of both previous *logoi.* Like Aristophanes', the ladder of *erōs* begins with the love of a single body. Like Agathon's, *erōs* culminates in the vision of beauty of the highest and best kind. The entrance and the speech of the beautiful, drunken Alcibiades at the end of Socrates' speech can be seen in many ways, but for our purposes here it serves to show how Socrates, after the manner of his own speech, attempts to redirect Alcibiades' desire for union of bodies. Alcibiades expresses wonder at Socrates' chaste treatment of him amid the closest physical contact. Thus guided by *erōs* for goodness, Socrates attempts to show by his action (*ergon*) toward Alcibiades what belongs to the best erotic life.[30]

"Everyone applauded after Socrates gave his speech, except for Aristophanes, who tried to say something about how Socrates referred to his own speech in his remarks . . ." (*Symposium* 212c). What can this "reference" (*emnēsthē*) be? According to Alfred Geier in *Plato's Erotic Thought,* it is an "intended rebuttal of Socrates and [a re-presentation] of Aristophanes' view of body-love."[31] As such, it begins to break the *sunousia* ("Being-together") established by Socrates' speech, a breakage that is furthered toward its completion by the speech and deeds of Alcibiades. But isn't it just as possible that Aristophanes, instead of insisting on body-love, would remind them of the divine nature and contribution of *erōs* in his speech, and his role in bringing about at least some measure of that very gathering (*sunousia*)? In that case, the sudden entrance of Alcibiades immediately thereafter would constitute at the same time both the break (looked at one way) and the continuity, according to which Plato has Socrates illustrate in deed what he has just said.

I am claiming that Plato has shown Aristophanes to be someone who understands Socratic beliefs and Socratic activity. In terms presented in the *Symposium,* we would do well to interpret the "*sunousia*" that is named "Socrates" as consisting of both earthboundness and transcendence. In *Clouds,* by warping his earthboundness and mocking his transcendence to such ridiculous degrees, Aristophanes affirms both.

"There is no Zeus": *oud' esti Zeus.* So Socrates tells his startled pupil, who soon learns that Clouds, rather that Zeus, make it rain. (Strepsiades previously supposed that rain was caused by "Zeus pissing through a sieve" [373].) Zeus' thundering in, another falsehood, becomes the Clouds that are set in motion by a mechanical cause called *dinos* (whirl). Socrates explains the crash of thunder by giving Strepsiades the Socratic-style words, "I'll teach you from yourself" (*apo sautou' gō se didaxō*), and then likening this crash to the flatulence experienced after overeating soup at the Panathenaea (385–387). Becoming more adept at *phrontistērion* discourse, Strepsiades likens Zeus' thunderbolt to a sausage that exploded when he forgot to cut a slit in it before cooking (and that also frightened him enough to cause him to defecate on another fearsome occasion). For his new wisdom,

Strepsiades' new goddesses praise him and promise him a blessed life . . . but only upon fulfilling a demanding series of conditions of which he seems unaware in his enthusiasm. The first two conditions, that he be "retentive and a cogitator (*phrontistēs*)" disqualify him already, and some of the later ones, which command physical and dietary asceticism, are no doubt beyond him as well. Upon promising Socrates that he will have no gods but "Chaos, the Clouds, and the Tongue" (424),[32] Strepsiades seems to contradict himself at once by also promising not to speak a word (*dialekhtheiēn*) to "the others" or to sacrifice, pour libations, or light incense to them! But shouldn't this apparent contradiction not also be read as a latent acknowledgement of the ongoing presence of the Olympian gods, and his renunciation as a function of the desperate straits in which he finds himself? In this context, the Clouds request that he "tell" (*lege*) (428) them what he wishes, and he replies that he wishes to be the "best speaker" (*legein . . . ariston*) (430). He does not wish to discourse (*legein*) on motions before the court, but only in "twisting lawsuits to my own advantage and giving my creditors the slip" (433–434). The Clouds seem to grant this to him but point out, in a manner that Strepsiades cannot yet grasp, that "it is nothing great that you desire": *ou gar megalōn epithumeis* (435).

The Greek word for "twisting law suits" is *strepsodikēsai,* which can be read literally as "to turn justice aside" or "to twist justice, to twist the right."[33] Henderson's translation follows many of his predecessors and, once again, cannot be called mistaken. But given Strepsiadian innocence and desperation, and given his knowledge that what he is proposing to do transgresses all accepted norms, I think that this more literal translation presents a more faithful echo of his soul. He knows both that the suits are just and that the creditors are right under the law. He does not, however, feel responsible for Pheidippides' behavior, and sees no other recourse than this sophistry he knows to be wrong in some deep way. By accepting the divinity of the Clouds and pledging to ignore the gods that had guided him in the past, Strepsiades accepts a course that requires the kind of orientation (as well as skill) of which he had never been in need before. Little does he foresee how the acquisition of this skill will affect the "innocence" of his soul.

LINES 475–516

These few lines give the preliminary indication of Strepsiades' unsuitedness to comic-Socratic questioning, and seem (but perhaps only seem) to seal his fate as a "non-cogitator." He mistakes the sense of words (e.g., he mistakes an educational "attack" for a literal one [478–483]). He "remembers" debts owed him but not ones that he owes (483–485). He likens "snapping up" cosmological insight to doglike behavior (491). Once again, these exchanges can be read in two ways, perhaps even simultaneously: (1) as the demonstration of the stupidity and bad character of a man with a manipulative soul, and/or (2) as the efforts of a naïve man who is trying to grasp a way of behavior that is both beyond him intellectually and at odds with a nature that was fundamentally just at one time. As he enters the *phrontistērion* with Socrates at the end of these lines (which shall continue after the choral interlude), we certainly find ourselves in no position to say which is the better reading, or even if the two readings represent real alternatives.

Yet there is a great deal at stake in such a decision. The *logoi* of the comic Socrates and their ability to seduce the at least semi-credulous Strepsiades seem to suggest that *logos* indeed has a strong ability to mislead. Even if we take a position that the main thrust of my interpretation rejects—that Socrates indeed talked nonsense and misled his followers—this strong ability is proclaimed. A more innocent interpretation yields the same result, namely that the comedy was intended as a mockery of sophistry only and that the figure of Socrates was used in an intentionally ironic fashion. The outcome seems to be nothing other than the following: *logos* has enormous power to mislead.

However, this conclusion flies in the face of the hilarity and laughter that surround the performance of the comedy. The laughter of the spectators bears witness to their grasp of the exaggerated distortions presented in the comedy, in this case to their consciousness of the ridiculousness of comic-Socratic discourse and the (apparently) inept Strepsiadian response. In other words, their laughter testifies not nearly so much to the power of *logos* to persuade as it testifies to the transparency of false and misleading *logos*.

One can surely point to examples of the supposed power of *logos* to mislead. There are the dark examples in recent history, such as Hitler's ability to rally Germany to the Nazi cause. There are such frivolous examples as the ability of beer advertisers to draw sharp distinctions between quite similar brands, and of cosmetics advertisers to convince women that a good appearance involves looking younger, and requires many products to do so. But do these examples truly bear witness to the power of *logos* to mislead? Or are they not rather instances in which there is awareness of some *need* or weakness, large or small, in another human being, or group, or in a state, and fashions a *logos* in accord with that need. A nation that is confident of itself will not fall victim to the eloquence of a vicious tyrant, just as an intelligent man or woman understands the function of the advertisements—whether they yield to their persuasion or not.

The point is that by itself, *logos* takes its measure *from what is spoken about,* and *from the context in which it is spoken.* The Dionysian performance provides both a vicarious sighting and a context in which *logos* can be measured. The comic situation, which is clearly preposterous, enables the spectators to exercise both their insight into this measure and their enjoyment at its presentation within this measure. Its obvious excess *announces* this measure. In terms of the way it leads the soul (its *psuchagōgia*), *logos* can lead wisely or mislead only when the context of need (or vulnerability) in which it occurs is well understood. Thus, its measure is found elsewhere than in itself. Once need, weakness, object, and context are bracketed, either in thought or in deed, *logoi* can be evaluated in terms of their truth and goodness, or their lack thereof. As we will see, *logos* can reveal—just as it can conceal—only so much and no more.

LINES 518–626

The next section, which seems to occur as a structural necessity and as an interruption of the dialogue between Socrates and Strepsiades, may appear to contradict the claim briefly argued above, concerning laughter and hilarity. This section, included as a revision in the newer edition and perhaps never performed, seems to indicate Aristophanes' frustration and disgust with both his audience and his judges for giving *Clouds* only third prize when it was initially performed. As I hope to show in what follows, this Choral Interlude must have its language and its chief *logoi* interpreted no differently than any other language and *logoi* in the comedy to which and in which it belongs.

First of all, I disagree strongly with those who hold that the long speech of the Chorus Leader (KORUPHAIA) presents Aristophanes' direct reproach to his audience for giving *Clouds* only third prize at its first staging, his losing to two "vulgar men" (*andrōn phortikōn*), and blaming the "sophisticated" (*sophōtat'*) ones for this poor showing. We do not have complete texts of the plays that received first and second prizes.[34] But while less than certain, another conclusion can be drawn that is more than merely speculative—and clearly better than the conventional wisdom.

The first premise for my conclusion is that nothing said in the context of Aristophanes' comedy ought to be interpreted as anything other than comic![35] The second premise concerns Aristophanes' appeal for a better judgment this time around: he is certainly aware that there can be no worse way to court votes than to insult his audience, more particularly to call one segment "vulgar" and to accuse the other of exercising "vulgar" insight. Thirdly, as to content at least, it is difficult to imagine that any of his competitors could be any coarser than Aristophanes. Consider just a few of the juxtapositions thus far: an oblique one at lines 177–179 likening Socratic food-gathering to stealing a jacket from a passive homosexual;[36] rain is likened to Zeus pissing through a sieve; Zeus' thundering is likened to farting; and Zeus' thunderbolt is likened to exploding sausage and defecation. Recall also our earlier discussion of the quite careful distinction of farting and defecation in the determination of hubris and excess. In this light, Aristophanes' calling this comedy "decent" (*sōphrōn*) is hilarious in itself.[37]

My conclusion is rather that *Clouds* is a *Socratic play in the Platonic sense*! Nietzsche writes, "I know of nothing that has allowed me to dream of *Plato's* secrecy and sphinx nature than that happily preserved little fact: that under the pillow of his deathbed there was found no 'Bible,' nor anything Egyptian, Pythagorean and Platonic,—but rather Aristophanes. How could even Plato have endured life—a Greek life to which he said 'No'—without an Aristophanes!—?"[38]

I contend that in this light, the friendship between Socrates and Aristophanes was—as represented in the *Symposium* and elsewhere—*at the time of the performance of Clouds,* a most genuine one. As Gilbert Murray has argued, "the whole trouble and danger came from a change in atmosphere, in 423 [BCE] were jokes. In 399," i.e., at the time of Socrates' trial, "they were not jokes at all."[39] Thus, the playful/serious harmlessness of *Clouds* in 399 BCE could be employed as dangerous evidence ("old accusations") at the prosecution of Socrates.

In the speech from lines 518–562, Aristophanes is not throwing the sophisticates together with "the many" (*hoi polloi*) in order either to bash them or to court their votes. Instead, he is throwing them all together much as Socrates placed the statesmen, poets, and artisans together in the *Apology:* the members of all three groups proved to be alike in that all professed a wisdom that they did not have. What Plato essayed in philosophy, Aristophanes attempted a short time earlier in poetry. His lines are musical, calling out to one and all, in their poetical way, to attempt to discern the seriousness that sits at the heart of all worthy play.

More fundamentally, as the activity of Socrates and the dialogues of Plato were designed to provoke the kind of self-reflection belonging to an examined life and the recognition of ignorance that belongs to it, the comedy of Aristophanes—at least *this* one, as I have been at pains to show (though I believe it holds for the others as well)—is designed to provoke similar self-reflection, by means of laughter-producing images rather than by means of questioning (and through consideration of philosophical images such as the sun, the divided line, and the cave). Far from precluding reflection, the often puzzling and always all-too-human behavior of its comic figures makes possible a kind of vicarious participation that can lead to conclusions regarding one's own essentially comic traits. Just as in the Platonic dialogues Socrates invites his interlocutors to join him in the questioning, Aristophanes in his long poetic *logos* invites his audience not merely to judge him worthily, but to "take pleasure in me and my creations": *emoi kai toisin emois euphrainēsth' heurēmasin* (562).

To those who might have been offended by the portrait of Socrates (it has been reported that Socrates was present, and was not offended at all), *Clouds* is a call to recognize the image precisely *as* a caricature and as false to his nature in every way. To those who have forgotten the real importance of the Dionysian festival as a celebration of the life forces of nature, including those of human nature, *Clouds* serves as a reminder. The recognition of human limits is built into *Clouds* as an integral part of that celebration.

Like Socrates and Plato, Aristophanes here *challenges* those who come in contact with his work and in so doing *selects* them in a sense. There are no pre-given classes called "the excellent ones" (*hoi aristoi*) and "the many" (*hoi polloi*). As in Plato's *Apology*, the term *hoi polloi* refers to all of those who are incapable of unbiased judgment, regardless of social class. Indeed, Socrates' prophecy to his condemners, that they will not escape future consequences for their injustice, can be seen as a reverse mirror-image of the final line of the Chorus Leader at 563: "[but if you take pleasure in me and my creations] you will be respected in ages to come for your good sense": *eis tas hōras tas heteras eu phronein dokēsete.*

Following this lengthy *logos,* the Chorus of Clouds invites the supposedly nonexistent "highguardian of the gods" and "great chieftain Zeus" (*Zēna turannon*), "first of all" (*prōta*) (565), to their dance, and follows this with an invitation to the equally nonexistent Poseidon. After appealing in their song to Aether and Sun, two natural beings, one can only say that the Clouds have clouded the atmosphere such that orientation remains either difficult or impossible and absurd: either there are no gods or there are, and the Clouds are the true ones—but both contradictory claims are affirmed in their song of Aether and Sun.

The Chorus Leader reappears, speaking as the voice of the unappreciated Clouds, who have done so well by Athens.[40] The Chorus and its Leader close this section by recollecting both particular goods with which it has blessed the Athenians, and some of the consequences of the Athenians' folly. Of particular interest here is the Clouds' song of "the Moon" (Henderson's interesting translation of *Selēnē*). *Selēnē* broaches both the divine and the natural regions. She is first of all a goddess, descended from the Titans Hyperion and Theia. However, she at once shines down on the earth, conferring benefits—as the Clouds remind—"not with mere talk but with plain action (*ou logois all' emphanōs*): first of all, she saves you at least a drachma per month in torches" (612–613).

Such crossing of the highest with the most common and earthly is a recurring theme of the comedy, and the source of both its seriousness and its hilarity, or rather its hilarious seriousness: its ridiculous thoughtfulness. We human beings find ourselves located between a dimly discernible realm beyond us and an all-too-earthbound realm around us. Our orientation occurs in this *mixed realm,* where "above" and "below" are both accessible and withheld. By this I intend several interrelated features: (1) that we attempt to bring together "principles" as guides to actions and the actions we perform; (2) that we attempt with our finite intellect to discern the best life (here I agree with *Republic* 505d5–9 that all people want the "real good," although the way of their—our!—pursuit might well lead them astray); and (3) that we attempt to deal with our fear, whether this fear be of something short term (e.g., impending personal rejection, financial difficulty somewhat in the manner of Strepsiades), damage to one's place in society (e.g., bad reputation), fear of bad character (e.g., doing injustice, a fear that Socrates called worthy in the *Apology*), or the ultimate fear to which we are all in some sense subject, namely, fear of death.

In every case, we find ourselves without sure guidance either from what lies at our feet or from what is beyond us. The Dionysian festival, which we are privileged to visit particularly through the remaining texts of the plays that were performed there, announces that this condition of ignorance *calls for no lament.* As the tragedies of Aeschylus and Sophocles allow us to contemplate the precariousness of human fortune, the comedies of Aristophanes allow us to take vicarious pleasure in and to contemplate the folly to which we are all given over. Both belong to *our* condition, the human condition, and the necessarily foolish side of our nature is celebrated uniquely and best of all in Aristophanes.

LINES 627–812

The scene opens with a thoroughly frustrated Socrates invoking "Respiration," "Air," and "Chaos" as he lambasts the rusticity, stupidity, and weak memory of Strepsiades. Indeed, Strepsiades seems to find the subtlety of Socratic questioning far beyond his ability to answer or even keep up with. Once again, however, a more careful reading reveals the seriousness at the heart of this hilarious play.

All along the first part of this section, Socrates calls for the elements that will presumably develop later in the presentation of impressive *logoi.* These elements, like those discussed in *Republic* books 3 and 4, concern *mousikē,* music, what we would today call a "cultural" or "fine arts" subject. Strepsiades, of course, has no interest in such pursuits, and the poet gives us very strong evidence that this immediate lack of interest has its justification (633): his bed in the *phrontistērion* is riddled with bedbugs (*hoi koreis*)! The confounding of words by Strepsiades that first occurred in the "Socratic Dialogue" before the Choral Interlude both sharpens in wit and increases in philosophical significance here. On measure (*metron*): "The other day a corn dealer shorted me out of two quarts" (639–640). The most beautiful measure, three-measure or four-measure? "I say nothing beats the gallon" (643). When Socrates calls this answer nonsense, Strepsiades offers to bet him that a gallon is indeed a four measure.

In addition to the nonsensical Platonic dialogue that preceded the Choral Interlude, this section recalls the central matters first taken up in lines 126–214. There, Strepsiades sought the "applied logic" that would enable him to escape his debts in court, but instead found preposterous arguments from Socrates' students such as the one concerning whether gnats hum through their mouths or through their anuses. These arguments had the character of "pure knowledge" or "knowledge for its own sake," however ridiculous they were. The treatment of *phrontistērion*-geometry, which dealt not with "land for settlers" but only "land in general" so far as the students were concerned, suggested a meeting of "pure" and "practical." Pure geometry was seen there as the silent presupposition of many other arts.

Here, Socrates' treatment of "pure music" and its beauty bears resemblance to pure geometry and its capacity to measure space. Knowledge of musical measures would surely be helpful for persuasive *logos*—especially to temper the liberated bombast of Strepsiades, which would not serve him well in a courtroom. Some knowledge of rhythms would also serve, such as the rhythm "shaped by the finger" (i.e., dactylic, *daktulon*—line 651), as Socrates says. Strepsiades gives Socrates his middle finger in response, and the latter asks in complete exasperation, *ti dai*? "What *do* you want?" (657). His answer: "That one, the most unjust argument (*ton adikōtaton*)" (658). Socrates tells him that there are other things he must learn before getting to that argument.

There are several matters in this exchange that are worthy of note. First, unlike people driven solely by greed and a sense of their right to attain and avoid whatever they can and by any means, Strepsiades *knows* that the argument he seeks is unjust, indeed most unjust of all. Also, in a manner akin to the now popular "case study" method in applied ethics courses—a method that often yields opinions already held but which become buttressed by the language of more or less "erudite" philosophical language, a.k.a., sophistry—he does need at least *some* exposure to that presupposed knowledge (here of the elements of pure music) in order to make him a more effective speaker and sophist. So at least in this one aspect Socrates plays a role similar to the one he plays in the Platonic dialogues. To be sure, invective replaces irony, and effective *logos* at least *seems* to replace *logos* aimed at truth and goodness. But in turning attention toward pure matters, this is a Socrates we can recognize from the Platonic dialogues, even if "what is best" (*ō Beltistē*) is replaced here by "boorish . . . and stupid" (*agroikos . . . kai dusmathēs*) (646).

Finally, the discussion of measures (*metron*) raises the issue driving this entire interpretation. Socrates speaks of musical measures, asking Strepsiades which of the two measures, the trimeasure or trimeter (*trimetron*) or the four-measure (*tetrametron*), he considers more beautiful (*kalliston*). His aged student answers that to him nothing beats a gallon, and challenges Socrates to a bet that a gallon isn't a tetrameter (i.e., a four-measure). The comic confounding of a musical measure with a liquid measure takes place in a *logos* lacking proper measure entirely. Yet the recognition by spectators and readers of this lack obliquely acknowledges that indeed *logos* within proper measure is possible, and foreshadows the end of the comedy, where measure moves explicitly to the forefront.[41]

Lines 658–693 seem to concentrate on the parsing of obscure matters of the genders of words in a manner that holds Socrates' teacher Prodicus up to ridicule. This material, Socrates claims, belongs to Strepsiades' preparatory education toward his "ascent" to the most unjust *logos.* Though these distinctions seem (and are) often very foolish, they address two matters of importance for *logos* as it has been developing throughout the play. First of all, taking Strepsiades through this exercise does seem designed to alert him to the possibilities of using "fine" distinctions in grammar to mislead someone. It is also worthy of note that Strepsiades' irony suggests that, at bottom, he is not misled at all. For example, when Socrates makes the distinction between "fowl-ess" (*alektruainan,* female fowl: the word is an Aristophanic neologism) and "fowl" (*alektora,* referring to both male and female, but here restricted by Socrates to the male), Strepsiades sarcastically replies: "Fowl-ess? By Air that's good" (666–667).

However, the central matter of "pure" and "applied" *logos* is once again at play in these lines. Socrates speaks as though *linguistic* gender can be directly imported into *actual* determinations of gender. For example, the name "Amynias" is the name of a man, but when one calls out to this man, one will call "Amynia." The vocative case gives the name a feminine shape (mocked by Strepsiades as appropriate, on account of Amynias' supposed reluctance to go to battle). A similar exercise is performed on the word for "kneading-trough" (*hē kardopos*). When Strepsiades asks Socrates about the particular point of his learning these grammatical matters since everyone knows them, Socrates replies: "None at all, by god": *ouden ma Di'* (693).

There is, then, a break between the Greek language and that about which it must speak. This break, presented comically in these lines as (in some instances) a break between the gender of words and the gender of the human beings about which they speak, bespeaks a greater and more fundamental break between *logos* and its subject matter. Into this break enter sophists and philosophers alike. Even Socrates' comic swearing to the uselessness of these distinctions, "by god," indicates such a break: later in

Clouds, Strepsiades will demonstrate their "usefulness" by employing such a sophistical stratagem to fend off one of his creditors successfully.

How strange this entire exchange is! Strepsiades is fully aware of the bogus nature of Socrates' manipulations. That is to say, he is aware that they are fundamentally *unjust* in a way that, it appears, Socrates is thoroughly unaware. The discipline and the hardship are undergone by Strepsiades not because he cannot discern injustice, but only because he thinks it is the only avenue that is available to him for his survival. But by virtue of the conscious decision to preserve himself in this way, he has no awareness of its costs.

The aforementioned bedbugs take center stage, so to speak, for the next part of this dialogical section. Just as a breach occurs from above, that is to say from the gap between pure *logos* and *logos* applied to life in the city, another breach occurs from below, between excessively earthbound matters and genuine *logos.* Before he exits, Socrates has Strepsiades recline on his bed in order to do his own thing, but the old man's first "thought" is "Ouch! Ouch!" (*attatai attatai*), which is hardly a thought at all. When the Chorus of Clouds asks him what the matter is, Strepsiades screams that the bedbugs are chomping on his flesh, his testicles, and his anus (in far less decorous terms), and in so doing are killing him (709–715). What advice does he receive from the Clouds, in whom he has put such trust? Henderson translates (again correctly): "Well, don't make such a fuss about it": *mē nun bareōs algei lian* (716).

However, the Greek admits of another, more philosophical, interpretation: "Now do not place excessive weight upon your suffering." This accords with the earlier expression of tragic pain (*attatai attatai*), and provides a more serious edge to the comedy of the Clouds' casually brushing off the distress of their charge. As Socrates has said in the *Phaedo,* the trust of the pleasures and pains of the body causes the soul to suffer "the greatest and most extreme evil" (83c2–3), namely the belief that the object that causes these pleasures and pains "is most distinct of all and most true of all" (83c7–8). This belief cements that same bondage to the body that works against the strongest *logos*[42] as the measure of truth (83d4ff.). The most remarkable feature of this bondage is that, in significant measure, it is freely chosen: "and philosophy sees (*katidousa*) that the most dreadful (*deinotēta*) thing about the imprisonment is that it occurs through desire (*epithumias*), so that the prisoner himself is the chief assistant (*xullēptōr*) in his own imprisonment" (82e5–83a2).

Of course, Strepsiades' course of life was freely altered by his decision to enter the *phrontistērion.* He entered in order to learn how to do what he knew to be unjust, but he is receiving an odd, comically presented kind of philosophical education. Neither exposure to the purest "erudition" from above nor exposure to the most "earthy" provocations from below have proven helpful to his quest—in this case for the most unjust *logos.* One might say that in one very important sense, Strepsiades has indeed undergone genuine Socratic education: he has been brought before his ignorance, and no longer thinks that he knows anything worth knowing.

Upon returning to Strepsiades on the bed, Socrates asks him what he has (*ekheis ti?*), and his pupil can answer: "Nothing other than my cock in my right hand": *ouden ge plēn ē to peos en tē dekhia* (734). In addition to being a delightful play on Socrates' "have," his penis is the only place the bedbugs had not gotten to in his earlier report. We may read this as Strepsiades' effort to preserve the basic and final essence of his (embodied) manly identity amidst the tribulations he has found himself undergoing. That it is held in his right hand may indicate the "justice" of this comic attempt at self-preservation.

Socrates then "encourages" Strepsiades to think for himself, to let ideas and problems flow and to "rightly sort and investigate them": *orthōs diairōn kai skopōn* (742). On one level, Strepsiades fails utterly. The schemes he devises to evade his payments are nonsensical: buying a Thessalian witch to hide the moon for him in a mirror, thus forestalling any dawns of new and (due) days; holding a glass stone under the sun so that the stone's heat would melt the lawsuit papers; finally (if he has a lack of witnesses), hanging himself. A thoroughtly disgusted Socrates berates him and turns his back on him. One of the epithets he hurls at Strepsiades is *skaiotaton,* "most moronic" as Henderson correctly has it, or "most crude." However, the word also has overtones of "most left-handed," which contrasts markedly with Strepsiades' able use of his right hand as noted above. Perhaps again, Aristophanes is subtly showing an abiding hidden strength of his remarkable hero.

With Socrates refusing to interact with Strepsiades any longer, the Chorus Leader advises him to exercise his paternal prerogative—"if you have raised a son (*ei soi tis huios estin ektethrammenos*) send him to learn in your place" (795–796)—and to do so whether his son wants to attend or not. Strepsiades agrees, and the Chorus of Clouds sings to Strepsiades that he will soon get "a great many rewards / from us of the / gods alone": *pleista di' ē / mas agath' autikh' exōn / monas theōn* (805–807). As Socrates enters the *phrontistērion,* he remarks that this sort of business "has a way of taking / unexpected turns": *philei gar pōs ta toi- / auth hetera trepesthai* (811–812). One could also translate this passage as reading that a matter such as this "likes to turn otherwise," taking *hetera* as "other" and perhaps as "other in kind." The sentence pointedly does not specify for whom, in what way, or to what effect. Regarding the future, it foreshadows nothing but our ignorance regarding it.

There may be, however, a specific and deeply concealed foreshadowing if, once again, the *logoi* are attended to with care. The rearing of the son is at least obliquely attributed to *Strepsiades* (*soi*). (Henderson just has "grown-up," which is accurate but perhaps omits the overtones of *ektethrammenos* [795], that imply being reared from childhood.) Recall that Strepsiades has had virtually no impact on the shaping of his son's character, which has taken on the traits of his aristocratic wife and seeks refuge from his misdeeds in the protection of his wealthy uncle Megacles. Strepsiades' speaking of his son as having, in addition to his inherited physical strength, nobility and goodness (*kalos te kagathos*) (797), surely refers to his wife's lineage and not his own.

However, *genuine* nobility and goodness are at stake in this Aristophanic comedy of Socrates, just as they are in the Platonic dialogues of Socrates. In the *Meno,* Plato's Socrates demonstrates irrefutably that inheritance has nothing to do with genuine virtue. With no difficulty, he leads the self-important Meno and Anytus to admit that men whom they all agreed were virtuous had sons that fell far short of their virtue, despite the care that these fathers would surely have taken in rearing their sons. In Anytus' case, this encounter may have proven fateful: Anytus seemed to clearly suppose that Socrates implicitly grouped him with the unworthy sons of virtuous fathers, and later became one of his principal accusers.

LINES 813–867

The reentry of Pheidippides and the exchange between father and son provide an enactment of the breakdown in *logos* between them that was treated in the reflections of the opening sections of *Clouds.* After the goading of the Clouds, Strepsiades attempts to control his son by means of threats and insults. ("By fog, you're not going to stay in this house a moment longer!"—*outoi ma tēn Homikhlēn et entauthoi meneis* [814]; "stupid"—*mōrias* [818]; "get a move on and take my place at school"—*all ōs takhist' elthōn huper emou manthane* [839]; "you'll find out how ignorant and thick you really are"—*gnōsei de sauton hōs amathēs ei kai pakhus* [842].) In response, Pheidippides calls his father "crazy" in four different ways ("not of sound mind"—*ouk eu phroneis* [817]; "mad"—*maniōn* [833, 846]; "off his rocker" —*paraphronountos* [844]; "deranged"—*paranoias* [845]).

Once again, this direct and coarsely distorted caricature of Socratic dialogue possesses nuances that reveal themselves upon close attention. On its surface, Strepsiades presents as vivid a picture of inept fathering as one could envision, and Pheidippides continues disrespecting his father's wishes. However, this section shows that Strepsiades has plunged even further into his desperation. His sophistical ability is pitifully incompetent. To demonstrate the value of his learning at the *phrontistērion,* he presents the aforementioned ridiculous example of calling a male fowl "fowl" (*alektora*) and a female fowl "fowl-ess" (*alektruainan*). Aware of his incompetence (he lost both his cloak and his shoes to the *phrontistērion*), he needs Pheidippides to learn the art of making the weaker *logos* appear stronger in order to escape the debts incurred by the latter. At this point, desperation has all but entirely obscured the question of the justice of this goal.

This reenactment of the earlier breakdown in *logos* takes the following textual form: within this exchange between father and son, there is no occurrence of the word *logos* at all. In both senses of the phrase, then, the exchange is an *alogia logos,* both an "irrational" talk and a *logos* in which "*logos*" is absent. The comic *logos* in which this *alogia logos* appears, then, in its own inimitable way exposes the way of genuine Platonic argument in the *Meno* in an analogical fashion: if there is neither direct refutation nor some point of agreement from which the interlocutors can begin, nothing of value can come forth.

In this case, a thoroughly frustrated Strepsiades turns the education of his son, against the latter's will, over to Socrates. Their relationship mocks the aforementioned mutually respectful one required for progress. Pheidippides tells his father, "You'll come to regret this in time" (865), indicating not a shred of compassion nor a trace of responsibility for his father's plight. Where Strepsiades has shown a keen sense that *logos* can be enlisted on the side of both justice and injustice, and opts for the "unjust" *logos* only out of extreme anxiety, his son has no care for *logos* at all. Wealth and indulgence have relieved him of the need for it. This stripping of the need for *logos* has not only contributed to Pheidippides' obnoxiousness. It has robbed him of his humanity as well.

LINES 867–1130

After a similarly disrespectful exchange between Pheidippides and Socrates, Strepsiades pleads with Socrates to see to it that Pheidippides "learns that pair of *logoi,* the stronger, whatever that may be, and the weaker, the one that argues the unjust and overturns the stronger. And if not both, at least teach him the unjust" (882–885). It seems clear to me that, despite the practice of many able translators, it is very important especially on philosophical grounds to call the *logoi* "Stronger" and "Weaker."

Many translators of Aristophanes choose to render *kreitton* and *hētton* in terms that are not literal: "better" and "worse" (Henderson); "right" and "wrong" (Dover and Hadas); "just" and "unjust" (the Avon Text edited by Teitel); "Unfair" and "Fair" (Webb); and even "philosophical" and "sophistical" (Arrowsmith). But for the sake of understanding the philosophical depth of Aristophanes' text, the literal rendering is clearly best. For example, in the above passage, it is clear that Strepsiades equates the "stronger" with the "just" (or "right") and the "weaker" with the "unjust" (or "wrong"), a crucial philosophical equation and distinction, as well as a wonderful comic effect. This becomes clear when a personified Weaker *Logos* does not argue that his position is just, but only that he can defeat its personified counterpart, Stronger *Logos*. Thus Weaker *Logos* is indeed—and ridiculously—the stronger *logos,* but Weaker *Logos* never suggests that it is the just *logos.*

Although Socrates has agreed to teach Strepsiades, he has Pheidippides taught by "the arguments themselves" (*autoin toin logoin*) (886) and absents himself (887). Socrates does not reappear until the closing moments (1502–1509). Before venturing into the contest (*agōn*), these two matters are worthy of note: (1) Weaker *Logos* and the comic Socrates are not identical. We can conclude this confidently both because of Socrates' absence, and because these "*logoi* themselves" are unlike any of the ones encountered earlier by Strepsiades in the *phrontistērion,* at least with regard to their subject matter. The earlier ones concerned such matters as entomology, astronomy, geometry, grammar, and linguistics. Here, the *logoi* concern themselves with sexual matters and their place in a social context. (2) Stronger *Logos* is helpless in the face of the sophistical "Socratic linguistics" treated earlier (658–694), but Weaker *Logos* shows himself to be quite skilled at this subject. This skill proves to be important to understanding the outcome of the *agōn.*

Clouds seems to crown Weaker *Logos* with an undisputable victory. After all, Stronger *Logos* capitulates to and even joins Weaker *Logos.* But just as Weaker *Logos* shows himself to be "stronger in *logos,*" the following must be noted: by *acknowledging* his inability to offer a stronger argument, Stronger *Logos* gives evidence of his superior strength according to another measure. This strength is an analogue to the Socratic practice that runs through the Platonic dialogues, according to which one must defer to a superior *logos,* as Socrates himself does in the *Parmenides*[43] and as he invites his interlocutors, both friendly and unfriendly, to join him in this practice.

Also, the presentation of Stronger *Logos* is itself ridiculous. As we shall see, it is hardly less lascivious, and in a sense even more so, than the presentation of Weaker *Logos.* Aristophanes has his entire comic and philosophical gifts at work in this splendid section. I will try to exhibit a small portion of them in what follows.

Weaker *Logos* does not claim greater wisdom, but only that it can defeat Stronger *Logos* "before a crowd," or more literally "before the many" (*en tois polloisi*) (891). It will do so "by inventing novel ideas" (896), which Stronger *Logos* acknowledges is in fashion "due to these idiots" (*anoētous*—the ones lacking intellect), gesturing to the spectators. These spectators are immediately called "wise" (*sophous*) by Weaker *Logos.* Stronger *Logos* claims it will win by "arguing justice" (*ta dikaia legōn*) (900). These following lines are similar to those of Plato's *Apology,* although they predate it historically. This suggests that Aristophanes was acutely aware of contemporary Socratic practice, and even of the vulnerability to which this practice might subject him.

The *Apology* is characterized by Socrates' reversal of the normal juridical procedure: although he is the formal defendant, as Sallis notes "he places Athens itself on trial."[44] He calls his jury not "judges," as was customary, but "men of Athens." He refers to his opponents and their supporters, for whom he shows little respect, as *hoi polloi.* Justice is his sole concern, not victory. In the *Republic,* he goes so far as to say "a multitude is incapable of being philosophical" (494a4). Although in this very same *Apology,* Socrates seems to ascribe responsibility to Aristophanes as an important source of the "old" accusations, this contempt for *hoi polloi* and this unwillingness to flatter his audience are practices that run through the Platonic dialogues as a whole. Further, this is not the *comic Socrates* articulating the Stronger *Logos.* That Socrates is absent! At the outset of the *agōn,* Stronger *Logos* reflects the practice of the genuine Platonic Socrates only to this extent, that he insists only upon seeking the just.

The first exchange results from Weaker *Logos*' denial that there is Justice (*Dikēn*), and on Stronger *Logos*' counterclaim that justice is with the gods. What follows is either a frivolous interlude, a misreading of the Socratic understanding of *muthos* or, as I strongly suggest, a brilliant comic reenactment of it. Weaker *Logos* wants to know: "If that's where Justice is, then how come Zeus hasn't been destroyed for chaining up his own father?" (904–906). Stronger *Logos* replies, "Ugh (*aiboi*), this vileness is going too far. Give me a puke pan!" (905–906). Interestingly, Stronger *Logos* both (1) respects the inspiration of the myth, and (2) honors what the myth shows. (1) The goddess *Dikē* is born of the union of Zeus and Themis. Thus, if there were no Zeus, there could be no *Dikē.* In terms of the myth, it is impossible for *Dikē* to destroy her father before she is born. (2) In terms of the more "earthbound" sense of justice upon which Weaker *Logos* plays, there can be no justice in any sense until order (represented by Zeus) overtakes the murderous chaos of his father's reign.[45] Both of these, however, are insights requiring some subtlety, some grasp of the interpretation of *muthos,* and some ability to discern the hidden premises of certain arguments.

The response of Stronger *Logos,* despite or perhaps even because of its rhetorical zeal, is appropriate. Weaker *Logos* has manipulated the *muthos* in a manner that disrespects both its origin and its wisdom. Further, it employs the very notion it would deny in that it accuses (however inappropriately) the gods of injustice for not punishing Zeus, an accusation that would be meaningless unless justice exists. A most revealing exchange of verbal insults occurs in lines 906–931. As Stronger *Logos* grows angrier and angrier and rains down insults upon the head of Weaker *Logos,* Weaker *Logos* ever more calmly receives them as compliments.

The effect, at least the superficial effect, upon a group of spectators experiencing such a debate is likely to be that one of the disputants is in control of himself—rational, measured, calm—while the other has lost his bearings. However, to one who can discern, an outrageous pronouncement calls for an outraged response. Such a furious response to reckless misrepresentation is an appropriately *measured* response, while calm confidence in the carelessly false declaration of matters that most affect human life is clearly unmeasured. Once again, I suggest an advance echo of the *Apology,* where the very challenging presentation of Socrates proved to fall short in convincing his jurors.

At line 932 the Chorus Leader intervenes, successfully urging the disputants each to give a presentation, with Pheidippides to choose his educator. Cleverly, Weaker *Logos* proposes that Stronger *Logos* go first. His plan, far from being the display of superior wisdom, is to "sting his whole face and eyes with debating points like hornets, and so [he will] perish" (946–949). If it is a contest of mere persuasion, it is a great advantage to be the final speaker, especially if one is without shame when it comes to distorting the *logoi* of one's opponent. After this order is tacitly agreed upon (and will be followed), the Chorus of Clouds then proclaims that Stronger and Weaker *Logos* will use all of their talents to see "which of them, by what he says (*legōn*) will reveal himself the better man" (953–954). The text allows for an alternate translation: "which *appears* (*phanēsetai*) better." Since the entire matter turns upon persuasion of an uneducated hearer, rather than upon genuine superiority, this rendering of *phanēsetai* seems to cohere much better with Aristophanes' text.

At line 958, the Clouds announce the debate as a contest for wisdom, "the greatest *agōn*" (957). To say it mildly, neither of the competing *Logoi* have much to offer in the way of wisdom.[46] Stronger *Logos* offers justice (*ta dikaia*) and moderation[47] (*sōphrosunē*) as the foundation of the old (*arkhaian*) education, but in his account these two qualities make themselves manifest primarily, if not exclusively, in (1) obedience to one's elders, and (2) customs of modesty, and especially in refraining from sexual displays that might cause unwholesome desires to awaken in one's elders as well as in oneself. The fruit of such an education, Stronger *Logos* argues, is victory in military combat and comfort in old age. There is not a word about the improvement of one's soul in any sense, no reasoning whatsoever as to why such a life might be preferable to the newer, less austere one.

Still further, the text suggests that on stage Stronger *Logos* is arousing *himself* sexually by speaking of the "parted thighs" (964–965) of the boys marching naked through the street following the music master, of their "crossed thighs so as not to reveal anything to torment their onlookers," and their mindfulness in "smooth[ing] the sand and tak[ing] care not to leave behind an image of their pubescence for their lovers to find." Thus, to a spirited and unruly young man, Stronger *Logos* offers not only a *logos* that in both form and content does not fit with Pheidippides' soul, but also displays by his actions that this education in justice and moderation did not fully "take" in the soul of Stronger *Logos*.[48] The result, once again, is ridiculous.

However, if we consider the comic reversal, we recall that justice, moderation, and modesty are not qualities that are easily won. These qualities often require much effort and struggle, and are surely worth acquiring. In this light, the comic *agōn* of Stronger *Logos* with his baser and quite human desires deserves respect. The laughter that this ridiculous figure inspires in the spectators is at once an acknowledgement of his ridiculousness, and an acknowledgement of the ridiculousness that belongs to all of us in our struggle toward the best life.[49] In Aristophanes, the most severe ridicule and laughter is united with the greatest respect and honor.

However, Stronger *Logos*' demonstration is easy pickings for Weaker *Logos*, who explains that he has earned the name among the "educated ones" (*phrontistaisin*)[50] since he "pioneered the idea of arguing what's contrary to established ideas of custom and justice" (1038–1040). (This apparently casual claim will prove significant in the conclusion of this chapter.) His direct appeal to Pheidippides, however, has nothing to do with the intrinsic value of his new style of argumentation. He turns directly to the boy, saying, "And it will repay you more money than you can count, this ability to adopt the *weaker* arguments (*tous hēttonas logous*) and yet win" (1041–1042). He begins by giving two specious arguments similar to his earlier ones. The first confounds the mythical realm and the human realm, arguing for Heracles and his association with warm baths. In so doing, he refutes Stronger *Logos*' recommendation of cold baths (1047–1050). Weaker *Logos* plays on an equivocation on the word "agora." Weaker *Logos* employs it as Nestor used it in the Homeric epics, where it had the meaning of "public assembly."

Before proceeding to the heart of Weaker *Logos*' case, it is once again important to remember that Stronger *Logos* clearly does not speak for the genuine Socrates, and not only because the genuine Socrates had no difficulty controlling his sensual lust regarding wine or boys. The genuine Platonic Socrates *loved* the agora, hardly ever wishing to leave it. Further, as a lover of *logos*, he always maintained that he preferred "question and answer" to lengthy speeches like those to which Stronger *Logos* agreed in

Clouds. This is another important effect of the absence of even the comic Socrates from this scene. The comic Socrates, as the antipode of the genuine Socrates, also works by questioning and answering instead of long speeches, in accord with the ridiculous thoughtfulness ascribed to him by the gifted Aristophanes.

Weaker *Logos* then condemns as "very bad" (*kakō megistō*) both the idea that the young should be silent, and that they should be moderate, challenging Stronger *Logos* with the question: "have you ever seen anyone get anything good by being moderate?": *epei su dia to sōphronein tō pōpot' eides ēdē agathon ti genomenon*? (1061–1062). Once again, the appeal is crassly utilitarian, and clearly effective upon a boy who is already predisposed toward selfishness. What is striking is the inability of Stronger *Logos* to withstand this attack, and it is an issue worth considering more closely.

Recall the education the comic Socrates earlier provided, or attempted to provide, to Strepsiades. It consisted of a number of ludicrous but clever musical, linguistic, and (dare one say) philosophical moves preparatory to the mastery of courtroom rhetoric. At line 658, Socrates told him "there are other things you must learn before [learning the most unjust *logos*]." At 740–745, Socrates instructed him to release his thinking so as to treat the problem systematically and, if one of his ideas comes to a dead end, to start over and bring the earlier idea in later, as appropriate. Here is a clear case of the comic Socrates as the reverse of the genuine Platonic Socrates: the pedagogical methodology is generally the same, although the comic material resembles a reverse amusement park mirror of the genuine.

After giving two more specious arguments, Weaker *Logos* succeeds in having Stronger *Logos* both capitulate and join with his conqueror. The more blatant of the two specious arguments is the refutation of Stronger *Logos*' example of moderation, claiming that this quality enabled Peleus, a mortal, to wed Thetis, a goddess. Weaker *Logos* misstates Thetis' purported abandonment of Peleus (it occurs only in Sophocles' version, not in Homer's or in any other) as caused by the latter's not being a "roughneck (*hubristēs*), and no fun to spend the night with between the sheets" (1068–1069). Properly stated, Thetis left Peleus "as a goddess well might, when he spoke harshly to her."[51]

First of all, the word Henderson translates as "roughneck" also translates as "outrageous one," or "one who transgresses beyond the appropriately human limits." Dover interprets this, Weaker *Logos*' hubris, "as an ideal—naturally, since it is the opposite to moderation."[52] But Weaker *Logos* is all for keeping up appearances of propriety for purposes of gain. Hubris, for him, occurs only within the outer shell of moderation. When caught in an outrageous act, one does not publicly revel in it, but rather one makes excuses for it by appealing to similar behavior of the gods who dwell in another region and act in accord with other practices. Further, Stronger *Logos* is unable to counter even this weak argument from analogy.

Once again, this lack of resource distances Stronger *Logos* definitively from the genuine Platonic Socrates, who has all of Homer committed virtually to memory and who can easily see through the misuse of mythical material (see especially the *Protagoras*). Also, the genuine Socrates was trained by the prominent sophist Prodicus, known for his supreme ability to make sharp distinctions and connections and who, according to Henderson, "pursued interests ranging from natural science to semantics and ethics . . . [and] enjoyed a reputation comparable to Einstein's today."[53] The Platonic Socrates, then, was as far as possible from helpless at *logos.* He was splendidly prepared to meet the arguments of the Sophists, whatever they were, and could argue for justice and moderation more effectively than anyone—just as the comic Socrates could argue ridiculously and could lead an apparently quite successful school in which this sort of argumentation was its selling point.

The *coup de grâce* consists once again of a blurring of a word's connotation in the second and decisive specious argument. The word is *euruprōktos* (rendered by Henderson, mixing literality with a trace of delicacy, as "wide-arsed"). Weaker *Logos* argues that moderation entails the "loss of such pleasures as boys, women, fine food and drink, laughs," without which life would not have value (1072–1074). And if caught with another man's wife, he would appeal to Zeus' inability to control his lust. Stronger *Logos*' last challenge: the right of a cuckolded man to violate his rival with a radish and hot ash that would make his rival unable to argue his way around becoming "wide-assed."

Weaker *Logos* concedes this point, but then speaks in favor of "wide-assedness," noting that prosecutors, politicians, and other prominent men are wide-assed. (However, these have become so by virtue of their sedentary occupations rather than by virtue of their having been punished for being cuckolds.) Stronger *Logos* notes helplessly that most of the spectators are similarly "wide-assed," and so deserts to the side of Weaker *Logos.* Strepsiades entreats Weaker *Logos* to "teach and discipline [Pheidippides] well" (1107), and is assured that his son will emerge from the *phrontistērion* a "handy sophist."

This "greatest *agōn*" has turned out not to be a contest for wisdom, as the Clouds earlier announced, but a contest between one *Logos* who could name justice and moderation but could offer no account in their behalf nor show any concern for being able to give such an account, and another *Logos* who could defeat his inept opponent, but could only affirm an unbridled hedonism under the cover of respectability. Weaker *Logos* asks Strepsiades, "Do you want us to teach him to speak[54] for you?" (1106). This is the precise profession of the Sophists who, like Gorgias, claim only to teach people to speak well.[55] In Weaker *Logos,* then, it can be said that there is little pretense to wisdom—or else wisdom and the power to manipulate and persuade are one and the same.

LINES 1115–1130

The Chorus Leader then turns to the spectators judging the comedies and delivers a most striking *logos* to them. Justice occurs in this parabasis as a direct threat. If you do what is just (*ek tōn dikaiōn*) and support the Clouds, they are told, you will benefit. Fair weather for your crops will come your way. But dishonor us goddesses and we'll destroy your crops and your buildings. Also your festivals will be subject to torrential rain, such that the one who votes against this comedy may wish he were in (arid) Egypt. As we saw earlier, in our treatment of lines 475–516, it is likely that such provocative passages as this would be repugnant to the group that would allot the prizes for the comedies. But once again, it is also likely, and far more plausible, to interpret this *logos* as itself *comic.*

Thus far, we have experienced many different instances of *logos* in *Clouds:* Strepsiades' initial laments, and his plea to his son to enter the *phrontistērion;* Pheidippides' "self-contradictory" refusal; the *phrontistērion* students discoursing on their ridiculous "academic" pursuits; the entry from above, followed by the bombasts of Socrates; the over-the-top poetic entrance of the Clouds; the unequal and hilarious dialogue between the helpless but canny Strepsiades and the exasperated sophistical Socrates; the *agōn* between inept Stronger *Logos* and able Weaker *Logos.* To this point, there has not been one rationally defensible *logos.* Every single one has been ridiculous.

However, there have been glimpses of profound thoughtfulness in all of the above: how desperation can lead one to injustice, and into an ever-downward spiral in its pursuit, such that one only seeks the kind of unjust *logoi* that will further it; how carelessness and riches can lead to an avoidance of *logos* altogether; how the practice of abstruse *logoi* carries with it a danger of forgetting one's bond to the earth; how uncanny the call of the voices of authority (here the Chorus of Clouds) can be, and how easily misinterpreted; how dialogue must seek and secure a common ground; how a contest of *logoi* can take place with one side apparently enjoying a clear victory, but in fact establishing nothing. (Perhaps there is more honor in even the too-hasty concession than in the victory.)

In the comic *logoi* of Aristophanes, and in the comic *logos* that is *Clouds,* one discerns the outlines of genuine *logos* within all of the ridiculousness. Through the immediacy of laughter, the depths of insight shine through brightly.

LINES 1130–1320

Strepsiades spirals further into the abyss of injustice. Instead of viewing his son's education in the Weaker *Logos* as an act of desperation, he revels in it. Instead of showing genuine affection for his son (such affection being the other side of his earlier laments at having little impact on the boy), he positively revels in his new skill at "beating whatever lawsuit (*dikēn*) you like" (1151). With the greatest pleasure, he notes Pheidippides' innocent expression even when he is "guilty, even of a serious crime" (1173–1174). He rejoices when his son teaches him to fool his creditors by playing on the nominal doubleness of the "Old and New Day," which in reality is only one day, pre- and post-moon, designed so that lawsuits could be settled the day before the moon rose and so avoid court proceedings. Strepsiades is so delighted with his son's prowess at *logos* that he berates the spectators for being a gaggle of imbeciles compared to "us wise ones" (1205–1213), and takes Pheidippides into the house from which he previously ejected him and throws a feast (*hestiasai*) in his honor. No such feast was forthcoming when his son refused education or had nothing monetary to offer him.

Two creditors serially enter Strepsiades' house to be paid on Old and New Day. Both creditors are rebuffed by a mixture of specious argumentation and (mostly) by force. Strepsiades unsays his oath to Zeus, to the First Creditor, on the grounds that "back then Pheidippides hadn't yet told me the irrefutable *logos*" (1228–1229), and that "Zeus is a joke among the knowing": *Zeus geloios omnumenos tois eidosin* (1241). After humiliating the First Creditor by rubbing the latter's large belly, Strepsiades challenges the creditor to name correctly the mortar jar he has produced. When the man says *kardopos* (1248), Strepsiades uses the sophistical grammatical dodges he learned much earlier from Socrates (675–679), announces that he would never repay anyone foolish enough to say *kardopos* (masculine) instead of *kardopēn* (feminine), and shoos the creditor away from his door. The Second Creditor, distressed by a recent chariot accident, is also rebuffed with some ludicrous but effective sophisms, and is chased from Strepsiades' house with a goad.

In this section, we seem to be dealing with a Strepsiades reborn. He has no fear whatsoever of his creditors. His memory, earlier denounced as pitifully weak not only by Socrates but also by himself, has suddenly returned. And his *logoi,* such as they are, possess a surprising effectiveness. What is the source of this rebirth? I suggest that the primary source cannot be the *logoi,* which he apparently could have learned earlier, nor any awakening of his powers on their own. Only the newly established bond that he perceives between his previously estranged son and himself can account for this sudden and remarkable burst of confidence.[56]

However, the *logoi* he espouses with such confidence are weaker *logoi*—*logoi* that are in service to injustice. The creditors are treated with the same contempt which Strepsiades had heaped upon the spectators shortly before. As to his addition of force in his meetings with them, might Aristophanes not be hinting that sophistical *logoi* have their own peculiar force, such as the force we saw earlier when Weaker *Logos* succeeded in effecting the capitulation of Stronger *Logos,* who lacked preparation for the former's sophistical onslaught? It is that same exploitation of human weakness spoken of above, toward the end of the treatment of lines 475–516. It seems clear that Strepsiades has taken up the hubris proclaimed by Weaker *Logos* at 1068 with hubris of his own.

But the Clouds now proclaim the trouble that lies ahead. "How momentous it is to lust for villainous business: like this old man, in the grip of this lust": *hoion to pragmatōn eran phlaurōn: ho gar / gerōn hod' erastheis* (1303–1304). They announce that Strepsiades will regret all of his "success": his own training as a sophist (1308–1309), and his son having become so "formidable at arguing positions counter to what is just, so that he can beat anyone he may meet, even if he argues what's totally bad": *einai ton huion deinon hoi / gnōmas enantias legein toisin dikaiois, hōste ni kan hapantas, hoisper an xuggenētai kan legē pamponēr* (1313–1316).

This is the first direct condemnation by the Clouds of Strepsiades' path. As we have seen, they have been presented earlier by Socrates as "goddesses of idle gentlemen," "nourishers of sophists," and as able to shift their shapes into whatever form might be required by circumstance. The Clouds say that they will make Strepsiades a terrific speaker "because you desire nothing great" (433), and in a roundabout way they have made good on their word, since sophistry is nothing great at all. But with this denunciation, we realize that not once have the Clouds referred to themselves as goddesses, nor have they ever denied the existence of Zeus. In his capacity as chief educator in the *phrontistērion,* the comic Socrates has entirely separated Zeus and the Olympian gods from the Clouds. Never once do the Clouds offer a clear statement of approval either of Strepsiades' choice of injustice or of Socrates' *phrontistērion.*

Further, the appeal to the spectators by both the Choral Leader and the Chorus of Clouds had nothing whatsoever to do with the praise of sophistry, and even included an appeal to the Olympians Prometheus (567–568), and Apollo and Artemis, children of Zeus (595–600). In other words, there are hints, traces all along that the Clouds are not what they may at first seem, whether to Socrates or to Strepsiades.

Here, one can see—perhaps through the Clouds—that the choice of sophistry and injustice has unsuspected deleterious consequences, consequences indicated poetically by the dramatic downward spiral of Strepsiades, and what will soon be an even greater downward spiral for the comic Socrates. The Clouds, then, are indeed "cloudy," difficult to read. When one attempts to exploit the cloudiness inherent in many human things, one commits hubris. One thinks one can both see and control that which surpasses the capacity and the right of humans. The punishment for hubris is a visit from Nemesis, the daughters of Night who bring merciless vengeance and ruin. This punishment is how *Clouds* seems to conclude. It will remain for us to treat the question, *ti legeis*? What does this say?

LINES 1321–1451

These lines present the well-known beating of Strepsiades by his son, and the clever, sophistical *logoi* Pheidippides uses in defense of his actions. The section reenacts three of its predecessors: the two heated disputes between father and son (one that occurred at the beginning of the comedy, and the other at 813–867, just before Pheidippides enters the *phrontistērion*), and the *agōn* between Stronger and Weaker *Logos.* As a result of his sophistic education, Pheidippides is more reprehensible than ever. He acts out his disrespect violently, only here with the same calm self-assurance that Weaker *Logos* showed in his demolition of Stronger *Logos,* as if self-control while perpetrating a great injustice serves to make it individually and socially acceptable.

This fight began during the feast Strepsiades had prepared for his son, and concerned the son's refusal to play and sing from the works of Simonides and Aeschylus, and the father's dismissal of the son's preference for Euripides. While clearly Aristophanes in *Clouds* has Euripides representing the "novel" and Simonides and Aeschylus representing the "established," one should not be too quick in reading the author's own preference into this use.[57] On grounds that Strepsiades could not stomach Euripides' *Aeolus,* where "a brother . . . was screwing his sister by the same mother" (1370–1371), and his refusal therefore to ascribe to Euripides the title of *sophōtaton* (very wise) (1378, 1379), the verbal fight begun by the father soon evolves into the physical attacks of the son.

With the recently acquired confidence (inspired by his bond with his son) now broken, Strepsiades is once again powerless not only to repel the son's physical assault upon him, but to offer anything like an effective response in *logos* to his son's outrageous arguments. He can offer only vile curses and deep regrets. He faces the argument that a son can beat his father "out of concern," because the father has beaten his young son for such reason during the latter's childhood. If the son does not himself have a son, this would deprive him of a kind of equal right to beat a family member. At line 1437, Strepsiades capitulates in analogous fashion to Stronger *Logos*' earlier capitulation: "it seems just to me, you gentlemen of my own age, that he speaks justly, it seems that we should agree that these youngsters have made a valid point" (1436–1437).

But there is one concession Strepsiades will not make. When Pheidippides says he will beat his mother just as he beat him, his father has a fiery reaction. He calls it "a far greater evil" (*au meizon kakon*), and when Pheidippides threatens to bring out the Weaker *Logos* as before to prove the rightness of this action, he says "if you do, nothing will save you from jumping into the Pit along with Socrates and the Weaker *Logos*" (1447–1451).

The sophistical education of Strepsiades has come to an end. His son is now entirely estranged. We can assume that he will have to face his creditors unaided, i.e., without the temporary confidence he had gained, and without the taste for that injustice he had so eagerly sought. From being a desperate man at the beginning of the play, he is now a contrite but ruined man. At this point, one might ask: what constitutes the *comic* element of this comedy, beyond the hilarity provoked by so many of Aristophanes' laughter-producing lines and situations? After all, everything seems broken at this point. Hegel's insight, that an imperturbable ordinary man traverses life's pitfalls and emerges victorious does not apply to this play, which Hegel certainly knew well.[58] Strepsiades is hardly imperturbable, and if it can be said that he achieves any kind of victory at the end, it is surely a profoundly mixed one.

LINES 1452–CONCLUSION

In his final attempt to dodge responsibility for his actions, Strepsiades addresses the Chorus: "Clouds, it's your fault that this has happened to me! I trusted you with all of my affairs (*pragmata*)" (1450–1452). But the Clouds point out that Strepsiades himself is the cause (*aitios*), since he took "the twisted path that leads to evildoing (*ponēra*)" (1454–1455). When asked, they tell him that they didn't reveal their deed at the outset because they do the same thing to anyone who lusts for evil doings, plunging him into "calamity (*kakon*) until he knows (*eidē*) to respect the gods" (1460–1461).

Strepsiades invites his son to join him in the destruction of Chaerophon and Socrates "for deceiving (*exēpatōn*) you and me both." ("Deceiving" here seems clearly better than Henderson's "cheating," for it is not only a matter of money, but of the corruption of soul that the leaders of the *phrontistērion* aided and abetted.) Pheidippides refuses, citing the nonexistence of Zeus and the need, earlier asserted by his father, not to harm his teachers as the reasons for his refusal. Taking advice from a statue of Hermes he sees in the neighborhood, Strepsiades decides not to sue, but to "burn down the idle talkers' house (*tēn oikian tōn adoleskhōn*) as quickly as I can" (1484–1485). He instructs his slave Xanthias to begin taking his hatchet to the roof, and has someone (who?) fetch him a lighted torch, so that he can "do justice" to "someone in there for what they've done to me, even if they are big-time blowhards (*kei sphodr' eis' alazones*)" (1491–1492).

Both succeed. As the First Student exits the burning house in panic, he screams the question "Man what are you doing!?" to Strepsiades, who sarcastically replies, "I'm mincing words (*dialeptologoumai*) with the rafters of your house." This marvelous word occurs nowhere else in the Greek language. It combines *dialeptos* and *dialogos:* to make fine or delicate, and to dialogue, neither of which are happening to the rafters, but both of which are perhaps oddly appropriate. When the Second Student protests twice, "You'll destroy us (*apoleis*)," Strepsiades replies that this is what he wishes to do, so long as his hatchet works and he doesn't fall (1500–1501).

Finally, when Socrates calls to him on the roof, "what do you think you're doing?," Strepsiades mocks him with the words he heard earlier from Socrates: "I tread the air and scrutinize the sun" (1503). Strepsiades and Xanthias descend from the roof to confront and to chase the burning students and the choking Socrates, with the comic hero delivering his concluding lines:

> Then what was the idea of outraging (*hubrizete*) the gods
> And peering at the back side of the moon?
> Chase them, hit them, stone them, many times over,
> Most of all for knowingly (*eidōs*) treating the gods unjustly (*ēdikoun*).[59]

As Strepsiades and Xanthias chase Socrates and the students offstage, the Chorus Leader seems to conclude succinctly: "we've done enough (*metriōs*) choraling (*kekhoreutai*) for today." Dover claims that "*Clouds* shares with *Thesmophoriazousai* a final choral utterance which is little more than the verbal equivalent of dropping the curtain (*metriōs* occurs in both), but is peculiar in being entirely colourless."[60] To a philosophical reader of the play, these concluding words are neither dramatically terse nor colorless, but harbor within them the entire arc of the comedy.

As the Clouds declare shortly before, it is their deed (*ergon*) to bring hubristic men to ruin, so that they will come to honor the gods. To be sure, Strepsiades is one such man. But the comic Socrates is an even more serious case, for he denies the gods altogether and has built a school that teaches others to do so. Unlike Strepsiades, the comic Socrates cannot claim any "mitigating circumstance." Perhaps one can venture to say that the downward spiral of Strepsiades served to conceal an even sharper one of the comic Socrates. Recall that Weaker *Logos,* and not the comic Socrates, claimed to originate the practice of arguing against the established ideas of custom and justice. In this light, the comic Socrates has freely chosen the pathway of the Weaker *Logos* just as, once removed, Strepsiades has. *Clouds*, then, seems to present us with a tragic outcome—with a furious, avenging Strepsiades playing the role of the closing tragic Chorus.

I would like to focus upon the *metriōs* and the *tēmeron*. We have choraled "in proper measure" for "today." Read closely, the Chorus of Clouds has accomplished all that it can in one day. However, this does not at all mean that it has accomplished all that can be accomplished. Perhaps the Chorus can achieve more on other days. Perhaps other ways might come forth that can instill greater attention to appropriate measure. Could this "something other" be indicated already in the depths of *Clouds*? Recall the Choral passage in which Aristophanes calls attention to the subtlety of this play. Its end is quite obviously not a traditional comic ending, nor is *Clouds* traditional in its subject matter at all, given its apparently straightforward tragic theme. But perhaps it is comic in a far more profound sense than what is normally regarded as "normal" for Old Comedy.

Is Strepsiades rightly conceived as a representative on earth of the Furies (*Erinus, Nemesis*)? Or is there, once again, a certain ridiculousness to his action? In one sense, this conception is correct. As Dover points out (though he does not draw the analogy to the Furies), burning down the house of a certain kind of offender is neither clearly illegal nor "an unprecedented revenge."[61] As it was the function of the Furies, sent by the gods, to punish those who committed hubris, it certainly does appear that Strepsiades represents them in this case. The Furies do not engage in contests of *logoi*. Rather, as shown in many Greek tragedies, they merely and directly exact vengeance.

However, can we read Strepsiades' vengeance here as entirely appropriate? He is, after all, a human being. He has, after all, only recently come to his senses. His anger at being deceived is more than merely residual, but consumes his soul. Further, he came to his senses not through an insight into the gods' right to respect from mortals, but rather as a result of a beating by his own son. His few moments of strength came from the short-lived bond he thought he had with Pheidippides, but once this bond was broken he apparently thought nothing of razing a house in which his son might, for all he knew, have been present. His condition at the end of *Clouds* is, if anything, worse than it was at its outset. He is still saddled with heavy debts incurred by his son, debts that loom large and threaten his financial survival. It seems extremely unlikely that his instinctive and liberating response to Pheidippides' threat to beat his mother will win Strepsiades any favor even from his mother's side. His distance from his son, earlier quite marked, is now total. He is a man all alone, full of rage but lacking resource and lacking prospects. Victory? Some victory!

The last *logos*-related word in *Clouds* is *dialeptologeomai,* the Aristophanic neologism that mocks the genuine Socratic *dialogia,* turning it into a practice that makes overly and improperly fine distinctions. Liddell and Scott offer "logic-chopping"[62] as one of the meanings (all of which are derogatory) that it carries. As we have seen, Strepsiades uses it to describe what he is doing as he sets fire to the rafters of the *phrontistērion.* While this is certainly a peculiar and ironic, as well as hilarious employment of a *logos*-related word, there is certain propriety to this usage: just as the *phrontistērion* was a place where genuine *logos* was perverted by means of the cultivation of overly and improperly fine distinctions, its demise is accompanied by an "improper" use of a *logos*-related word, i.e., no "speech" or "argument" or "reasoning" is involved in the action of a torch upon wooden rafters. And of course this is the only way Strepsiades would be capable of overcoming the spoken *dialeptologeomai* that was the coin of the realm in the *phrontistērion.*

Where is the *comedy* here? After all of the bombast and noise, after all of the sophistry, after all of the vulgarity and force, even after the destruction of the family that forms the core of this comedy, nothing remains except . . . genuine *logos,* the kind associated with Socratic practice as presented later in the Platonic dialogues. Socratic *logos* seeks truth and goodness rather than mere advantage, and almost always culminates in some way in a certain self-aware ignorance. The ridiculous excess of Aristophanes' *Clouds* and the lawful playfulness of the Platonic-Socratic dialogues mutually echo one another.

Aristophanes' ridiculous thoughtfulness is directly related to such *logos.* It seems clearly mistaken to call it "conservative"[63] here, both because all sides are presented as equally preposterous, and because there is hardly what can be called a noble victory of traditional values at its conclusion. It is not the reinstatement of proper measure accomplished by tragedy, but a measuring of another very important kind. *Clouds* measures *logos* precisely by bringing to light the excesses to which it is vulnerable and the excesses that it can provoke. On the page or on the stage, these excesses, to which we are all subject in some way, are brought forth masterfully and hilariously so that we can enjoy them and ourselves, live through them vicariously, laugh at them and ourselves, harmlessly. Our learning from them can occur unconsciously, through our immediate laughter at Aristophanic ridiculousness, or through conscious scholarly work like the study undertaken here, which is necessary on account of the loss of the spirit of ancient Greek theater. What remains for us on "another day" is to speak thoughtfully, with all play governed by proper measure.

Two

Wasps and the Limits of *Logos*

While the external similarities in plot between *Clouds* and *Wasps* seem unmistakable, close attention to the *textual* concerns in *Wasps* reveals a comedy that exposes quite different philosophical concerns. Obviously, we are confronted with a father-son conflict in which a wealthy son disapproves of his father's life or activities. Further, we are witnesses of debates that range from the ridiculous to the transcendently preposterous, as we were in *Clouds.* However, the differences even within these parallels are clear enough to preclude any hasty conclusions concerning these superficial similarities.

Unlike Strepsiades who seems to have little power and little pleasure, Philocleon treasures the power he wields as a juror. This power allows him to humiliate wealthy young defendants in their physical prime who hope to obtain a favorable verdict. Unlike Pheidippides, Bdelocleon seeks to express his sincere care for his father by offering him comfort and luxury. There are other, more important differences as well, which will become clear in the course of the interpretation.

One is Philocleon's status as a genuine dramatic *hero.* I understand a dramatic hero to be a person of a certain magnitude who discloses the nature and limits of human life in an exemplary fashion. By "a certain magnitude," I interpret heroism more broadly than Aristotle and the Aristotelian tradition. Noble birth is not necessary. The hero need not be better than us, nor have a flaw (*hamartia*) that brings about downfall. Rather, to merit the stature of a hero, the character's traits must be outsized so that they can be discerned very clearly, these traits must be consistently enacted until they reach their limit, and his/her exploits must ultimately transcend sympathy or blame. While Strepsiades' actions—taken in order to meet his obligations—could elicit at least some measure of sympathy from the beginning, Philocleon behaves odiously from the outset. Nor does Philocleon experience a reversal in moral insight like the one experienced by Strepsiades at the end of *Clouds*. I will argue toward the end of this chapter that Aristophanes' portrait of the boisterous, unruly Philocleon in *Wasps* is quite subtly drawn, and that the sense of Philocleon's heroism is both deeper and of greater philosophical significance than the hero of *Clouds,* the comedy that supposedly has philosophy as its foil.

Since this book is devoted to the *philosophical* yield of the Aristophanic comedies, I shall now state the general orientation of my reading of *Wasps.* As in the first chapter, historical matters will be considered only insofar as they contribute to a close and rigorous interpretation of the written work, with the focus upon purely philosophical matters. At first glance, *Wasps* might seem to resist such treatment. After all, it is well documented that Aristophanes and Cleon were bitter enemies. On account of the comic poet's negative portrayal of him in *Knights, Wasps*' two main characters, Philocleon (Lovecleon) and Bdelocleon (Hatecleon), take their names from their relationship to this prominent Athenian general and politician. The Athens of 422 BCE was indeed a litigious society. The comedy consists largely, it seems, of a mockery both of Cleon and of this excessive litigiousness. Henderson observes, "*Wasps* satirizes Athenian jurors and criticizes their staunch devotion to demagogic politicians."[1] Further, "Aristophanes exploits the parallelism between Philocleon's position in the city (in happy service to the vulgar Cleon) and his status in his own household (dependence on his cultivated son) in order to consider what would happen if men like Bdelocleon were to win the allegiance of Cleon's followers and introduce them to the finer things of life."[2]

I seek to examine the comedy through a different lens. Just as in the case of *Clouds,* it is both possible and fruitful to look away from the matters emphasized by Henderson—to the maximum degree that one can—and toward those that transcend historical, political, and social particularity. The comedy abounds with wondrous treatments of the perennial issues confronting all who seek to live a good life. Once again, I will look closely at the *logoi* themselves, and at "*logos*" and words related to it, as providing keys to the philosophical reading of the comedy. In order to isolate those concerns that *Wasps* is preeminently suited to illuminate, I will treat the issue of justice or jurying as peripheral to the philosophical yield of the comedy. The jurors (*dikastai*) are so far removed from even the most elementary concern for justice (*dikē*) as to render a discussion on justice like the one in the previous chapter unnecessary. However, this distance and difference between the name "justice" and the "jurors" called upon to act in its name will serve to frame many of the following readings.

LINES 1–135

The word that strikes the reader most forcefully at the outset of *Wasps* is *kakia,* "badness" in its most general sense. It occurs in many variants at its beginning, which I shall highlight. In the first line, the slave Sosias questions his fellow slave Xanthias (who is asleep on the roof during his night watch shift): *Houtos, ti paskheis, ō kakodaimon Xanthia:* "Hey, what's happened to you, evil-spirited Xanthias?" Here, *kakia* is a quality affixed to one's character. After the latter replies that he's learning to relieve the night watch, Sosias responds once again with a variant of *kakia: ara tais pleurais ti proupheileis mega:* "Great badness, then, will be owed to your ribs." Here, the variant of *kakia* indicates "pain." These two occasions foreshadow an ongoing theme of *Wasps* that is concealed from the surface of the play, namely the nature of *kakia,* of "badness." The early lines indicate that *kakia* can inhabit both the soul, here the soul of an irresponsibly sleeping watchman, and the body, here of the same man, who will experience "badness" in his ribs as a result of his sleeping on a roof.

Xanthias and Sosias are full-blooded and distinct characters. Their comic names—Xanthias means "yellow," and he wore a yellow wig; Sosias means "yours" in the sense of "your servant"—should not mislead us into thinking that they are mere ciphers that stand for interchangeable "slaves." Xanthias will show himself to be the more passionate of the two, and Sosias the more analytical. At *Wasps*' conclusion, this individuation of Xanthias proves to be of much importance.

Their exchange of *logoi* on their respective "amazing" (*thaumaston*) dreams displays two common themes: (1) the interplay of the divine and the human (in particular, in the realm of the polis), (2) the individual and more private issue of badness and the terrible (*deinon*). Both ascribe their rooftop sleepiness to Sabazius, "a Phyrigian god associated with Dionysus and popular with women and slaves."[3] This oblique invocation of the god in whose name the festival is held signals the comically "sacred" content of their dreams. The slaves' position on the roof locates them between the "heavenly" and "earthy" regions. Xanthias dreams of an eagle swooping away a shield, soaring up to the heavens, and then becoming Cleonymus, a reputed coward who "loses" his shield. He interprets his dream in a worrisome manner: the dream of Cleonymus' "badness" foreshadows "something *kakon*" that will come to the dreamer. Sosias reassures him. Although it is terrible (*deinon*) that a man should shed his gear, Sosias tells his colleague that nothing terrible (*deinon*) will happen to the fretful Xanthias as a result of his dream.

In the first part of Sosias' dream, Sosias imagines the Athenian assembly as a group of old sheep with tattered coats who have been "fleeced" by the words of the prominent demagogues Cleon, Theorus, and Alcibiades. Cleon appears in the form of a whale—*phallaina*—haranguing the sheep "like a scalded pig."[4] The whale holds a pair of scales and begins "weighing some fat (*dēmon*)." This first part of Sosias' dream strikes so much revulsion (*aiboi*) and fear into Xanthias that the latter urges his colleague to end his unbearable *logos: paue paue, mē lege: ozei kakiston tounupnion Bursēs sapras:* "Stop! Stop! Don't speak. Your dream reeks most foully of rotten hides" (37–38). Concerning the whale weighing out the fat, the much more anxious Xanthias hears "*dēmon*" ("fat"—accented on second syllable) as "*dēmon*" ("people"—accented on first syllable), and sees the dream as foretelling faction that the demagogues will introduce into their city.

In the second part of his dream, Sosias imagines that Theorus, an associate of Cleon, has turned into a crow (*korax*). "Crow" (*korax*) becomes "groveller" (*kolakos*) when pronounced with the lisp for which Alcibiades is known. Although Sosias finds it *allokoton* ("eerie," even "monstrous") that in the second part of his dream Theorus has turned into a crow (*korax* / *kolakos*), Xanthias calls this transformation "excellent" (*ariston*) (49). For the direction of this change, according to Xanthias, means that Theorus is "leaving us" and going "to hell" (*es korakas*) (51). The more ironically inclined Sosias offers Xanthias a "two obol salary" for his "wise" (*sophōs*) dream-interpretations (52–53).

In both parts of Sosias' dream, Aristophanes presents the intersection of the dream world through which the gods send their signs, and the so-called "real" world to which these signs supposedly pertain, by means of two inspired puns. ***Dēmon*** and ***dē****mon* connect not only in sound but in meaning as well: demagogues treat the people as if they were mere slabs of flesh to be "heated up" in calculated ways. Similarly, the appearance of the rhetorician Theorus as a "crow" connects with his arrogant oratory. In the second pun, Theorus' "descent" in *logos* from *korax* to *kolakos* displays an ordered regression from a bad state to ones that grow ever worse.

The dialogue between Xanthias and Sosias abounds with badness and horror. There is talk of *kakia, deinon, aiboi, allokoton, kolakos* / *korakos,* and *miara* (defilement by blood). The words themselves shift and metamorphose. The "bad" outcome of Xanthias' dream refers to the fate to which he fears the gods have in store for him. The "badness" of the ache in his shoulder refers to the much more prosaic pain resulting from his sleeping on the roof. Sosias' comforting words that nothing "terrible" will happen to Xanthias mean that the dream will not bring him harm. Xanthias' observation that it is "terrible" to flee from armed battle means that it is morally blameworthy. The "foulest" reeking of Cleon's hides refers to a noxious sensation, which occurs by means of the peculiarly direct descent from Sosias' "dream world" to the "real" world of Xanthias' "delicate" sensibility. Theorus' "monstrous" transition from a man addressing the assembly to crow, to groveller, then on to hell is seen as an ascent, a great gain, by Xanthias.

Several questions fundamental to a philosophical reading of *Wasps* occur from this initial exchange. First of all is the following: what is badness (*kakia*)? From the various senses that occur at the outset of *Wasps,* we can infer that *kakia* implies an *upsetting of order* of some kind. Such upsetting belongs to each and to all of its uses, whether they be physiological, psychological, moral, or aesthetic. Regarding the related question concerning goodness, not nearly as much can be gleaned. Xanthias regards Theorus' descent into hell as *ariston,* something very good. But Xanthias' sense of goodness is here directly tied to the demise, i.e., to something *kakon,* that happens to one of his and his master's enemies. This striking but isolated remark suggests that the region of political life is not a nourishing environment for disinterested philosophical inquiry concerning *to agathon,* the good.

The good cannot simply be spoken of as "order," for clearly order belongs to much that we would denounce. The most skilled evildoers, from murderers to embezzlers to pickpockets, proceed with great attention to the proper order of their activities. In Plato's *Republic,* the good is spoken of as "the greatest study," a study that must take place outside of the strictures demanded by political life. Socrates says that only "what looks like a child of the good" (*hos de ekgonos te tou agathou phainetai*) (506e3)—the sun in the visible region and the intellect (*nous*) in the intelligible region—can be considered within the scope of the dialogue. The good is not only beyond the dialogue's scope, but even "beyond being, exceeding it in dignity and power": *eti epekeina tēs ousias presbeia kai dunamei huperhekhontos* (509b9–10).

In contrast to the Platonic dialogues, Aristophanic comedy generally (and *Wasps* in particular) entertains *kakia* far more, and far more often, that it does *agathos* and *aristos.* However, Platonic philosophy and Aristophanic comedy concur in this, that both disclose those limits appropriate for the best life in a thoughtfully human manner. The former does so through the philosophical questioning it engenders. The latter does so through the laughter it provokes. The disclosure of *kakia* in all of its many guises serves to open up the realm within which this study can take place. Socrates holds that "the soul divines (*apomanteuomenē*) that [the good] is something" (*Re-*

public 505e2), but lacks it and must seek knowledge of it. The varied Aristophanic "appreciations" of *kakia* provide a worthy clearing for this necessary divination.

There is a second, even more fundamental question arising from this brief but memorable exchange: what does the art of Aristophanes reveal concerning *logos*? His comic *logos* functions in several ways. *Logos* can reach from the city to the heavens in a single sentence. (See lines 15–19, where the eagle takes the shield from the agora upward to heaven [*eis ton ouranon*] in one swoop.) It addresses moral concerns among humans in a straightforward customary fashion (Cleonymus' purported cowardice). It can describe physiological sensations so vividly that these *descriptions* have an effect akin to an actual event (the foul-smelling animal hide that produces real revulsion in Xanthias, and Sosias' "dream-whale" that produces physical disgust in his colleague). It can employ mockery and punning in order to transform the realm of the human into that of the merely animal and vice versa, as I have already shown.

The playfulness of Aristophanic *logos* within the human/divine range, a range that it shares with the deadly serious tragic *logos* of Aeschylus and Sophocles, is its distinguishing feature. The immediate visceral laughter provoked by Aristophanic comic *logos,* so different from the "fear and pity" provoked by its tragic counterpart, demands a different interpretive approach. It may seem that there are no limits in comedy other than those belonging to what is sayable at all, whereas tragedy is always concerned with the appropriately human limits and their transgression. However, this is not the case. In the chapter on *Clouds,* I concluded that *logos* is measured precisely by bringing to light the excesses to which it is vulnerable and the excesses that it can engender. The comic image of Socrates could not have been a more unmistakable philosophical foil. In *Wasps,* however, there is no recognizable figure upon whom to anchor the reflections. *Wasps* must therefore be approached in another way, but with the same goal in mind: to excavate those philosophical resources present in the comedy, taking them out of the joyous realm of inspired poetry and placing them into the different but equally joyous realm of philosophical *logos.*

To Xanthias, once anything can be brought to *logos,* it can traverse the realm of the gods, the earth, and the underworld virtually without distinction. This power of *logos* impresses itself on his excessively "soft-waxed"[5] soul, and is the reason both for his reflexive fearfulness and for his equally reflexive affirmative turn. It is as if Xanthias identifies the names themselves with the things that they name. The more "hard-waxed" Sosias playfully chides his colleague for the emotional excesses that directly inform his dream-interpretations. His playful offer of "two obols" to Xanthias for the latter's dream-interpretations (52–53) seems just about right: it is one obol less than his master "earns" for the ridiculously careless judgments he makes during his jury service.

Xanthias' recitation of the "plot" (*logos*) of the play yields a striking and surprising togetherness of two notions that seem to be basically at odds with one another. We learn that the master's "father suffers from a monstrous disease" (*noson gar ho patēr allokoton autou nosei*) (71), the diagnosis of which is unknown unless Xanthias and Sosias reveal it. Amynias is said to diagnose it as *philokubon* (love of dice). After Amynias' wrong guess, Xanthias does give the hint that the disease begins with *philo-*. Sosias supposes it to be *philopotēn* (love of drink); one Nicostratus has guessed that it is *philothutēn* (love of sacrifices) or *philoxenon* (love of guests). At last, Xanthias reveals that the master's father suffers, like no other man, from the disease of *philēliastēs,* love of jury service. Bringing *nosos* and *philia* together is Aristophanes' wonderful comic surprise.

The surprise is lost in Henderson's translations, which are accurate on other grounds. In every case, he translates *philo-* as "addiction to."[6] To readers of English alone and to potential producers/directors of *Wasps,* Henderson's renderings surely capture a good deal of the sense of the comic drama, as perhaps my "love of playing dice," "love of drink," "love of holding sacrifices," and "love of entertaining guests" might not. In his actions, Philocleon shows himself indeed to be "addicted" to jury service. But just as surely, many *philo-* words bespeak nothing like addiction: *philozōos* (lover of animals), *philogrammatos* (lover of books), *philoditēs* (lover of travelers), or *philozephuros* (loving the west wind). To readers attending to Aristophanes' philosophical gift, the more neutral translation of *philia* as "lover of . . ." is superior, not least because of the word that orients this entire inquiry is ***philosophia,*** philosophy, the love of wisdom.

The activity of philosophy involves careful attention to words (*logoi, onomai*[7]). In the Platonic dialogues, this attention shows itself in the frequent *ti legei* questions: "what does it say?" or, more loosely, "what does it mean?" For example: "what is virtue?," "what is justice?" Socrates himself speaks of matters that are beyond the earthly (see, e.g., the great myth of love [*erōs*] in the *Phaedrus* [243e9–257b6]), and beneath the earthly (see, e.g., the myth of Er in the *Republic* [614b2–621b7]). Further, in a manner perhaps most in accord with Aristophanes in *Clouds* (I refer to the Socrates/Strepsiades "dialogue" on "linguistics" at lines 635–699), and also here in the early part of *Wasps,* Plato's *Cratylus* has an "inspired" Socrates speaking oracles (*khrēsmōdein*) (*Cratylus* 396d3), and deriving the names of the gods from natural phenomena.[8]

According to Sallis, the comedy of the *Cratylus* consists "in the sense that perhaps every dialogue stands near, and at certain points becomes, comedy by virtue of the fact that each abstracts its subject matter from the whole on which this matter, nevertheless, depends, hence omitting something that, strictly speaking, cannot be omitted."[9] We can see quickly how *Clouds,* in having Socrates suspended in a basket as if humans were not bonded to the earth, fulfills this condition.

But further, something decisive comes to light in the course of the comedy regarding the relation of names and things, namely that "the unfolding of the comedy proves to be such that names both serve to make things manifest and, on the other hand, are in need of being limited by what they themselves first make manifest."[10] In the comic context of *Wasps,* the incongruous *philia* that will make Philocleon's condition manifest will at once show itself within its limits by means of that very manifestation. That is, it will display Philocleon's obsessive love of jury service against the absence of justice itself. But it is only the presupposition of justice that gives the activity of jury service any meaning at all, and thus indicates its *proper* limits.

The express measuring that takes place within the Platonic dialogues is appropriately absent in *Wasps.* After the derivation of the divine names in *Cratylus,* Socrates exhorts Hermogenes: "Then for the gods' sake, let us leave the gods, because I'm very afraid to discuss them": *ek men oun tōn theōn pros theōn apallagōmen, hōs egō dedoika peri autōn dialegesthai* (407d6–7). This statement is ridiculous and sober simultaneously. Given both the preceding extensive and confident discussion of the naming of the gods, and the invocation of the gods with which this discussion began, this exhortation is comically excessive. But the unease Socrates expresses concerning his speech about them at once acknowledges the appropriately human limits, including the awareness that he speaks from ignorance regarding these matters.

By contrast, Aristophanes implicitly presupposes this philosophical modesty in his very deed of purposefully—often bawdily, always hilariously—transgressing it. Never do his characters in *Wasps* reflect upon the nature of their activity. Nor do they need to, since the measure is already "written into" the comedy. This measure is disclosed to the members of the audience and to readers through the laughter provoked by the juxtaposition of the words and deeds of the characters, and by this presupposed standard of appropriate human speech and action. Thus, Philocleon's *philēliastēs* (love of jury service), later also called *philodiken* (love of litigation), needs no express and obvious distinction from its genuine source, *philodikaios* (love of justice).

The remainder of Xanthias' introduction of the plot details the extent of Philocleon's obsession with hearing cases at the law court. Among other symptoms, Philocleon never sleeps. He regards the ballot box as the ideal of beauty. He stands watch at the courthouse after dinner. He keeps "a whole beach" of voting pebbles in the house, in order to be certain that he won't run out. Bdelocleon, his son, tried "soothing words" (*logoisi paramuthoumenos*) (115). He tried exorcism. He tried joining him to the Corybantes. He took him to Aegina and had him bedded down at the temple of Aesclepius, the god of healing. Nothing helped. In a single word, Philocleon is *aluei* (111)—he is "crazy," as Henderson has it. However, given that the word *luō*—to loosen, to unbind, or to come apart—is at its root, we may read *toiaut' aluei* as "this is how he has lost it." This more literal translation is a superior *reading* translation, in my opinion, because in the course of *Wasps* we will find that earlier in his life, Philocleon *had it.* It will also become clearer as to what this philosophically crucial *it* refers. In the meantime, Bdelocleon has instructed his slaves to keep his father confined to the house on account of his "illness." This proves to be no easy task, as Philocleon strives mightily to escape by every means, even the remotest, at his disposal.

Xanthias' recitation of the plot concludes with the presentation of the comic names of the their masters, the two protagonists. "I swear by the gods (*nai ma Dia*) the old man is named Philocleon and his son is named Bdelocleon" (133–134). Recalling the discussion of naming above, Aristophanes' poetic gift has the gods *straightforwardly* vouchsafe two names that are at both suitable to their characters as we first meet them, but also entirely impossible in principle: Philocleon is older than Cleon, and there is no way to determine the son's political orientation at birth!

However, the closing line of Xanthias' recitation foreshadows a more nuanced account of the father-son relationship. It reveals that Bdelocleon may have some dubious traits himself, which we later discover are tied to his father's legacy. Xanthias attributes *tropous phruagmosemnakous tinas* ("some high-horsical traits") to Bdelocleon (135). Like *dialeptologeomai* in *Clouds, phruagmosemnakos* is an Aristophanic creation that appears nowhere else in Greek literature. It combines the neighing of a horse both semantically and onomatopoetically. As Henderson effectively conveys, it has the sense of someone "high on his horse," affectedly superior. This raises the question: how did it come about that the father has become so "crude" and his son has become so "snobbish"? Unlike in *Clouds,* there are no debts incurred by the son to explain the wretchedness of the father's condition, nor any aristocratic mothers and rich uncles to account for the affectedness of the son. Philocleon is no Strepsiades, and Bdelocleon is no Pheidippides.

LINES 135–229

These lines juxtapose two discordant images of the desperate father Philocleon. First, he is described as *smaller than human.* He is in the kitchen of the house "scurrying about like a mouse" (*muspolei ti katadedukōs*) (140). The slaves are concerned that he will find an exit through the drain. After unsuccessfully trying to pass himself off as smoke coming from out of the chimney by means of an outrageous pun (as Henderson notes, *sukinou,* "figwood" puns on *sukophantēs,* "malicious prosecutor"), and failing to break out through the door, Philocleon attempts another, more complicated and revealing stratagem.

He curses his son most severely but suggestively as well. *ō miarōtatoi* (156) means "you who are most disgusting of all" (Henderson has "you utter scum"). But as indicated earlier, it also has the sense of "stained with blood." With whose blood might Bdelocleon, who has led a life of carefree luxury, be stained? The staining may well issue from the blood of his father. In other words, perhaps Philocleon has some sense that his son's attitude toward him has its origin somehow in Philocleon himself. At this point, we have only this suggestion. Of course it is too early in *Wasps* to see precisely how this may be so.

In the next part of this subsection, we have Philocleon presenting himself as a reader of oracles. It had been prophesied to him (*manteuomenō*) (159) by the Delphic oracle that he had better not acquit anyone, or else he'd "dry up and wither away (*aposklēnai*)" (160). However, the Delphic oracle never makes such clear and specific prophecies. The Pythia's pronouncements at Delphi were always ambiguous. They were "a result of the ambiguity inherent in the god's signs and in the Greek perception that ambiguity is the idiom of prophecy, that there are limits to man's access to knowledge of the future: the god speaks ambiguously and man may misinterpret the messages."[11]

There is more than the one obvious way to regard Philocleon's report on the oracle, namely to claim that there was no such consultation and that he is grabbing at straws to persuade his "captors." However, another way of regarding his encounter with the oracle is that he indeed received a message, but misheard it on account of his "having lost it." Still more interesting is the possibility that the message has been correctly heard, but is indeed ambiguous in a way that escaped Philocleon's grasp.

The Greek word for "acquitted," *ekpheugō—ekphugē* in Philocleon's appeal at line 160—also means "to flee out," or "away." Thus, it can be interpreted, as the obsessed juror Philocleon reads it, as "do not acquit anyone or you will wither away," or otherwise as "do not flee away from *yourself* or you will wither away." According to the former reading, Philocleon is dutifully fulfilling the prophecy of the oracle, however "crazy" he may appear to his son and the slaves. According to the latter reading, the view of Bdelocleon, Xanthias, and Sosias represents the fulfillment of the prophecy in the other sense: Philocleon has lost *himself* and is behaving most irrationally as a result. As Xanthias remarked in his rehearsal of the "plot," Philocleon is *aluei,* loose.

In the first part of this subsection, Philocleon appeared as a mouse in the *logoi* of the others. In the second, and for reasons that we are still unaware of, he appears as all-too-human. In its final and longest part, Philocleon presents himself in the guise of Odysseus, the most resourceful of Greek heroes. Aristophanes' comic appropriation of the hero of the *Odyssey* begins, I suggest, at line 162, where Philocleon exclaims: "Come on, I beg you, let me out, or I'll explode": *ith', antibolō s', ekphres me, mē diarragō.* Perhaps this is a reach, but it is nevertheless suggestive: the old man Philocleon begins his entreaty with the word *ith',* whose letters are, of course, the first two letters of Ithaca, Odysseus' home. The *Odyssey* opens with its hero "trapped" in the caverns of Calypso (the nymph who wants him for her own husband) while longing for a homecoming to his wife Penelope in Ithaca. Old Philocleon's "entrapment" in the house of his son is an amusement-park-mirror analogy in which he longs for the only place he feels at home, and that is in the courthouse along with his fellow jurors.

Bdelocleon accuses his father of setting out to commit some great "badness" (*mega ti . . . kakon*) (168)—Henderson has "crime," yet another sense of *kakia*—when the latter exclaims that he wishes either to kill or convict Xanthias (or perhaps his own son)[12] for forcing him inside. At that point, his father undertakes his ruse and proceeds to display his comic *polutropon* (many-way'd) Odyssean efforts to escape from the home of his son to his "true" home in the courthouse. Combining the image of the Trojan horse that led to the ultimate fall of Troy[13] with Odysseus' near-fatal encounter with Polyphemus the Cyclops, Aristophanes' "Trojan horse" is a donkey with Philocleon strapped to its belly beneath. His son quickly discovers Philocleon, and playfully asks his father's name. *Outis, nē Dia:* "Noman, by God," is the response echoing Odysseus' famous words to the Cyclops in *Odyssey,* Book 9. Where is *Outis* from? *Ithakos Apodrasippidou,* Ithaca, "Son [not of Laertes, but] of Runawayhorse."[14]

This part of the subsection should not be seen only as an inversion of the heroic exploits of Odysseus. Rather, a streak of Philocleon's heroism is also made manifest, albeit in a comic context. Like Odysseus, he wants to go "home," since he finds little that is "home-like" in his son's house. After having been forced back inside, Bdelocleon heaps abuse upon him, however well-motivated this abuse may—or may not—be. The son calls his father *miarōtatos* (187) ("most wretched," or again, "most stained with blood"), echoing the vile insult that the father hurled earlier upon the son: bad blood circulates between them here. "Further, you are rotten and a skilled deceiver": *ponēros ei porrō tekhnēs kai parabolos.* / "Me, rotten? No, by God, Don't you now know that I'm entirely excellent?": *egō ponēros: ou ma Di', all' ouk oistha su nun m' ont' ariston* (192–194). Read carefully, this exchange proves to be far more than a mere father-son spat.

First of all, has Philocleon threatened some "great harm"? He did say that he would like to kill (*apokteinaimi*) (166) his "jailer" son with a sword. But he followed this threat with "or better yet, with a penalty tablet" (167), a meaningless gesture outside of the courthouse. The sense here is that the old man lacks the power to do any serious damage in that context. The exchange with his son, however, reveals the following kernel of self-knowledge that Philocleon possesses. He denies that he is "rotten" (*ponēros*), but he does not deny that he is a "skilled deceiver" (*porrō tekhnēs kai parabolos*). Further, he asserts his own "real excellence." Odysseus' heroism consisted not of pure "goodness," but of a combination of *aristeia* and deceitful cleverness. Perhaps it would be more nearly accurate to say that Odysseus' peculiar excellence consisted precisely of the mixture of his courage, cleverness, and deceitful ways that helped bring ultimate success to the Greeks over the Trojans, with his (at least spiritual) fidelity to his family in Ithaca, where that same mixture destroyed the suitors and restored his house and his marriage to his loyal wife Penelope.

We will learn later in the play that Philocleon has his own just claim to excellence on the battlefield. His battlefield—though also brought forth in *logos* in a work of art—is human-size, unlike the battlefield of Hellespont in the Homeric epics, where heroes like Achilles wield shields far too heavy for any mere human to lift. The images of the epic and tragic heroes (most of the latter are drawn from the former) should be regarded in terms of their outsized natures and exploits. Like their comic counterparts, they are *vicarious* images, i.e., images through which we can experience ourselves. But the rage of Achilles and the adventurousness of Odysseus, for example, exceed our own through their *mere* magnitude. Through these poetic creations, our rages (and their quieting) and our risks (and their various outcomes) are enlarged by several orders of magnitude, as if presented on a large and minutely detailed viewing screen. As human beings seeking the best life, the heroic creations offer vicarious possibilities as well. Odysseus is one: excellence and cleverness (deceitfulness) focused (usually!) upon the goal(s) of victory and homecoming.

Aristophanes' genius presents magnitude in another, but equally compelling manner. The behavior of his comic hero exceeds our own by virtue of turpitude and ridiculousness far beyond any available to us. However, we experience our own qualities in a way analogous to that when we consider the tragedies. I regard the image of Philocleon hidden under the donkey as constituting nothing less (and nothing more!) than *an appropriate image of a human being,* at least of a certain worthy kind. In part *aristos* (having discharged his responsibilities and having faced danger bravely and well), in part "deceitful" (albeit with stunning ineptitude), Philocleon pursues the respect that is his due, and he believes he can find in no other role than that of juror.

But he is forced back into the house, from the eaves of which he rains down "dirtballs" upon Xanthias and Bdelocleon. "Oh, evil spirit (*oimoi kakodaimōn*): the man's becoming a sparrow: he's going to fly his way out" (207–208). The *kakodaimōn* has surely found its way into Bdelocleon's soul. Xanthias attempts to calm him down and suggests a nap, assuring his master that every exit has been firmly secured, and that the two could easily stand ready to pelt his father's fellow jurors with rocks should they arrive to pick him up on the way to the courthouse. At first, this only increases Bdelocleon's alarm, for "whoever riles that tribe of oldsters riles a wasps' nest. They've even got stingers, extremely sharp, sticking out from their rumps, that they stab with, and they leap and attack, crackling like sparks" (223–227). But Xanthias assures him that he can handle the jurors, and the two go off to sleep.

In this section, the many-sided *kakia* that made itself manifest in the first 135 lines becomes more particularized in this last group, where the capacity of *kakia* to bring *disorder* comes to the forefront. Philocleon scurries frantically to escape from his son's house. With similar frenzy, Bdelocleon and Xanthias seek to keep him indoors. Father and son hurl invectives at one another, but choose a word (*miarōtatos*) that not only slanders the other, but maligns their own blood as well. Philocleon's dropping down a dirtball (*bōlion*) on the head of his son proves to drive Bdelocleon *aluei,* i.e., to the point where he has "lost it," such that a *kakodaimōn* has taken over his soul. I might suggest that unlike Xanthias, who falls asleep in confidence that the house is secure, Bdelocleon falls asleep because staying awake has become entirely too difficult.

Finally, a short reflection upon the *bōlion* can produce a provocative philosophical result. A *bōlion* is a small lump of earth. There is a perspective other than Bdelocleon's upon its significance for him. Perhaps apart from (or even in addition to) the frantic efforts of an imprisoned father, the *bōlion* striking Bdelocleon on his head is poetically designed to bring the wealthy and conceited Bdelocleon to the recognition that he, like all other human beings, is bound to the earth.

Thus, the ridiculous side of the exchange of *logoi* between father and son is shrouded by the genuine disorder of *kakia,* introduced as inhabiting soul and body separately in the first lines of the play through the exchanges of Xanthias and Sosias, but now seen as producing an entire atmosphere of hostile *logoi,* in which father and son heap horrible curses upon one another, curses that involve their own heritage, their own blood. In these cursed *logoi,* their own *aristeia,* their excellence, becomes transformed into something *ponēros,* something wicked.

How did matters reach this sorry stage? The Chorus of old jurors, the "wasps," will reveal the first part of the answer.

LINES 230–390

No likeness of the assertive Chorus Leader in *Clouds* can be found in *Wasps.* Here, the Chorus Leader can only encourage his cohort of old men not to move quite so slowly toward the courthouse. The old men make their trek in the middle of the night, so that they can arrive at their destination by dawn. Their first appearance on the stage pointedly contrasts with Bdelocleon's image of them as a frightening phalanx of waspish attackers. To the contrary, when the Chorus Leader calls to his "best fellow-juror" (*beltiste sundikastōn*) Strymodorus, asking him to locate a few of the others that seem to be missing, he can only call to him while uttering sounds of pain and woe, *appapai papaiax* (235). The Chorus Leader himself seems to be nothing more than a weary old man leading other old men who are even more tired.

However, after recalling a playful exploit from their youthful past, the Chorus Leader's pulse seems to quicken. The trial schedule of the day, set by Cleon, features the general Laches, who is said to have plenty of money. They look forward to "three days' ration of rotten rage" (*orgēn triōn ponēran*) (243) against him, to punish him for his "crimes" (*ēdikēsen*) (244). He directs his fellow jurors to search, with their lamps, "for stones (*lithos*) waiting to hurt someone (*kakon ti*)" (247).

Philosophical matters emerge forcefully, once again, when this section is read closely. As we have seen, the forms of the words *ponēros* and *kakon* have played a major role in the comedy thus far. Until, they have been regarded negatively by all of the characters. Both slaves lament the kinds of *kakia* to which they are subject. Bdelocleon fears that his ranting father is about to commit some *mega kakon.* Philocleon does not object to being called *parabolos,* but he expresses visceral offense at being called *ponēros.* One might retranslate the last three words of line 243 as "three days of wretched rage" merely in order to heighten the moral overtone of *ponēros,* in a similar spirit. This moral wretchedness resounds further in the Chorus Leader's ascription of the *stones* lying about, waiting to harm someone. While they revel in their power to discharge their anger and to profit monetarily from its discharge, they seem here to wish to keep themselves at a distance from their own agency. Instead, they transfer it to the stones they will cast when, before hearing so much as a single detail, they convict today's defendant Laches. Their "service" consists of *kakon ti drasē* (doing harm) rather than of punishing *ēdikēsen* (crimes). The latter word can also be rendered as "wrongdoers" or "unjust ones," a rendering which would heighten the contradiction between the name *dikastai* (jurors) here and their obvious injustice. Thus, the Chorus Leader reverses the attitude toward badness and toward wretchedness that was established by the characters. Badness and wretchedness become goals to be pursued eagerly.

However, before we pass judgment on these jurors too quickly, their plight deserves an honest assessment. As the following lines demonstrate, both the Chorus Leader and the members of the Chorus suffer from agonizing poverty. Their only source of income consists of the three obols per day dispensed by Cleon, not enough for anything more than the barest subsistence. Recalling David Hume's philosophical fiction of unlimited scarcity, in such a condition—a condition that the lives of the old men in the Chorus approach, in its material and spiritual severity—there is no need for justice, hence no justice. While the Chorus members are not at such extreme need, their poverty and sense of dishonor is surely real and, as in Strepsiades' case, understandable. Once upon a time, as we will find out (and as has already been hinted), they were noble and prosperous young soldiers who were respected by all. Here in their old age, they find themselves reduced to a state in which their earnings are meager and their honor consists only of their title as "jurors" in a rigged court.

As a further image of their unhappy plight, Aristophanes has the Chorus members slopping through mud in the dark night, with their sons carrying the dimly lit lamps that light their way. Though the Chorus Leader hounds his son concerning the possible waste of scarce and expensive lamp oil, his son has no fear. The boy's ability to negotiate the mud while holding the lamp gives him the ultimate power over his father. If the boys were to go home, the men would be lost and in even greater distress. What about the mud? I suggest that it be seen both as the feeling that the earth has become unstable under their feet, and as an image of the spiritual mess and lack of clarity in which they live out their undeservedly difficult lives as old men.

We learn, as they approach Philocleon's house wondering where he may be, that their comrade is a "lover of singing (*philōdos*)." Thus, they try to "sing him out of the house" (271), hoping that he'll then be "pleased (*hēdonēs*)" to hobble outside (272). They praise his single-minded mercilessness toward defendants who entreated him for leniency: "'You're boiling a stone,' he said": *lithon hepseis, elegen* (280). They wonder whether an acquittal on the previous day had angered him. They urge him to put down whatever dissatisfaction he may have in order to join in today's prosecution of Laches, a deed that would profit them all. Thus, Philocleon is himself one of the stones they are seeking in the "mud" of their lives in order to bring *kakia* to a defendant whose preordained verdict requires only the automatic seal of the wasps.

Philocleon's having said (*elegen*) that he is a stone presents a further comic aspect. The text notes often that he is a *man,* and that he belongs to a Chorus of *men* (*hanēr*—269; *ōndres*—270; *gerōn* [old man]—274; *hanēr* —285). Men and women are distinguished from other beings by virtue of their capacity for *logos.* When Philocleon *says of himself* that *logoi* from defendants have no more effect upon him than boiling has on a stone, he renounces his status as a being with the capacity for *logos* . . . in *logos*! A short time later, Philocleon himself entreats his colleagues to "turn me into stone, the one they count the votes on" (*lithon me poiēson, eph' hou tas khoirinas arithmousin*) (332–333) as his ultimate fate, if he cannot be loosed from the prison of his son's house.

We learn in a funny and sad interlude between the Chorus Leader and his son (290–316), before the jurors arrive at Philocleon's "prison," that the Chorus Leader not only lacks the resources to supply the sweets (figs) his son desires, but fears that even a meager lunch and dinner for his family is beyond his reach unless court is in session. Upon learning this, the son sings a lament to his ornamental (*agalma*) shopping bag. Henderson has "useless," again surely correct, but the more literal "ornamental" better captures the comedy of describing an empty shopping bag with a word customarily used in connection with gifts and sacrifices to and statues of the gods. This entire section is ripe with playful imitations of phrases, meters, and gestures from tragedies, especially those by Euripides. The principal philosophical interest here, however, is this juxtaposition that comically undermines the "lofty" and/or "settled" from within.

Still another example of this self-undermining comedy is *philōdos* Philocleon's singing from a window to his colleagues: "since I am not able to / sing, what can I do?": *ou gar hoios t' eim' / adein, ti poiēsō* (318). If he cannot "do some badness" (*kakon ti poiēsai*), he believes that he is useless, and asks Zeus either to turn him into smoke, or bake him and throw him into "vinegar sauce" (Henderson has the more contemporary "hot salsa"), or as we have seen earlier, turn him into stone, more precisely into the stone upon which the votes are counted. Philocleon might well be seen as a hilarious version of Socrates' citizen of his first city in the *Republic,* in which "one man, one art (*tekhnē*)" is the governing practice, and each man minds his particular art and no other. In this regard, as long as the *tekhnē* of jurors is to convict enemies of Cleon and the ruling party, Philocleon is the consummate juror. Nothing else, not even his life, has any meaning for him. In his ridiculously noble song, Philocleon also resembles the guard in Kafka's *The Penal Colony* who impales himself on the cruel machine of death he had administered when he is barred from using it on others.

In answer to his colleagues' question as to the cause of his imprisonment, Philocleon moans, "Gentlemen, he will neither let me render judgment (*dikazein*) nor do *kakon*" (340). Once again, a discordant juxtaposition—*dikē* and *kakia*—reveals the morally confused status of the Chorus. Under pressure from the Chorus members, the supposedly toothless Philocleon (Xanthias to Philocleon earlier: "you haven't any teeth!" [164]) instantly gnaws through the netting that kept him indoors. A comic character, as we saw in *Clouds,* can flout the laws of physics at least occasionally, often to make a serious point. Here, the point is that the poor old man still possesses unsuspected resources.

Before leaving this section, two matters deserve closer attention. First of all, Philocleon has been offered an apparently attractive alternative to jury service by his son. The line that follows the lament in the previous paragraph reads: "He is eager to wine and dine me,[15] but that is not what I want": *alla m' euōkhein hetoimos est', egō d' ou boulomai* (341). I suggest very strongly that this preference for poverty and jury duty over comfort and luxury is a sign, albeit a ridiculously twisted one given the "moral standards" of his service as a juror, of the nobility of character than shone from him in his youth. Here I must disagree with Dover who (almost against his will) confesses sympathy for Philocleon, but follows this by documenting Philocleon's loathsome character and his reprehensible behavior: his desire only to do harm (*kakia*); his ability and enthusiasm for stealing; his willingness to escape from battle; his eagerness to seize property not lawfully his; his inclination toward incestuous gestures. Taken together, Dover regards Philocleon as morally beyond the pale of even comic heroes.[16] But upon close examination, these recourses seem to be all that are left to him. Further, Bdelocleon's offer to supply his father with a life of ease can easily be regarded as smacking of condescension and disrespect, especially by his father. Bdelocleon's *tropous phruagmosemnakous* are on display here, signaling his relatively effortless life, a life that was made possible by his father's bravery on the battlefield. The "moral standards," in other words, may be no higher on Bdelocleon's side—only different.

Secondly, Philocleon offers an unusual sacrifice to Lykos, "an Athenian hero whose shrine is next to a law court"[17] (389–394). He offers, in return for safe passage from his son's house, a promise "never to piss or fart on your fence": *kou mē pote sou para tas kannas ourēsō mēd' apopardō* (394). MacDowell explains that such coarse behaviors (especially the former) signal disrespect (farting can sometimes express "fear," other times "self-pleasure," and occasionally mere "enjoyment") and that Philocleon's recourse to them "is evidence that he is so poor that he cannot promise Lykos any more expensive kind of honour."[18] I suggest rather less strongly, however, that there may be another reason for Philocleon's particular choice of sacrifice. Once again, this may be a reach, but given Philocleon's miserable condition, perhaps in the past he *has* urinated and broken wind at Lykos' shrine. Three obols per day in order to do something *kakon* to someone in an Athenian arena, for the honor of which he fought: at some level, perhaps an unconscious or a semi-conscious one, it is surely not hard to imagine Philocleon expressing disgust at the injustice that has been perpetrated upon him.

At the end of the previous section, we saw that the disorder of *kakia* disturbed the appropriate conduct of *logoi* between father and son. In this section, with the advent on stage of the Chorus, further disorientation infects *logos.* The sad existential fate of the Chorus is mirrored in their compromised moral state. Their existence is so miserable that one would have a difficult time holding them fully accountable for their moral lapses. The *logos,* like the Chorus, is mired in mud. Their only compass is the corrupt courthouse, in which they play their corrupt part. Their only guides are dimly lit lamps, helping them look for stones that can accomplish *kakia* as if they were not responsible for casting them. On stage, their satires of tragedies well-known by their spectators, their rantings, and their exploits are laughable. Their lives are hardly amusing to *them.* Aristophanes' ridiculous thoughtfulness succeeds in displaying both of these aspects at once, playfully/seriously respecting their humanity.[19]

LINES 394–479

For the sake of the liberation of their colleague Philocleon, the Chorus members take off their cloaks in order to ready their stingers for action against the newly awakened Xanthias and Bdelocleon. One aspect of the Chorus' call to action includes: "run and shout, and report this to Cleon": *theite kai Boate, kai Kleōni taut' aggellete* (409). While running is out of the question, shouting remains within the old men's competence. They scream that Bdelocleon is "a man who hates his city (*andra misopolin*)," and who will be destroyed for "proposing the *logos* that lawsuits be abolished": *tonde logon eispherei, / mē dikazein dikas* (413–414). The first claim is characteristic demagoguery at any time and in any culture. The second is somewhat more interesting, and bears closer study.

Here again, I believe that for purposes of this book, a more literal translation is desirable. Henderson translates *logos* as "idea." MacDowell suggests "'theory', 'rule.'"[20] But the Chorus here makes a factual claim: the claim is that Bdelocleon actually *said,* i.e., gave a *speech,* a *logos,* in which he proposed the abolition of lawsuits. This claim is entirely implausible, and probably outright false. The implausibility is further suggested (as if further suggestion were needed!) by the phrase *mē dikazein dikas.* It could almost be heard as saying that Bdelocleon wanted no more justice, at the same time as the Chorus expresses its outrage at the possibility of having no more opportunity to render their customary injustices in their judgments.

The Chorus' penchant for demagoguery shows itself once again and foreshadows a future discussion. It does so by referring to Bdelocleon's refusal to release his father as "manifest tyranny" (*turannis . . . emphanēs*) (417). However, in the sentence that immediately follows, the Chorus implies that one of their very own champions, Theorus, is a *kolax* (419). *Kolax* was the ascription heard by Sosias in his dream recounted in the first section (41–45). Once again, Aristophanes makes an oblique but clearly discernable suggestion that the Chorus members, once noble fighters for the Athenian cause, have at least a semi-conscious sense that their current "political benefactors" are *kolakoi,* i.e., unworthy—these "political leaders" are, in fact, lesser people than were the Chorus members in *their* primes as brave soldiers.

The abiding courage of the old men shines forth even in the ludicrous image that follows. They remove their cloaks, reveal their stingers and, under the direction of the Chorus Leader, they charge. They aim toward Bdelocleon, toward the other young slaves that Bdelocleon summons from the house, and toward the terrified Xanthias: *xustaleis, eutaktos, orgēs kai menous emplēmenos:* "With ranks closed, in good order, filled with rage and spirit" (424). But their charge is easily repulsed and they retreat—as objects of laughter, but also as a group of men who deserve respect. When they fought in their prime, their opponents did not ridicule their *orgēs kai menous.*

Further, both the Chorus Leader and Philocleon raise compelling issues regarding both old age and fatherhood. The Chorus Leader observes that old age truly holds "many terrible 'evils'": *poll' . . . deina tō gēra kaka* (441). All of the painstaking care and protection that the father had given is forgotten, e.g., how "in wintertime he saw to it that their feet would not be frozen. But in their eyes there is no shame in regard to their former footwear": *alla toutois g' ouk eni / ouden ophthalmoisin aidōs tōn palaiōn embadōn* (446–447). In Bdelocleon's "high-horsical traits," a proper sense of shame (*aidōs*) may be indeed missing in an important way.

After spitting venom at his son—"O most 'evil' beast" (*ō kakiston thērion*) (448)—Philocleon recalls his conscientious parenting, which included the infliction of a frightful beating after Bdelocleon was caught stealing. *Akharistos*—ungrateful, ungracious (451)—this is the charge leveled by the father against the son! The ridiculous thoughtfulness of Aristophanic comedy once again playfully juxtaposes the outrageously ludicrous with the most sensitive and nuanced. To expect gratitude to a father for "flaying you raw" when you stole grapes (450), even as the father celebrates his own joy taken in stealing when younger, is preposterous. Yet showing concern for both the physical and moral wellbeing of a son does deserve gratitude. So does the life of ease that the son enjoys as a result of his father's courage.

The "evils of old age" (*deina tō gēra kaka*) of which the Chorus here speaks refers in its most fundamental sense neither to moral nor even to physical "evil" or "harm." The "evils" are the mere consequences of *powerlessness.* The approach of death, to which all human beings are subject, is depicted here as *kakon* not because it signals the end of life on earth, but because of the vulnerability to which the aging are given over. Aristophanes layers a raucous comic veneer atop this painful truth. By means of the instinctive laughter provoked by the pathetically brave Chorus of wasps, this dark truth finds its way to the spectators. However, vulnerability belongs to our condition. Disrespect for the aged on account of their loss of power is identical to thoughtless disrespect for one's own humanity.

After retreating, the Chorus lambasts Bdelocleon, calling him: *ō ponō ponēre kai Komētamunia:* "O 'rotting rot' and long-haired Amynias" (466). *Ponēros,* as we have seen, has *aristos* as its opposite. In both *Clouds* and *Wasps,* the name "Amynias" signaled cowardice. "Long-haired" implies luxury and, perhaps, effeminacy. These charges, when leveled against Bdelocleon, may indeed have some merit. Also not entirely without merit is the Chorus' claim that Bdelocleon has not permitted his father to take his place along with them, having bound him *oute logon eutrapelon, / autos arkhon monos:* "without dexterous *logos,* but by one autocrat alone" (469–470).

As we will soon see, the Chorus' skills at dexterous *logos* are considerable. Bdelocleon offers to "enter into discussion and compromise" (*es logous elthoimen allēloisi kai diallagas*) (472), but the Chorus declines the offer forcefully. After regarding his proposal with disdain ("Discuss with *you*?"), the chorus members call Bdelocleon "enemy of the people and lover of monarchy and buddy of Brasidas," a leading Spartan general: *soi logous, ō misodēme kai monarkhias erasta / kai xunōn Brasida* (475). Again, even granting the character flaws that Bdelocleon seems to possess, not a single piece of evidence warrants these accusations against him. No wonder Bdelocleon exclaims that he'd do better to write his father off altogether rather than "battling day after day in such a sea of *kakois*" (478–479).

From these lines, we can discern another, much more positive dimension to the father-son relationship. Bdelocleon, the loather of Cleon, loathes such demagoguery both out of concern for his father and out of concern for Athens. Here, the *kakia* consists of the depredations of his father's fellow jurors. However frustrating and time-consuming, Bdelocleon constantly attempts to shield what is left of the moral integrity of his father from this *kakia.* Though Bdelocleon swears that he'd do better to write his father off completely (478), he does not, nor does he ever consider doing so. His exasperated exclamation is a cry issuing from his love.

Careful attention to the comic content of this section of *Wasps* reveals both a morally complex landscape and a deepening of those issues that have come forth earlier. Philocleon has earned the right to enjoy a comfortable old age, as have his fellow "wasps," but lives in poverty. He had done his part to secure Athens, but now must perpetrate many injustices at the behest of a shameless and selfish demagogue in order to receive his pittance. Bdelocleon will affect the snobbishness of the privileged, but has enough genuine feeling both for Athens and for the honor of his father to detest the demagogue Cleon and to take the unpleasant measure of keeping his father housebound by force. The sad result thus far can be seen in their mutual hurling of the expletive "*ō miarōtatoi*" at one another. A depth of love, concealed within the comic venom, provides the origin of this sad exchange.

Toward the end of this section of *Wasps*, a new and truly central philosophical issue arises: what is the nature of "discussion," of *logos* as a means to reach some reasonable compromise or solution? The wasps claim that *logos* with a traitor and scoundrel such as Bdelocleon is impossible—but their claim takes place *in logos*! Nevertheless, their response raises the question: are there certain conditions required for the possibility of agreement or compromise? If so, what are they? Under the best conditions, what can be accomplished, and what—if any—are its limits? In the earlier discussion of these questions in the *Clouds* chapter, we saw how, in Plato's *Meno*, Socrates presents two legitimate dialogical options. The first is direct refutation (*elegkhein*) of an answer given by one's opponent. The second is finding a common ground, using agreed-upon terms known to the questioner: *di' ekeinōn hōn an prosomologē eidenai ho erōtōmenos* (*Meno* 75d7–8). If there is neither direct refutation nor some point of agreement from which the interlocutors can begin, nothing of value can come forth at all.

In *Clouds*, the procedure of dialogue took place in exchanges that could only be characterized as entirely *willing*, however ridiculous and hilarious their subject matter. Even the exchanges between Weaker *Logos* and Stronger *Logos* were undertaken with gleeful enthusiasm. In this section of *Wasps*, however, the hostile demagoguery of the wasps violates the condition of willingness, and does not even approach the securing of a common ground of agreement. In lines 394–479, the *logoi* occur in an arena in which all of the characters have been badly compromised both existentially and morally. (In Bdelocleon's case, too much easy wealth is as compromising as poverty.) To our earlier questions and answers regarding the nature and limits of *logos*, we must append the following further question: given the conditions under which the characters in *Wasps* live, what does Aristophanes' comic art disclose concerning the possibilities and limits of *logos*? What is the philosophical yield of these comic disclosures?

LINES 480–649

After a brief interlude during which Bdelocleon denounces the Chorus' accusation of him as a tyrant, father and son begin their *agōn* (contest) of *logoi*. In a most unexpected way, Bdelocleon fulfills the dialogical requirement that a common ground of agreement must first be established: he allows the *Chorus*, Bdelocleon's accuser and enemy, to decide the winner.

The confidence of Philocleon and his fellow jurors could not be higher, given both this condition and given the self-certainty of their position. Philocleon would rather judge for a tiny allowance than be given a luxurious life (508–511). He cannot so much as frame the thought, in this exchange, that his jurying could be a fault (*examartanō dikazōn*). Upon being told, "you are a laughingstock (*katagelōmenos*) to men you all but grovel to. You're unaware that you've been enslaved," Philocleon retorts that he is "master of everyone" (*arkhon tōn hapantōn*) (515–518). If he gives the weaker *logos*, Philocleon promises, he'll fall on his sword (523). He agrees to "abide by the arbitration," and "never again . . . toast the good spirit (*agathou daimonos*) with unmixed[21] jury pay" (525).

In lines 531–545, the Chorus proclaims what is at stake for them in this great *agōn* of *logos:* virtually everything. If Philocleon, their representative, loses, then the "elderly crowd" will have been shown to be worthless (*ouketi . . . khrēsimos*) (540–541) and will become an object of mockery everywhere. But Philocleon steps forth fearlessly, claiming that no life is as happy (*eudaimon*), most-blessed (*makariston*) (550), more well-fed (*trupherōteron*), and "terror-inspiring"[22] (*deinoteron*) (551) than that of a juror, despite his old age. These four qualities issue one and all from the perceived power of the juror over the supplicants to the court who "beg and grovel, pitifully pouring out their pleas" (555).

To this sense of power, Philocleon adds a "grace note" of meanness and cruelty: after raising the hopes of the supplicants, even taking a bribe from some (such as a piece of pork) and promising them a sympathetic hearing in return, he breaks all of his promises and rejects every entreaty. This, he claims, is great authority (*megalē arkhē*) and mockery (*katakhēnē*) of wealth. Once again, however, one finds a comic hint of self-knowledge even in Philocleon's encomium to the juror's life. In its midst, he claims, "Some of [the supplicants] bewail their poverty and go on exaggerating their *kakia* until they sometimes seem as bad as my own" (564–565). The *kakia* he suffers in his son's house is related to his self-perception that he is powerless. Human power, he believes, is manifest only in its external exercise. It consists of the ability to effect something in the city or upon his family members. Given his current state, power can be defined as the ability to do harm to others. Perhaps it is not very much of a reach to suppose that Philocleon's desire to do *kakon* things to innocent others is a mere reaction to the *kakia* that he believes he has undergone, whether by nature (aging), by political outcome, or by both—and on some level, he is aware of this propensity and of its cause.

Further, somewhere in the depths of his soul Philocleon knows that his *logos* is wildly excessive. In no sense is he "most well-fed" as a juror, either in or out of the courthouse. His happiness and his blessedness are evanescent, and come at the cost of what is best in him. As for his capacity to inspire terror, this extends only as far as the courtroom. Given his "definition" of power and his awareness that he has none outside the courtroom, it is small wonder that he revels in the only position that, to him, affords him a feeling of value—at this point, power and value are directly related in Philocleon's soul. But even as his *logos* unfolds further, we begin to see at least something of a "deeper Philocleon," and the ravages that political folly and cynical rhetoric have had upon him.

What are "the goods" (*tagatha*) the jurors gain from their rule (*arkhein*) (577)? First of all, they get to look at boys' "private parts" (*aidoia*) when the boys are examined for registration. Bdelocleon responds to his father's declaration of "goods" by blessing this first one, as he blesses several others that range from the ludicrous to the disgraceful (588). The worst of them concerns the jurors' ignoring the will of a dying father, and selling his heiress daughter to the highest bidder (in Aristophanes' text, they "award the girl to whoever talks us into it" [586]). Bdelocleon affirms even this "benefit," but calls it "unjust" (*adikeis*) to "remove the seal cap (*anakogkhuliazōn*) of the heiress," i.e., open the will of the father for inspection. But as MacDowell points out, Aristophanes has folded a pun into the word, for *kogkhē* means "vagina."

Read carefully, the aesthetic treatment of *women* in *Wasps,* even an oblique and apparently casual one such as this, reveals a surprising philosophical dimension. It occurs in the midst of others: the public solicitude of powerful men as Cleon and Theorus toward the jurors; (the former swats flies away from him and his colleagues [592], the latter sponges them off [592, 596]); the favorable attention heaped upon him from his wife and daughter when he brings his jury pay home; and authority that can only be likened to Zeus' (619–629). Each one of these benefits is wretched, ridiculous, or both at once. So, too, then is the callousness toward the daughter of the dying father, and the cruel pun uttered "in jest" by Bdelocleon. By means of this darkest of comic inversions, Aristophanes affirms the dignity of women.

The Chorus praises Philocleon's *logos* for its unmatched clarity (*katharōs*) and intelligence (*xunetōs*) (631–633). Neither Chorus nor spokesman show the least concern with Bdelocleon's claim that "when you do [stop your *logos*] you'll stand revealed as an asshole (*prōktos*) that can't be washed clean with that authority (*arkhēs*) of yours" (604). Both Chorus and spokesman speak with assurance of victory. However, the "serious" subsoil of the comedy is fully present even before Bdelocleon's response. The same Philocleon who would carelessly and unblinkingly sell the rightful inheritance proceeds of a fatherless daughter to the highest bidder has a daughter of his own. His daughter's good opinion of him matters to him a great deal, and is one of the great benefits of jury duty that he has cited! This utter inability to connect the effect of his judgments upon the lives of his victims bears witness to what might well be irremediable damage to his humanity. Has he been so morally debased by his jury service that he cannot make any connection between the importance and the sacredness of his own private affairs to him and any similar regard that others might attach to theirs?

He has no difficulty, however, in connecting the most divine and the most human matters in the likening of his powers to those of Zeus. Recalling a similar motive in *Clouds* where Zeus' thundering is likened to Strepsiades' farting, Philocleon exults in his ability to frighten the "fat cats and the VIPs" to "say a prayer and shit in their pants": *poppuzousin / kagkekhodasin m' hoi ploutountes / kai panu semnoi* (625–628). In *Clouds,* Socrates provided Strepsiades with a Zeus-denying education, claiming that Zeus' thunder is nothing more than the farting that ensues from overeating the soup served at the Panathenaea. The distance between the human and the divine is thereby completely closed. A totally mechanical cause called *dinos* (whirl) replaces Zeus, and to its efficacy the motion of the clouds is ascribed.

Even more brazenly and more ridiculously than Strepsiades' "learning from himself" in *Clouds,* Philocleon arrogates the thundering power of Zeus to himself, equating it to his own control over the fate (and the bowels) of the hapless defendants who appear before him. Regarding his own private matters, he acknowledges his sacred and traditional relationship to family, at least in his own fashion and at least when he has his jury pay. But in his public duties, he has regard only for his "superiors" who flatter him, and none for his fellow citizens who come before him in court for judgment. Though there are traces of subconscious awareness, Philocleon's obliviousness to this radical discontinuity is as striking as it is riotously funny. In the very same soul in which we find a split identity with regard to private and to public matters, one finds total immersion in the "civic" identity as juror, *dikastēs.*

This too-radical division, together with its too-thoroughgoing immersion, indicates a soul out of balance with what is appropriate for a human being. This image of an unbalanced soul provokes the thought of what might belong to a *properly* balanced human soul. Perhaps we can here trace further echoes of Plato's *Republic.* At the end of book 6, justice in the soul is defined in analogy with justice in the aristocratic city in *logos.* At many points, Socrates denies the actual existence of such a city, but perhaps most strikingly at *Republic* 497b1, where he says, in answer to Adiemantus' query as to which regimes are worthy of the philosophic nature: "None at all": *Oud' hēntinoun.* Nevertheless, in the city in *logos,* justice consists of the guardian class (*phulakes*) allied with the class of auxiliaries (*epikouroi*) ruling over the class of artisans (*dēmiourgoi*), with each of the three classes *minding its own business* (*en autē prattein triōn ontōn genōn*) (441d8). Arrived at by analogy with justice in the city, justice in the soul is defined as calculation (*logistikon*) allied with spirit (*thumos*) ruling over desire (*epithumia*), with each of the three parts of the soul minding *its* own business.

After the "interlude" concerning philosophy and the soul in *Republic* books 5–7, the discussion of the cities resumes. Books 8–9 narrate the inevitable decline of the cities, from the aristocratic, to the timocratic, to the oligarchic, to the democratic, to the tyrannical. The *typical* ruling soul in each of the kinds of cities reflects this decline: in the timocratic city, one finds timocratic souls; in the democratic city, democratic souls, etc. By holding fast to the characteristics of the *just* soul, however, the decline of an *individual* soul need not take place in accord with the decline of the cities and the typical souls of their citizens. In what might be considered another amusement-park-mirror analogy to *Wasps,* Plato has Socrates (in book 9) attribute the prefix *philo-* to the objects of the various parts of the soul: *philokhrēmaton* (money-loving) and *philokerdes* (gain-loving) to the desiring part (581a6–7); *philonikon* (victory-loving) and *philotimon* (honor-loving) (581b2) to the spirited part; *philomathes* (learning-loving) and *philosophon* (wisdom-loving) to the calculating part (*logistikon*). Socrates concludes that although the just city may indeed occur nowhere on earth, "it doesn't make any difference whether it is or will be somewhere. For [the just man] would mind the things of [the regime in his soul], and of no other" (592b4–5).

As suggested earlier, Aristophanic comedy tends very often to present and to support a genuinely philosophic life precisely by exhibiting its opposite. A sophistical Socrates in *Clouds* found swinging in a basket in the air is the direct opposite of the genuine Socrates of the Platonic dialogues. The Aristophanic Socrates disdains contact with the affairs of the city and its inhabitants. The Platonic Socrates remains earthbound both physically (his regular habit is to walk barefoot) and existentially, by conversing with anyone and everyone who wishes to speak with him honestly (and many who would prefer not to!) on those matters pertaining to the best life for a human being. In the lives of Philocleon and his cohorts, we have a delightful artistic presentation of the reverse of such a life: there is no meaningful conversation (*logos, diallagē*) at all, nothing aimed at truth or justice, only a collection of souls whose *philia* aims toward exercising their power to make many of their fellow citizens miserable, and toward the pleasure that they derive from this power.

LINES 650–798

Accordingly, his colleagues express rapture at Philocleon's words: *kan makarōn dikazein / autos edoxa nēsois / hēdomenos legonti:* "and I saw myself judging / in the Islands of the Blessed / taking pleasure in his *logos*" (639–641). This appraisal hardly bodes well for Bdelocleon, for the wasps warn: *emēn orgēn pepa- / nai khalepon neania / mē pros emou legonti:* "to soften my anger / is hard for a youth / if I don't like his *logos*" (646–648). However, Bdelocleon shows no fear, responding instead with self-assured irony. He repeats the wasps' self-descriptive "hard" (*khalepon*), but adds that his retort will provide "wondrous," "marvelous," or perhaps even "terrifying" (*deinēs*)[23] insight (650). Such insight occurs "beyond the scope of comedians" (*meizonos ē 'pi trugōdois*) to heal an "inveterate sickness endemic in the city" (650–651).

In the most literal sense, the *meizonos ē 'pi trugōdois* suggests that the *logos* of Bdelocleon will somehow echo Aristophanes' own "serious" views of the cause of a major Athenian ailment, namely excessive litigation and corruption of the courts. However, in my reading I will proceed in another direction, both because I find serious difficulty with this one, and because once again the reading I shall offer keeps faith with Aristophanes' text and yields a richer philosophical harvest.

Phruagmosemnakous ("high-horsical") Bdelocleon, not Aristophanes, speaks here. The insight "greater than that of comedians" is spoken from *within a comedy.* Accordingly, the rationality and persuasiveness that will mark Bdelocleon's speech falls entirely within the scope of the comedian, and of comedy. The apparent declaration of modesty is at once a claim that the comedian's art can sufficiently mark out the contours of the weightiest of matters. This gesture is reminiscent of its philosophical analogue in the *Apology* in which Socrates at once denies that he knows anything worth knowing, but affirms that he may indeed be the Greek than whom no one is wiser.

In another "semi-Socratic" gesture, Bdelocleon addresses his father as "*ō pappidion,*" and asks him to relax his anger. This relaxation of anger is the necessary *existential* precondition for rational procedure, just as the agreement on a common ground is the necessary *epistemological* procedure, as we saw in an earlier discussion. When these are present, Bdelocleon can present his *logos.* He and his father together are then obliged to "calculate" (*logisai*) (656). From taxes and other fees and sources, Athens' income is nearly 2,000 talents. All of the jurors together, in the most generous estimate[24]—"for never yet have more dwelt in this land" (663), Bdelocleon intones in a mock-epic manner—receive a grand total of approximately 150 talents. The astounded Philocleon asks where the rest of the money goes, and his son details the sordid and all-too-common corruption and duplicity of the rulers, together with the gullibility of the ruled (665–679). The most stinging line is, "You choose them to rule you, father, because you've been buttered up (*peripephtheis*) by . . . slogans" (667).

And slavery? While the rulers and their flunkies (*kolakas*) have grown wealthy and enjoy the bounty made available by the courage and excellence of the Chorus members who were once soldiers, these now-aged veterans depend totally upon their base and dishonest rulers. Each of the "wasps" is kept poor and desperate so that he will obey his "trainer" (*tithaseutēn*)[25] when called upon to attack one of his trainer's enemies. Philocleon shakes with self-recognition from his son's *logos:*

> *Tauti me poious': oimoi ti legeis: hōs mou ton thina taratteis,*
> *kai ton noun mou prosageis mallon, kouk oid' ho ti khrēma me poieis.*
> (696–697)
>
> Is this what they do to me? Oh, me, what are you saying? You're shaking me
> to my depths, and you are turning me around more to thought (*nous*), doing I know not what to me.

In the previous section, persuasion of the jurors by means of rational argument was virtually impossible. Their only interests consisted of the exercise of power in order to make many of their fellow citizens miserable, and the derivation of pleasure from this power. The *philia* of the jurors therefore did not allow for their being led to consider (*prosagōgē*) any other point of view. Here, the son's *logos* itself serves to cause the father to reconsider. Further, the son explains that his *philia* for his father led him to lock him in the house: "I wanted to feed you / and I didn't want these blowhards to make a chump (*egkhaskein*) of you" (720–721).

The transformation of both Chorus Leader and Chorus by means of *logos* takes place almost instantly. The former reveals his long-lost nobility of character when he agrees that it is "wise" (*sophos*) to withhold judgment until both sides are heard (725–726). Still more significantly, he says in his concession that his "anger has slackened": *tēn orgēn khalasas* (727). *Logos* as rational discourse, as "argument" in the sense of providing accurate premises that support a conclusion, serves as a means to quiet anger as well as a means to arrive at truth. The Chorus takes up its leader's conversion, entreating Philocleon to "listen, listen to the words (*pithou pithou logoisi*), and don't be stupid, / too unyielding and tough a man" (729–730). Its members ascribe the *logos* of Bdelocleon to "the advent of some god (*theōn*)" (733), and conclude their entreaty by urging their colleague to "accept his help" (*su de parōn dekhou*) (735).[26]

Bdelocleon offers his father a series of blandishments to entice him, ranging from the mundane ("a cozy coat"—738) to the more exotic ("a whore to massage his cock and his tailbone"—739–740), but notes that his father is silent, not even offering a grunt. His colleagues in the Chorus offer an optimistic interpretation of this silence. It is an interpretation that rewards close attention:

> *nun d' isōs toisi sois*
> *logois peithetai*
> *kai sōphronei mentoi methistas es to loipon ton tropon*
> *peithomenos te soi.* (747–749)
>
> Maybe now he's listening
> to your arguments
> and really being sensible, changing his ways from now on,
> and listening to you.

In their metamorphosis from a loud, angry, resentful mob of jurors whose actions contradict their titles to a thoughtful assemblage of reflective human beings, their interpretation of Philocleon's non-response shows the way that *silence* belongs essentially to *logos.* Their own silence, as they heard Bdelocleon's arguments, showed itself to be a silence of the most *active* kind. By means of their silence, their humanity became transformed into something better. Qualities were reborn that the Chorus members once likely possessed, but which had withered and been swept under by the malevolent manipulation of the crooked rhetoricians in power.

Of course not all silence belongs to this splendid variety. That silence that stubbornly refuses to engage in dialogue in order to stand firmly upon an unexamined opinion clearly does not so belong. Nor does the silence deserve praise that cleverly refrains from dialogue in order to seize a vulnerable moment for merely personal advantage. What can be said, then, about the silence of Philocleon in the face of his son's *logos,* and in the face of his comrades' reversal of the point of view they held before? What relationship can Philocleon's silence have to this "silence" spoken of by the Stranger in Plato's *Sophist:*

oukoun dianoia men kai logos tauton: plēn ho men
entos tēs psukhēs pros hautēn dialogos aneu
phōnēs
gignomenos tout auto hēmin epōnomasthē,
d i a n o i a. (263e2–5)

Well then aren't thinking and speech the same, except that the soul's inner conversation with itself, when it arises without voice, has been given the title by us—"thinking"?[27]

As his comrades noted earlier, Philocleon was not merely one juror among others. He was never late (268). He was by far the fiercest of all. Further, he was the only one who couldn't be persuaded to relent (278). His own *logos,* in the face of entreaties by defendants, was "You're trying to cook a stone": *lithon epseis* (280). If one may so characterize him, Philocleon was comedy's Platonic embodiment of the form "juror," before the Chorus' "purification" by means of *logos.* For one so habituated to the life of the "unpurified" wasps, one must wonder what kind of hold argument and dialogue, *logos* and *dialogos,* can take in a soul like Philocleon's. Can such a soul attune itself to the silence that belongs to *logos* and *dialogos*?

The "intellectual content" of his initial response, despite its exclamatory nature, is not difficult to read. No longer does he call his son "you who are most disgusting of all." Nor, however, does he accede to the urgent promptings of his colleagues that he accept the divinely inspired words of his son. Philocleon shouts: *iō moī moi:* "Oh! Woe is me!" (750). Aristophanes' comic appropriation of a tragic motif has the most serious role of exhibiting a soul in genuinely pained perplexity. The *logos* of his son has clearly penetrated his soul, and at least *something* along the lines of that inner dialogue spoken of in Plato's *Sophist* has taken place. However, this inner dialogue has not been silent, *aneu phōnēs,* like the one spoken of in the *Sophist.* The loud voice that Philocleon has both acquired by habit and cultivated in order to deny all inner ambiguities and/or misgivings cannot be so easily quieted, if it can be quieted at all.

Thus, the "intellectual content" might be read thusly: "I am a juror and can be nothing else. But I am thoroughly persuaded by the evidence that I must cease to be a juror . . . but I cannot!" The existential content could not be clearer: Philocleon is a man torn between what his reason tells him is true and what his long-held identity tells him is "dignified." He offers a compromise: he will do anything except give up his role as juror. The latter is so dear to him that he says: "Before I do that, death (Hades) will decide between us": *touto de Haidēs diakrinei proteron ē 'gō peisomai* (763–764). Bdelocleon seals the compromise with his own offer: Philocleon may continue as a juror, but only within the walls of his son's house. Philocleon will decide accusations of household transgressions, such as a maid opening a door without permission. He will now do so "with good reason" (*men nun eulogōs*), outdoors when it's warm, by the fire if it snows, indoors if it rains. He may sleep as late as he likes. He may chew his food while deciding cases, thereby "getting to the meat of the matter by chewing it over," as Bdelocleon explains. Bdelocleon will pay him. Philocleon happily accepts (767–785).

Several crucial Platonic themes echo in this section. I will refer to the Platonic interlocutors who best reflect Aristophanes' art. The first concerns the influence of *logos* upon Meno and Anytus. These men cannot be reached because their identification with their role in the *city* is total. They are wealthy and influential citizens who are psychologically either unable or unwilling (or both) to entertain the healthy confusion that Socrates attempted to instill by means of testing their views and subjecting them to cross-examination (*elegkhos*). Though both wealthier, more influential, and (in a certain limited sense) more articulate than Philocleon, the genuine philosopher gives the wreath to the latter if one were to imagine a philosophical *agōn* between them.

On the other extreme, and at the outset of the dialogue that bears his name, Phaedrus uncritically admires the *logos* of Lysias. In this *logos,* Lysias argues that the benefits of yielding to non-lovers (*mē erōsin*) (*Phaedrus* 231b1) are far greater than those received by yielding to lovers, basing his argument on the general premises that lovers behave imprudently and depart when their passion has been spent, while non-lovers are both prudent and will continue to offer goods of all kinds that are lasting. Through a series of mythical and rational *logoi,* Socrates turns the soul of Phaedrus around to the view that *erōs,* a species of divine madness, bestows the greatest gifts upon humanity, and to a disposition that might make him less likely to be persuaded by artfully constructed, manipulative, and false *logoi,* such as Lysias'.

Glaucon and Adeimantus, in the *Republic,* must be placed somewhere between these extremes. They regard justice as an intermediate good, beneficial for its consequences such as good reputation and protection from rampant injustice, but as drudgery otherwise. This view about justice, also held by the majority of those in their class, holds that it is a compromise between what would be best (doing perfect injustice, never suffering for it, and enjoying a reputation for justice) and what would be worst (being just, suffering perfect injustice, and having a reputation for injustice). Adeimantus gives no evidence of coming around to Socrates' view, namely that justice is one of the unalloyed goods, enjoyed both for itself and for the benefits it brings. Glaucon gives *some* evidence of accepting the Socratic view, but it is not entirely convincing.[28] These two are "quieter" analogues of

Philocleon. Apollodorus' melodramatic external behavior (see *Symposium* and *Phaedrus*) resembles Philocleon's, but this resemblance hardly makes him a better analogue than Adeimantus and Glaucon.

Another crucial Platonic issue is the shift, agreed upon by both father and son, from the determination and enactment of one's identity primarily in terms of the *polis* (i.e., publicly), to its determination and enactment *privately* (in one's own soul). The comic image of this privacy is the house of Bdelocleon. Its Platonic counterpart occurs at the end of *Republic* book 9 (alluded to earlier), where Socrates concedes that the good city does not seem to exist anywhere on earth, but adds:

> "[I]n heaven," I said, "perhaps a pattern (*paradeigma*) is laid up for the man who wants to see and found a city within himself on the basis of what he sees. It doesn't make any difference whether it is or could be somewhere. For he would mind the things of this city alone, and of no other." (*Republic* 592b1–5)

It appears to be quite a leap from mindfulness of the Platonic heavenly paradigm to mindfulness of the implicit but vaguely drawn paradigm in Bdelocleon's convincing refutation of his father's *logos.* The preposterous matters that arise in the house of Bdelocleon seem equally far removed from the lofty matters that occupy Socrates in the *Republic.* Nevertheless, I insist upon their close accord. In the comic inspiration of Aristophanes, I discern a marvelously careful presentation of those matters that affect our humanity most of all. The fundamental philosophical task is *not* intellectual proficiency, and could not be further from the rhetorical ability to win arguments. The task indeed involves the determination of the strongest *logos,* but the penetration of this argument into the soul and the actions—into the identity, the very being—of the human being constitutes its essence. In this sense, Philocleon is a vicarious image for *all of us,* as we attempt to fashion our lives by allowing the "divine advent" of *logos* into our souls in order to clash with our habituated, cultivated, established, unreflective identities and so seek a life that is best.

Aristophanic comedy shares another deep and fundamental kinship with Platonic philosophy. In both, one finds unstinting recognition of human *kakia.* One finds frequent acknowledgement of the inefficacy of *logos* in many situations and in many human beings. Yet both retain a steadfast *optimism,* and a steadfast *cheerfulness.* One can discern this optimism in the turning-around of the Chorus leader and the Chorus members in the face of Bdelocleon's superior *logos.* One can just as surely discern it at the end of the *Apology,* where Socrates addresses his would be acquitters with the words: "And you too, judges (*dikastai*), must face death hopefully (*euelpidas*), and believe this one truth, that no harm (*kakon*) can happen to a good man, either in life or after death" (41c8–d1). In the face of his own conviction and death sentence, the hopefulness of Socrates remains unruffled. In the same sentence, a provocative argument occurs that echoes the artistic presentation in *Wasps:* the way to overcome *kakia* is the truth-seeking way of *logos.*

Socrates reserves the word "judges" or "jurors" (*dikastai*), the same word employed by Philocleon and his cohorts, for those who deserve the name by virtue of their demonstrated capacity to render judgment based only upon the evidence revealed through the *logoi.* Before their verdict was rendered, he put his "only nominal" jury on trial, calling them merely "men of Athens" until they proved worthy of the name *dikastai.* The lack of such differentiation in *Wasps* affirms rather than contradicts this difference. The philosophical distinction so sharply drawn in Plato's *Apology* and the confounding of this distinction in Aristophanes' *Wasps* point to one and the same phenomenon by different means. What Socratic *logos* reveals through painstaking reflection, Aristophanic comedy reveals through its ridiculous thoughtfulness.

LINES 799–892

This section, hilarious from a dramatic point of view, serves to prepare Philocleon's first astonishing trial. A few matters are of particular concern to my purpose. First of all is Bdelocleon's almost casual, surely careless reference to some *kakon* that might have been done by one of the household staff, perhaps "the Thracian girl who scorched the pot yesterday" (828). Once again, we have a blurring of the issue of justice and judging—here in the new and supposedly better and purer private domain, and by the supposedly "more just" Bdelocleon. Once again, Aristophanes creates a more subtle character than one might suppose upon first encounter. A servant girl has made an innocent mistake. Bdelocleon has no moral compunction about subjecting her to a "guilty" verdict at the hands of his father for the sake of his, Bdelocleon's, own tranquility.

The "purified" Chorus Leader and Chorus also contribute to the thought revealed in this section. After the "respectful silence" called for by Bdelocleon in response to the Chorus' initial celebration of the father-son truce (863–868), the Chorus members—along with their leader—pray for a similar concord to occur once they return to *their* houses. Bdelocleon then offers a prayer to Sidewalk Apollo, a god of roads and traveling,[29] to whom he makes several entreaties: to soften his father's hard heart; to influence him to treat people more gently; to be more sensitive to their pleas; to quiet his anger (875–884). The Chorus Leader sings of Philocleon's "new regime (*neaisin arkhais*), on the strength of your pronouncements (*proleleg-*

menōn)." (A form of the word *logos* resides within *prolelegmenōn*.) Philocleon's response upon hearing the announcement of the first defendant: "So who's this defendant? He's really going to get it!"[30]

The loud voices in the soul of this committed wasp "juror" does not seem to have been quieted at all by the *logoi* of his colleagues and of his son. Entering his first trial (and what a trial it is!), he appears to have arrogated even more power and hubris than he had before. In his son's house, unlike the courthouse, he is provided with greater comforts to enjoy and with far fewer obstacles than those with which he previously dealt. He seems ready to do *kakia* with even greater relish than before.

Seating him in his own personal juror's chair and giving him the sole vote has turned Philocleon away from the "*iō moi moi*" that indicated some potentially fecund confusion (*aporia*) that might lead to questioning and self-reflection on the way to the betterment of his soul. Instead, the comic wretchedness of Philocleon, given encouragement in the past both by his now "purified" colleagues in the Chorus and by the behavior of his son, returns in all of its magnificence. The shift from public to private—analogically from city to soul—only serves to show, in a mock-Platonic fashion, that indeed one and the same *eidos* ("form"[31]) can be seen in each domain.

LINES 893–1008

With his son as presiding magistrate, Philocleon conducts a trial between two dogs! Demadogue (*Kuōn*), the watchdog of Cydathenaeum, is the prosecutor. Grabes (*Labēt*) of Aexone is the defendant.[32] The charge: Grabes did not share a Sicilian cheese, but devoured it all by himself. The proposed penalty: a collar of fig-wood.[33] Though obscure to us, the local political overtones of this trial are unmistakable and, as MacDowell points out, would be obvious to even the dullest member of the audience.[34] However, looking away from these political matters and toward philosophical ones, I believe that the philosophical lens allows aspects of the Aristophanic text to come forth that escape even such trenchant, sophisticated, and witty political commentary.

The penalty of fig-wood is, for Philocleon, far too lenient. The greedy consumption of cheese by a dog is a capital crime: "No, he'll get death, a dog's death, when he's convicted" (898). In his habitual manner, Philocleon excoriates Grabes as a thief and a manipulator as soon as this defendant appears. Prosecutor Demadogue then comes forth, indicting his presence by barking (*au au*) (903). The prosecution begins with the statement of the aforementioned facts, with Demadogue denouncing Grabes for hiding and eating the cheese under cover of darkness, for most outrageously (*deinotata*) withholding a share from him and from "the whole yo ho ho (*to rhuppapai*)" (909). (The latter locution refers to the sailors, who were drawn mostly from the poorest classes and who strongly supported Cleon.)[35]

In the course of this utterly ridiculous trial, issues are broached that thoughtfully probe the human condition. Philocleon brings Grabes into the domain of *kakia* when he reports direct and present evidence of a "most horrible (*kakiston*) cheesy belch" emanating from the dog and toward him. The capacity to belch is a well-known staple of Old Comedy, but it serves here to point both to the unbreakable bond between humanity and animality, and to the way excess makes itself manifest in both. Another of Philocleon's noteworthy objections occurs at line 917, where he says of Grabes: "He didn't even share it with the public, me!": *tō koinō, emoi.* As sole juror, it is with a certain (albeit *very* limited) propriety that Philocleon considers himself and his city to be one and the same. However, in asserting *his own right* to a share of the cheese (a matter clearly not at issue in the trial) Philocleon nevertheless obliquely reveals the juncture between animal and citizen. While the quality of citizenship is possible to human beings alone and requires both a measure of rationality and also of moral responsibility in return for the privileges it confers, citizenship never leaves animal desire and animal fear behind. After all, laws and customs concerning property can ultimately be traced back to these characteristics.

The nature of this bond finds further reinforcement in Demadogue's confounding in the other direction. "Now don't let him off, because of all the many dogs [Grabes] is the most selfish-eating *man* of all (*andra monophagistaton*)" (922). *Monophagistaton,* according to MacDowell, seems to be another Aristophanic neologism. He suggests "most solitary-eating" or "lone-eating-est";[36] Henderson has "most hoggish."[37] I prefer to interpret *phagon* (infinitive *phagein*) as *already* suggesting excess, i.e., not just "eat" but "devour." In Homeric Greek *phagon,* applied to such "monsters" as Polyphemus and Scylla, meant precisely that.[38] What, then, does the addition of the prefix *mono-* contribute to the comedy? In addition to the image of a "selfish" dog "unwilling" to share its cheese, it suggests a kind of selfishness over and above ordinary selfishness, namely hubris. But mere animals cannot commit hubris. Such outrage lies even outside the scope of monsters. Hubris can only be ascribed to human beings. This is why Demadogue's discourse refers to Grabes as *andra monophagistaton,* the man whose excessive aggrandizement surpasses all measure.

Juror Philocleon entertains no doubt that Demadogue the prosecutor has proven its/his case, and takes a brief respite to urinate. After Bdelocleon asks him whether he's done pissing and is ready to be seated and hear Grabes' defense, Philocleon indicates his juridical certainty by saying, "No, but I think this one will be shitting himself today!" (941). Grabes takes the stand, but when directed to present a defense (*apologou*) and to speak (*lege*), he says nothing. Philocleon immediately concludes, "This one seems to have nothing to say for himself." He soon calls Grabes "a thief and a conspirator" (953).

Earlier, I raised a question regarding the capacity of a soul like Philocleon's to attune itself to the silence that belongs to *logos* and *dialogos.* These early returns are hardly encouraging. He fails to notice the clunky pun in which dog (*kuōn*) sounds something like Cleon (*Kleōn*). He also fails to see the parallels between Demadogue's inflated rhetoric and the rhetoric of Cleon and his ilk. More discouraging still, however, is Philocleon's interpretation of Grabes' silence as an implicit acknowledgement of his guilt. I have no quarrel with Henderson or other scholars who have likened the silence at this Aristophanic trial to that of Thucydides, son of Melesias, who "became tongue-tied at a trial."[39] However, I suggest that much more is at stake here than a literary allusion to a historical event.

Demadogue's prosecutorial remarks not only echoed the sentiments of demagogue Cleon, an echo that Philocleon—supposedly alert to the injustice of Cleon and his circle—should have noted at once. But further, Philocleon failed to recognize that most obvious anomaly, namely that dogs do not have *logos*! The very deed of speaking is inappropriate for a dog. By contrast, Grabes' lack of *logos* is entirely in accord with his nature. This dog's silence in the trial images the appropriate silence belonging to *logos* and *dialogos.* Philocleon has made *some* progress. He is content to serve as juror in his son's house. The trial of Grabes seems to suit him well. He shows no nostalgia for his days of hoodwinking and humiliating wealthy defendants. In this regard, he is indeed a *philēliastēs estin hōs oudeis anēr: era te toutou tou dikazein:* "a lover of jury service, whose *erōs* is to judge" (88–89). In this particular, he resembles Socrates' first and soon discarded characterization in *Republic* book 5 of the philosophic nature as a lover of learning who is not "finicky about learning" (*ton . . . peri ta mathēmata duskherainonta*) (475c1) but who is "insatiable" (*aplēstōs*) (475c7). But he has not even begun to understand the phenomenon, or even the need, for silent thoughtfulness that is so crucial to any pursuit of wisdom.

The kinship between the Platonic and Aristophanic texts is once again signaled by the precise character of their difference. Regarding the former, the philosophers are not mere "lovers of sights," like the insatiable ones who are "not finicky." Such lovers of sights are "not at all" philosophers, "but they are like philosophers": *Oudamōs, eipon, all' homoious men philosophois* (475e2). Philosophers are "the lovers of the sight of the truth" (475e4). If one were to suggest a parallel, *judges* are distinguished from lovers of jury service by virtue of their love of the sight of justice. Once more, this issue recalls Socrates' challenge in the *Apology* to "the men of Athens," at 18a3–6, to be worthy of the name "judges."

In Aristophanic comedy, one finds no lovers of the sight of either truth or justice. However, these qualities are affirmed through their very absence, and through the obvious and hilarious hypocrisy of the characters who proclaim them. This is yet another manifestation of the essential power of silence belonging to *logos:* those admirable philosophical traits, such as the pursuit of truth and of justice, shine forth precisely by means of their *not* being said or directly shown. The laughter occasioned by the ridiculous posturing of the characters vouches for their unmistakable disclosure.

An important conclusion regarding the limits of *logos* follows from both the preceding observations and from the entire action of *Wasps. Logos cannot* be understood lexically or even contextually. Not one of the scores of wide-ranging meanings of *logos* offered by Liddell and Scott takes account of the essential silence dwelling at its heart and making it possible at all.[40] Quite obviously, spoken words and the sincerity of their speaker can be at odds. Spoken words and sincerity can just as easily be in harmony, even when the speaker is somehow misled or honestly mistaken. The same capacity for error is present in "explanations," "narratives," "phrases," "myths," "formulas" and "definitions," "arguments," etc. If one were to speak "logically" (itself a comic locution in this context), *logos* is the necessary but far from sufficient condition for the discovery of truth, or justice, or wisdom. And if one were to extend this comically "logical" treatment of *logos* to, e.g., the noble labors of the lexicographers to whom every lover of the Greek language is so deeply indebted, this same silence at the heart of *logos* made their astonishing work—as they, with their exceptional erudition, sorted and pored over an untold number and assortment of documents—possible at all! *Logos* as somehow express or articulate meets its limit in one way or another. Only when silence belonging to *logos* allows the inner *dialogos* to occur (with its own silence) can anything genuinely philosophical take place.

Bdelocleon's "successful" defense of Grabes consisted of an odd claim (without any evidence or substantiation) that Grabes knew how to read and write and so "submitted dishonest accounts to us" (***kakourgōn** enegraph' hēmin ton logon*) (961, emphasis mine), and an almost surely lying witness to support this testimony.[41] This witness might be the Cheesegrater who testified that he parceled out the cheese in question to the troops (doing so through the non-objective voice of Bdelocleon's). It might be Bdelocleon himself.

Philocleon soon finds himself besieged from without and from within. From without, he is presented with his son's cries for mercy, and by the sympathy-producing move of Grabes' potentially fatherless baby pups coming before him. From "within," he is plagued by all of the hot soup he has been drinking throughout the trial, which causes him to cry at their sight and so weaken his resolve.

The final "success" occurs by means of Bdelocleon misleading his thoroughly disoriented father into dropping his pebble into the "acquittal" vase. Upon discovering this outcome, Philocleon is mortified. He frantically asks the gods for forgiveness. His plea bears close scrutiny: *akōn gar aut' edrasa kou tou'mou tropou:* "I did it unintentionally, it was unlike me" (1002). I will focus once again on the question of the identity of Philocleon, the "it was unlike me" in the above passage. Although he came to recognize the duplicitous manipulations of Cleon and the destructive consequences for his life and comfort, he still carries and deserves the name "Philocleon."

The influence of Cleon pervades the entire household. To break the habits instilled by Cleon in his father, Bdelocleon's manipulations may themselves be spoken of as mirror images of Cleon's, i.e., as Cleon-like. Although Philocleon has undergone what appears to be a major change of venue, Philocleon still looks to convict a defendant regardless of evidence. There are no three obols for a reward, but the son offers his profoundly distressed father its direct analogue as recompense for his aching bewilderment —not justice, not truth, but *luxury: hēdeōs diagein se ton loipon khronon: kouk' egkhaneitai s' exapatōn Huperbolos:* "You'll spend the rest of your time in pleasure; and no longer will Hyperbolus make a fool of you with his lies" (1006–1007). For Bdelocleon, *pleasure* is the antidote to sophistry. The question "who is Bdelocleon?" will soon rise to prominence as an equally compelling philosophical question.

LINES 1009–1121

Scholars have interpreted the beginning of this parabasis the same way they regarded the parabasis of the revised *Clouds.* That is, they suppose that the *logos* of the Chorus, as it denounces the spectators for their stupidity, is the means whereby the voice of Aristophanes declares his resentment at *Clouds'* third-place finish in its first production. They take lines 1015–1045 literally and at face value. Toward the beginning of his *logos* the Chorus Leader indeed says, "The poet now desires to blame (*mempsasthai*) the audience" (1016). While this naïve trust is touching, it fails to account both for the nature of the speaker *as a comic character,* and for what else is said in his *logos.*

Whatever went on in the mind of Aristophanes will, of course, never be known. It is extremely unlikely that even the most acute scholar can measure up to the sublime creativity and insight of Aristophanes. What is certain is that such words as *skaiōn theatōn* ("crude spectators") (1014), and *touto men oun esth' humin aiskhron tois mē gnousin parakhrēma* ("So you're all disgraced for failing to appreciate it right away") (1048), issue from the mouths of the Chorus and the Chorus Leader. Both the song of the Chorus and the speech of the Chorus Leader are the Muse-inspired renderings by the ***Wasps,*** men who once constituted a mighty and heroic collective military force but who have been grievously wronged at the hands of the generation they fought to protect. Their consciousness of this injustice, as characters in the comedy, is as recent as a few hundred lines ago.

What, then, can be made of their remarks urging the spectators not to be stupid but to "take care that the good words now don't simply fall to the ground": *nun ta mellont' eu legesthai. mē pesē phaulōs khamaz' eulabeisthe* (1011–1012)? Once again, if Aristophanes is competing for a prize, the stratagem of insulting his audience, or of obliquely suggesting that they might fall victim to stupidity, by means of false flattery,[42] hardly makes such a goal more achievable. I suggest strongly that—far from being a complaint concerning the fate of *Clouds* and concerning the lack of intelligence of his audience—the "poet" spoken of here as Aristophanes is hardly the actual flesh and blood human being competing with other such human beings at the festival, but is *one comic character among others* in *Wasps,* just as he was in *Clouds.* As such, his claims of superiority are hardly personal statements of resentment *but take on the comic hubris of the other characters* in *Wasps.*

At lines 1046–1047, the Chorus Leader says of the poet: *kaitoi spendōn poll' epi pollois omnusin ton Dionuson mē pōpot' ameinon epē toutōn kōmōdika mēden akousai:* "And yet over and over again he swears making libations to Dionysus that no one heard any comic poetry better than that." Henderson, following MacDowell, interprets *spendōn* metaphorically as "solemnly." MacDowell argues, "in the present case we can hardly believe that Aristophanes is actually making repeated libations."[43] I say that it is not only easy to believe this, but likely, once the poet is regarded as a comic character. Even if the "solemnly" is admitted as a possibility, it is difficult if not impossible to regard the *poll' epi pollois* ("again and again") with any straightforward seriousness. (Speaking for the poet at line 1024, the Chorus Leader said, "his head didn't swell," an odd locution when placed beside the aforementioned claim.)

But again, this is the song and the *logos* not of Aristophanes but of the wasps and their leader. The stinger on their rumps signifies their elite status as "the sole justly regarded indigenous autochthonous Athenians" (*Attikoi monoi dikaiōs eggeneis autokhthones*) (1076), who so impressed the defeated barbarians everywhere that they "insist that there's nothing manlier than an Attic wasp" (*mēden Attikou kaleisthai sphēkos andrikōteron*) (1090). That was, however, long ago. Their military victory, as we have seen, brought them neither honor from their city nor a fair share of the tribute from other lands that their military prowess and courage made possible. Close attention to the brief choral interlude at lines 1091–1100 reveals the reason why such honorable service went so unfairly without reward.

The Chorus sings that in the days of their military exploits, "I was terrifying then" (*ara deinos ē toth'*) (1091), the "I" indicating the unity belonging to these "indigenous Athenian" men. But "no, in those days we didn't care about getting ready to make a good speech (*eu lexein*) or to trump up a charge against someone, but only about who would be the best oarsman" (1094). To this carelessness regarding *eu lexein* in favor of concentration on military matters, they ascribe "the tribute's being brought to Athens, for the younger generation to steal" (1099–1100). Throughout this section, the limits of *logos* have shown themselves repeatedly. Silence, as I have endeavored to show, must belong to *logos* for *logos* to have efficacy for the human soul. In this song, the Chorus eschews *logos* disproportionately in favor of action (*ergon*). There is *silence,* but no *logos* and/or *dialogos* within which this silence might work. Calculative and sophistic *logoi* can take advantage of such silence, and indeed have already done so in order to deprive the noble wasps of their just due.

The Chorus Leader's final speech (1111–1121) reveals a great and ironic comic sadness. After stating the three reasons that the men are called wasps (their sharp temper, their gathering in swarms, and their resourcefulness in making a living), he laments the "drones" without stingers who have slipped in among them as jurors (men who avoided military service), and who receive an undeserved three obols as a share of the tribute that they did not earn. Given that the demagogues have duped the real veterans by several orders of magnitude, the resentment aimed at the "drones" (however merited) is out of proportion to the much larger injustice they have suffered.

Insofar as the earlier *logoi* of Bdelocleon exposed both this larger injustice and its source to the Chorus and its Leader, this failure of recollection belongs to their disregard of *logos.*

The theme of *war* is never far from *Wasps'* surface, and the relationship of *logos* to war and peace in this Aristophanic comedy finds both deep resonances and remarkable accord with its treatment in Plato's *Republic.* In the education of guardians—i.e., the warrior class—*logos* and *dialogos* were strictly regulated. Socrates has the founders of his city in *logos* censor and excise passages in Homeric poetry and Sophoclean tragedy deemed unsuitable for a guardian. Fear of death is not permitted to guardians, so passages that seem to reflect this emotion are censored. So too are passages that might suggest crying, laughing, *erōs,* and a large number of other all-too-human responses.[44] And what of the outcome in *logos* of this city? Three classes of citizens comprise it: guardians (the most able of the warrior class), auxiliaries to the guardians, and artisans. Where is *dialogos* in this city, i.e., where is the activity belonging to genuine thought, to *philosophy*? There is none. There is no philosophy in the so-called (and wrongly called) ideal city. Insofar as philosophy involves precisely such dialogue and such questioning, no philosopher would be permitted anywhere near it.

However—as was suggested in the Introduction—to the human being liberated from the cave and its shadows, i.e., to the one who is freed from the images (opinions) that he is permitted to see and to hear, the previously censored passages are not only permitted but take on central significance. The famous Achilles-in-Hades passage from *Odyssey* book 11—the very first passage censored in the education of the guardians—turns out to be the first one heard and affirmed by the liberated one. His surroundings are entirely new, very puzzling, and also radically alienating. Still, he "would rather be on the soil, a serf to another, / to a man without lot whose means of life are not great, / than to rule over all the dead who have perished" (*Republic* 516d10–11). That is, he would rather dwell in a state of utter puzzlement in the truth-revealing light than receive highest honors in the truth-concealing darkness of blind ignorance.

In this light, can the Chorus and the Chorus Leader of *Wasps* be held accountable for their neglect of *logos* and *dialogos* in favor of the deeds required for their difficult and successful military service, deeds that not only saved Athens from what appeared to be certain defeat but substantially enlarged its influence? If we allow for the kinship between Aristophanic comedy and Platonic philosophy, the answer has to be "no." In terms of *logos* and its limits, this "no" bears with it a particularly disagreeable aspect. In time of war, there appears to be little or no place for *logos* and *dialogos,* at least among the soldiers. However, once war ends and peace takes its place, those with skill in *logos* have every advantage and know how to garner the spoils. What about the genuine philosophers and poets who have such skill? They can challenge the demagogues and sophists. They have no desire for the spoils of war, but for a wisdom that exists beyond all price. There are no such characters *on stage* in Aristophanic comedy. But Aristophanic comedy accomplishes their nameless and essential work.

LINES 1122–1264

Touto toinun to tēn alētheian parekhon tois gignōskomenois kai tō gignōskonti tēn dunamin apodidon tēn tou agathou idean . . .

Therefore, say that what provides the truth to the things known and gives the power to the one who knows, is the *idea* of the good.[45] (*Republic* 508e1–2)

The reflection of Platonic thought in the amusement-park-mirror, comic distortion of Aristophanes reaches its high point—which is to say at once its low point—in this section. The "high-horsical traits" attributed by slave Xanthias to Bdelocleon shine forth in all their deformity, guided by one "idea," *his* idea of "the good." While he opposes Cleon and seems to feel genuine sympathy for the damage caused to his father's soul by the cupidity of Cleon and his associates, Bdelocleon seems just as little able to ask the question concerning his own identity. He does not recognize that he is a full-fledged member of the generation that enjoys a luxurious life by virtue of the military excellence and the sacrifices made by men such as his father, and not as a result of its own efforts.

One cannot read this section without being struck by Bdelocleon's appeal, direct and indirect, to *goodness.* I shall list them all:

agathon eoikas ouden epithumein pathein (1125): Bdelocleon to his father, offering him a new coat: "You don't seem to desire anything good."
pothen, ōgath' (1145): "Where did you hear that, good sir?" Bdelocleon speaking to his father like the latter is a "gentleman," in response to Philocleon's comment that the cloak looked like a woolen sausage.
ekh', ōgathe (1149): "Take it, good sir." Bdelocleon urging his father to accept the coat like a "gentleman."
All', ōgathe (1151): "But good sir—." Bdelocleon pleading with his father to cooperate in his transformation into a "gentleman" by means of a fashionable new wardrobe.

The final attribute of one who deserves the adjective *agathon* is the social hypocrisy that passes for "sophistication." Bdelocleon—"Cleon-hater"—is preparing his father for an imaginary dinner engagement where the despised Theorus will sing and the loathsome Cleon will be present. After having his father "step out as the wealthy do, like this, with a sort of voluptuous swagger" (1169), Bdelocleon asks Philocleon whether he will "know how to tell impressive *logoi* in the presence of very learned and righteous men": *andrōn parontōn polumathōn kai dexiōn* (1175). Philocleon quite honestly provides a *logos* he knows, concerning someone named Lamia who farted after having been captured (1177). After offering a further "unsophisticated" tale about a mouse and a cat, his son denounces him harshly:

You badly-educated shadow[46]—as Theogenes said
to the dung-gatherer, and this when quarreling:

ō skaie kapaideute—Theogenēs ephē
tō koprologō, kai tauta loidoroumenos:
mus kai galas melleis legein en andrasin (1183–85)

A *skia* is a shadow. Bdelocleon here regards his father *as lacking the substance of a man,* or at least someone who falls short of the "manliness" of his stylish associates. What is the measure of a man, according to Bdelocleon? For one, it is the abandonment of *muthoi,* in favor of *logoi* that have *anthrōpinōn* (1179), i.e., that tell of "human affairs." However, before anyone can conclude—whether in his audience or among his readers, then or at present—that a replacement of myths with rational accounts is here called for, it immediately becomes clear that Bdelocleon wants his father to *lie through his teeth.*

He instructs his father to tell "magnificent" (*megaloprepeis*) *logoi,* such as "how you went on an official embassy with Androcles and Kleistheses" (1187). But Philocleon went on no such embassy nor any resembling it. Nor could Philocleon accurately recount a certain wrestling match—he had not seen it! When asked to speak about the bravest deed of his youth, all Philocleon had to offer was his theft of some vine poles (1200). In aristocratic company, other skills are called for as well. Philocleon is instructed by his son on how to recline and how to make superficial conversation about the decorations and art objects in the room. Then some "role-playing" begins. Bdelocleon prepares his father for an actual feast by pretending to be present at one in which "dreams" are served. When non-existent wine is poured into a non-existent glass, Philocleon asks: *pros tōn theōn, enupnion hestiōmetha:* "By the god, are we feasting on dreams?" (1218).

Careful attention to the concluding portion of this section yields a subtle shift in the moral positioning of father and son. Imagining a feast with Cleon and his associates, Bdelocleon asks his father to respond to Cleon's singing of the Harmodius Song: "Never was a man in Athens born . . ." Philocleon responds at once: ". . . so great a scoundrel and such a thief!" (1226–1227). Instead of rewarding his father both for the identification of the one who swindled him and for his courageous confrontation of the swindler, he blasts Philocleon for his dangerous imprudence.[47] When Philocleon expresses his desire not to drink wine at the feast (*mēdamōs. / kakon to pinein*) (1254–1255) because his propensity for wild drunkenness leads to property damage, assaults, and consequent payments for these offenses, Bdelocleon asserts the exception: "not if you're in the company of men who are noble and good": *ouk, ēn xunēs g' andrasi kalois te kagathois* (1256). How will the company of such men provide a measured milieu for a drunken Philocleon? If indeed he causes damage, they'll intervene successfully on his behalf. The other option: Philocleon can relate something ludicrous (*geloion*) he heard at the symposium (*sumposion*),[48] so the victim will laugh the incident off as a joke.

Who is Bdelocleon? He is first and foremost the spoiled, wealthy son of a father who has been at least partially ruined by the injustices he has suffered. Having convinced his father of Cleon's treachery, he shows no inclination to entertain even a mock challenge of the man he loathes, this same man who bears such large responsibility for his father's fate. His father, knowing his propensity to cause harm when inebriated, wishes to remain sober at Philoctemon's feast. But his son urges him to join him in what Henderson translates as having a "booze up" (*methusthōmen*) (1252), telling him that he need not worry either about responsibility for the damage he might cause or the expense he might incur: the "aristocrats" with whom he will drink will get him off the hook, one way or another. If one were to categorize Bdelocleon, he is little more than a self-indulgent hedonist, having scarcely a shred of concern for what is genuinely noble and good (*kalon te kai agathon*).[49] This "little more" and that "scarce shred" consist only of his desire to provide some pleasure to his father (though these qualities do distinguish him from the dreadful Pheidippides).

While it may stretch a point to say that Philocleon here shows considerable ethical thoughtfulness, this is what I maintain. After all, I am writing about comedy. He has grown in order to become, in the context of Aristophanic poetry at least, a *comic* ethical man. He is a man who knows his weakness and seeks to avoid the dire results that are likely to flow from his indulgence. Of course his truth-telling and his desire for sobriety are rooted in consequentialist concerns. But both decisions, the decision to tell the truth to Cleon in the "thought-symposium" and the (at least initial) decision to refrain from drinking at Philoctemon's feast, were decisions based upon what he knew to be unquestionably best.

Aristophanes has created two masterful portraits. We encounter what here may appear to be a "morally evolving" Philocleon. Although he is far from leaving his past behind, he begins to show evidence of making responsible choices, at least in *logos.* Among these choices is a denunciation of Cleon, the demagogue and self-serving manipulator who is the genuine source of his woes. We also meet a "morally regressive" Bdelocleon, who urges his father to drink excessively in spite of the bad results this causes, and who claims that any damage thus caused can be managed either by the influence of his powerful friends or by sophistical use of *logoi.* Among his exercises is a caution to his father that involves treating Cleon with respect. By the end of this section, one must wonder whether the two have become unhinged from their names, indeed whether it would be proper to exchange them altogether.

But one must wonder further: are human beings capable of such thorough and rapid moral change as is here represented, at least in Philocleon? Recalling the earlier discussion, Philocleon was the most hardened juror of all. For such a person, the degree to which he could change his life outlook remained questionable. Additionally, one must admit that *any* human being, however well educated and habituated, is always capable of moral weakness. Even Kant, the quintessential ethical deontologist, believed that the human will is imperfect and could never achieve holiness, even when guided by the very best of intentions. What, then, could one hope for in the case of the benighted Philocleon, who knew of his own weakness for drink, who sought to stay sober in order to shield himself from this weakness . . . but whose son offers him all the pleasures of wine coupled with a free pass for any negative consequences?

LINES 1265–1363[50]

Shortly before Philocleon makes his astonishing entrance, the Chorus Leader informs the spectators that far from making peace with Cleon, the performance of *Wasps* is his occasion to turn the tables on him and to attack him anew (1284–1291). Classical scholars seem to share universal agreement that the Chorus leader is Aristophanes as both author and actor, speaking in his own voice. Cleon "showered abuse upon me" (*me* ***kakisas*** *eknise*) (1286), but now it is the poet's occasion to return like for like. The documentation of the acrimony between Cleon and Aristophanes leaves little doubt of their distaste for one another. MacDowell, in his summary of this part of the parabasis, writes, "the author declares that it was a mistake to imagine that he had ended his attacks on Kleon."[51] However, the *poetical* Chorus Leader must once again be separated from the author of the play, regardless of whether the author acted this part. First of all, it is hardly necessary to declare any personal resumption of attacks at this point in the play. Cleon's influence by virtue of his sophistical *logoi* has already disappeared—*in the comedy.* Secondly, the pedestrian fact that the name "Aristophanes" appears nowhere in the cast list militates against such an assumption. Further, the Chorus Leader depicts himself in ridiculously helpless terms, as a victim both of flayings by Cleon and by the indifference of a cold-hearted public.

In the midst of the speech, Cleon was said to have heaped *kakisas* (abuse) upon the Chorus Leader. Here, if we experiment by allowing the dramatic character to incorporate the aforementioned view of the scholars, an intriguing result obtains. Cleon's unsuccessful prosecution of Aristophanes for libel in his comedy *Knights,* regarded here as *kakisas,* strongly suggests the following: that the Chorus Leader has come to understand false accusations as *kakia.* What was once *agathon* has been transformed into its opposite.

The transformation of Philocleon seems to be another matter entirely. His self-knowledge regarding the effects of wine upon him proves to be impeccable. Xanthias, the slave who accompanies him to the feast and who has been the victim of constant beatings at drunken Philocleon's hands, speaks of the latter's behavior in superlatives: *atērotaton . . . kakon* (1299); *paroinikōtatos* (1300); *hubristotatos* (1303): "the most recklessly bad"; "the most drunk and disorderly"; "the most hubristic." I argue that these superlatives at the head of Xanthias' report serve a critical function in the understanding of Philocleon's philosophical significance. For this interpretation, the translation of "*atērotaton . . . kakon*" must be more literally rendered in the way that I suggest, despite its awkwardness. (Henderson has "an utter calamity"; Liddell and Scott have "an outrageous nuisance," which is echoed in MacDowell.[52]) For Philocleon has shown himself to be no ordinary man. He was, according to his wasp colleagues, "by far the fiercest (*drimutatos*) of us all / and the only one who couldn't be persuaded to relent[53] (*kai monos ouk anepeithet'*)" (277–278). Philocleon, I insist, is no mere old, resentful, irresponsible, immoral drunkard and purveyor of *kakia.* Above all, he is a *hero* whose very excesses expose the limits appropriate to human action.

I shall divide these excesses into two rough groups, those issuing from the outrages he has suffered and those issuing from the outrages he perpetrates. Concerning the first group, he is the victim of the excesses in word (*logos*) and in deed visited upon him by Cleon. Philocleon, a worthy military man, was fooled into serving this unjust demagogue as a juror for his crooked court. While the tribute from the conquered city-states pours in and provides the next generation with a luxurious life, Philocleon lives in virtual poverty and second-class citizenship in the house of his own son. The military virtues of comradeship, unity for the sake of a difficult and dangerous campaign, and indifference to frills prove to be useless in a time of peace and prosperity. I claim that all of these wrongs done to Philocleon involve outrage, hubris. All of them show thoroughgoing contempt for the humanity of a person who has served nobly, if naively. In so doing, humanity as such is degraded.

Philocleon's outrageous moral wretchedness should be seen as the other side, the mirror image, of the outrages he has suffered. The list of offenses is long: he hurls murderous curses at his son; he punishes innocent defendants with pleasure, doing so even after accepting their bribes; he claims the blessing of the Delphic oracle for his treachery; he proudly maintains that he would sell the rightful inheritance proceeds of a fatherless daughter instead of seeing that she receives them; he drinks to excess knowing the deleterious effect upon him, so long as he will bear no responsibility for the *kakia* he causes; he destroys property; he starts fistfights; he sexually harasses a young woman. Each of these singly, and all of them taken together, bear witness to his hubris. These outrages should also be seen as measure-disclosing. The negation of all of these actions, when generalized, would serve as a worthwhile contribution to a primer of basic human conduct.

At this point, further attention to the *names* given to the two main characters yields considerable and important new light upon this comedy. "Strepsiades," "Socrates," and even "Pheidippides" belonged to their bearers in such a way that their identities were clearly distinguishable from the identities of others. By contrast, "Philocleon" and "Bdelocleon" define their bearers entirely in terms of their relation to another, Cleon. Philocleon has paid a terrible price for his name. He cannot shake his namesake's pernicious influence upon his humanity though he tries on several occasions, once he has discovered the truth about Cleon. Lacking both the honor and the intensity of his father, Bdelocleon falls far short of heroic stature. Despite his correct assessment of Cleon's nature, Bdelocleon's own superficial unreflectiveness indicates the steep price that he has also paid. He equates goodness with luxury. One finds no recognition at all that he belongs to the generation that prospers thanks to the courage of men like Philocleon. He "educates" his wronged father by teaching him social hypocrisy.[54] He celebrates their new union by encouraging his father to drink to excess. He assures his father that the wealth and influence of his feasting partners will protect him from the easily foreseeable consequences of his drunkenness.

The decidedly negative characterization of Bdelocleon seriously calls into question the view that *Wasps* is primarily a biting satirical attack upon Cleon, if it does not give the lie to this conventional wisdom altogether.[55] The character who bears the name of the one who hates Cleon is at least as comically depraved as Philocleon. This is no mere scholarly quarrel, but goes to the heart of Aristophanes' artistry, to the thoughtfulness embedded in his comic genius. A human being, in order to be fully human, requires *a name of his or her own.* More particularly, one must be self-defined insofar as this is possible and appropriate for a human being. Of course the proper discharge of one's familial, social, and political obligations belongs to one's identity. The Greeks surely understood the nature and the complexities of these relations. The Dionysian festivals at which the tragedies and comedies were performed served precisely to present and to celebrate these relations in all of their glory, horror, and complexity, just as the Panathenaea did for the Homeric and Hesiodic epics.

In the tragedies and the epics, the heroes were surely given over to familial, social, and political matters that played significant roles in their identities. But *they all had their own names,* and consequently their behavior, their speech, and their actions were clearly individuated. By contrast, in *Wasps* the two main characters lack such individuation. By virtue of their respective relation to Cleon *in* their names, they do not reveal the appropriately human limits by virtue of the "pity and fear" they inspire in the spectators. Instead, they reveal these limits through the laughter they provoke. Philosophically speaking—that is, speaking in terms of the love of wisdom—defining oneself in terms of someone else is *folly,* begetting ridiculous humanity.

Philocleon's ridiculous "liberation" from Cleon shows how a human soul can be deformed by having suffered injustice and how thoroughly hubris can root itself in the human soul. The consequences of his drunken actions will even exceed the excesses from which Philocleon supposed he was immune! He tells *logoi* that are indeed "completely inappropriate to the situation": *proseti logous legōn amathestat'* (1320–1321). However, these *logoi* occur in the context of direct, personal insults to those very "gentlemen" who were to protect him. Further, the liberation of this "new" Philocleon has produced a most surprising and self-destructive reversal. When threatened with summonses for the damage he has wrought in his drunken state, Philocleon calls his accusers "archaic" (*arkhaia*) (1336), since he "can't stand to hear about lawsuits" (1337–1338). "Throw out voting urns," he urges (1339).

Of course it takes only a minimum of insight to judge Philocleon's actions as being both outrageous and unworthy. But recalling that the Dionysian festival serves to effect a reunification of humanity with nature that overcomes all social convention,[56] and recalling that spectators and readers find themselves before a poem in service to the wine god, Philocleon enacts the movements of a prototypical Dionysian hero. As he waves his phallus in the face of the flute girl he has kidnapped—in this very outrage—he symbolizes and reenacts the phallic procession that characterized the original Dionysian festivals.

LINES 1364–1448

Father and son seem to have reverted to their relationship as it stood at the outset of the play. Noticing that Dardanis, the kidnapped piper girl, is in Philocleon's custody, Bdelocleon hurls a vile epithet at his father: *tuphedane kai khoirothlips:* "deluded cunt-chafer"[57] (1364). In response, and with an oblique allusion to his son's coarse imagery, Philocleon replies: "It would please you to eat up a sour lawsuit": *hōs ēdeōs phagois an ex oxous dikēn* (1367). Bdelocleon gets the joke at once: *ou deina tōthazein:* "How awful to make fun of me" (1368). Why this sudden discord? By stealing the flute girl away from the feasters, Philocleon has placed his son in a position in which his filial obligations divide him from his social ones. However, Bdelocleon instinctively moves to protect his father, even within the resurfaced acrimony. As MacDowell has observed, their places in the family structure have been reversed: Philocleon behaves like a reckless young man while Bdelocleon offers paternal protection.[58]

There are two significant encounters with women in these lines. The first is with the flute girl Dardanis, who is almost surely a slave. Philocleon's attempts at seductive charm fall somewhat short. He tells her that she owes him a cock-rubbing, since he kidnapped her just before she was to perform fellatio on the other guests. If she yields to his wishes and does not act like a "bad woman now" (*mē kakē nuni gunē*) (1351), he'll buy her when his son dies, and he could call her his own "little cunt" (*khoirion*). (*Khoiron* also has the sense of "pig.") Referring to himself as "young" (*neos*) and under the care of his overprotective son who worries about spoiling his father, he urges Dardanis to stand still while he attempts to trick Bdelocleon into thinking that it is not the flute girl, but a torch that he carries.

Here, MacDowell observes that Philocleon's associations with youth at this point are "not just an elaborate verbal joke. They imply a comment on the plot of the play as a whole: Philocleon's change to a new way of life has rejuvenated him."[59] As I indicated at the end of the previous section, much can be said in favor of such a view. However, I would add the following observation on the limits of his rejuvenation. Throughout both his "courtship" of Dardanis and his rancorous and ultimately physical conflict with his son, Philocleon remains aware that he can *no longer achieve an erection.*[60] Regarding the latter, he commands:

> Come up this way, my little blond cockchafer. (*offering his phallus*)
> Grab hold of this rope with your hand.
> Hang on, but be careful, the rope's worn out;
> all the same, it doesn't mind being rubbed.
>
> *Anabaine deuro, khrusomēlolonthion,*
> *tē kheiri toudi labomenē tou skhoiniou.*
> *ekhou: phulattou d', hōs sapron to skhoinion:*
> *homōs ge mentoi tribomenon ouk akhthetai.* (1341–1344)

However, as we shall soon see, Philocleon's impotence is both only sexual, and more than sexual.

This section concludes with the escape of Dardanis made possible by the argument between father and son, i.e., by their contest in *logos,* at the end of which Dardanis finds herself unattended. This intervening exchange features several provocative elements of Aristophanes' ridiculous thoughtfulness. Dardanis is ordered by Philocleon to stand still in the darkness, so that he might convince his son that a torch and not a woman stands before him. During the inspection, the father points to several features. He points to the place where the torchwood properly splits—its "cleavage" (*eskhismenēn*) (1373). He indicates the site at which the hot pitch comes out (*hē pitta dēpou kaomenēs exerkhetai*) (1375). When his somewhat dimwitted son begins to discern the truth—"And behind there, isn't this an asshole?" (1378)—Philocleon claims that it's only a knothole. But the suddenly sapient Bdelocleon grabs Dardanis away and calls his father "worn out and utterly unable to perform" (1380–1381). Undeterred, Philocleon tells a tale of Olympia in which old Ephudion knocks young Ascondas down. Then he "sucker-punches" his son to the ground, thus enacting the "moral" of the tale.

On Dardanis, who does not speak a word: the dehumanization she undergoes at the hands of everyone in the comedy, both on and offstage, is unmistakable. The despicable treatment, finally including the nonsensical "dialogue" on her nature between father and son, make her escape possible. Her humanity is quite alive to *her,* just as the humanity of the slave women of Achilles in the *Iliad* was very much alive, although permitted to show itself only under the cover of Achilles' grief at the death of Patroclus.[61] To speak of Aristophanes' *intention* at this point and in such an interpretation is beside the point (although few poets, in my opinion, have acknowledged womanly power more openly, as well as more subtly). In the play, her appropriate *silence* empowers her liberation, while the ridiculous prattle of two men who "have power" over her leaves them both to their "unempowered" selves. Philocleon's limp penis and hard fist, together with Bdelocleon's "potency" and his liking of embellished *logoi,* leave both empty-handed, and most deservedly so.

This section seems to move toward its conclusion in the same way as did the analogous section in *Clouds.* Two victims of old Philocleon's outrageous behavior confront him, threatening lawsuits if he does not make recompense for the damage he has caused. The perpetrator, newly "instructed" in the use of *logos,* fends his accusers off (at least temporarily) with the cleverness he has acquired. However, the differences are worth noting. In *Clouds,* Strepsiades fashioned his *logoi* by means of linguistic sophistry. Philocleon tells not-so-charming "charming stories" (*lexai kharienta*) (*Wasps* 1399). Myrtia, the beaten and cheated bread-seller, is treated to a pseudo-Aesopian, "Bitch, bitch (*ō kuon kuon*), if you'd trade that nasty (*kakēs*) tongue of yours for some flour, I'd think you'd be showing sense" (*Wasps* 1403–1405). Philocleon advises the man he assaulted to "practice the craft that he knows" (*Wasps* 1431), as if the victim caused his own injury the way an inexperienced driver falls from a poorly driven chariot.

Both kinds of defective *logoi,* linguistic sophistry and "charming stories," are designed to lead their hearers away from what is true. Both are unmoored from reality. And *in the comedy,* neither displays the slightest effectiveness in convincing their hearers. To be sure, the pain experienced by the victims has a great deal more influence than the ludicrous efforts of the perpetrators to mislead them. I suggest strongly, however, that the depth of *Wasps* on this matter consists in this, that the resistance shown by the victims to the sway of Philocleon's misleading *logoi* flows entirely from the directness and immediacy of the attack. The more indirect the situation, the easier it is for misleading *logoi* to succeed. Recall Philocleon's earlier high regard for Cleon, from whom he draws his very name! Cleon's *logoi* were neither direct nor immediate. They ably hid their exploitative hold on the wasps by means of flattery and by means of offering them bogus power. In this manner, the men who were responsible for the Athenian prosperity were cruelly led away from their rightful share of it.

In the final event of this section, Bdelocleon carries his fuming father into the house. He does so out of concern for the proliferation of legal witnesses his father's words and actions are creating, and not at all out of any sense of shame or justice. We are left with two wonderful characters. Aristophanes provides neither with an ultimately redeeming quality, but gives them a great many hilariously odious traits through which we can vicariously experience ourselves.

LINES 1448–CONCLUSION

The choral song with which the final section opens has occasioned different and opposed interpretations. It ascribes "good fortune" (*eutuxias*) (1449) to the old man. His colleagues sing: "he has learned other ways / and he'll make a great change": *hetera de nun antimathōn / ē mega ti metapeseitai* (1452–1453). Though there is a brief caveat ("But maybe he'll not want that"—1455), the tone is surely upbeat. A paean to Bdelocleon sounds within the song: "So kind a man I've never / met, nor with anyone's behavior / have I been so 'crazy about' (*epemanēn*)[62] and melted away" (1467–1469). He is praised for having "stronger rebuttals" (*antilegōn . . . kreittōn*) (1470–1471), and for leading his father to "classier" activities.

MacDowell reads this song as both appropriate to the plot of the comedy, and appropriately placed as well.[63] He reads the caveat as the Chorus' recognition that Philocleon is still a work in progress and that the outcome sought by Bdelocleon is not yet certain, although some clear gains have been made. Given the previous scene, however, the discovery of significant progress is not an easy task. Encouraged by the belief that the education in behavior and especially in *logos* provided by his son would exempt him from the consequences of his outrageous actions, Philocleon behaves far worse than he ever did when under the sway of Cleon.[64] Further, the example of Bdelocleon's sham cultivation has shown itself to be hardly worth emulating in the first place.

Therefore, it seems clear to me that the contents of the song are *ironic.* His thoroughly unmeasured actions in the company that his son referred earlier to as "noble and good" (*kalois te kagathois*) (1256) show clearly that Philocleon is far from ready for what the Chorus calls "a life of delicate luxury" (*epi to truphōn kai malakon*) (1454). Bdelocleon also merits no such praise. It was he, after all, who encouraged his father to drink as he wished and have no care for the consequences. The song is neither an accurate assessment of Philocleon's progress, as MacDowell argues, nor is it a misplaced item at odds with the rest of the plot, as Rogers and Zielinski maintain. Rather, it is a perfectly placed comic inversion of the moral status of this remarkable father-son relationship.

The comedy closes with a slave calling out to Dionysus, the god of the festival. "Some god (*daimōn*) has set our house awhirl (*eiskekuklēken*) with some confusing business! (*apora . . . pragmata*)" (1474–1475). Philocleon has danced the old tragic dances all night, and has called others—Carcinus and his sons—to join him on stage. The reconstruction of the actual choreography is impossible, though some interesting speculations might be made.[65] For this interpretation, however, other matters take precedence. First of all, the invocation of Dionysus and the wine-inspired dancing of the old tragic dance honors the god under whose aegis, and the setting within which, the comedy occurs.[66] To Xanthias, the more passionate and more reactive of the two slaves, the actions of Philocleon bespeak *kakia*— Henderson has "trouble," another variant of "badness."

Xanthias' appraisal quickly accelerates from "the beginning of madness" (*manias arkhē*) to a diagnosis of its full presence. He urges Philocleon to take medicine for this affliction, and warns him that he'll soon be pelted, which is a public reaction to public madness. To Philocleon's expression of pleasure in his own peculiar terpsichorean virtuosity—"Not bad?" (*ouk eu*) (1496)—Xanthias replies, "No, by god, it's mad business" (*manika pragmata*) (1497). Thus for Xanthias, madness equals badness, at least the drunken madness of Philocleon does. Xanthias, as we have seen, prizes quiet and order and is easily shaken by both actual events and by dreams. It is thus not difficult at all to follow the increasing intensity of his judgment.

However, as we have also seen, *divine* madness bestows the greatest gifts upon humanity. What kind of madness does Philocleon display in his spirited dancing? I return to Plato's *Phaedrus:* "That," i.e., avoiding lovers because they are mad, "would be fine to say if madness were simply bad (*haploun to manian kakon einai*): but the greatest goods come to us through madness, when it is given as a gift from the god" (244a5–8). Of the four kinds of divine madness listed by Socrates, the third reads as follows: "This madness takes hold of a tender soul . . . it arouses and fills the soul with a Bacchic frenzy (*ekbakkheuousa*)" (245a2–3). Such an inspired soul creates lyric songs and other kinds of poetry that recalls the deeds of the ancients and so "preserves these deeds as suitable models for the coming generations" (245a3–5). I maintain that the madness inspiring Philocleon's final dance is divinely inspired, along the lines of this third kind.

This distinguishes his behavior from the treatment of his victims recounted in the previous section. There, his actions were both *calculated* and *abusive,* two traits that are characteristic of human behavior that is unmoored from goodness and truth. It can certainly be argued that the fit with the Platonic third kind of divine madness is inexact. While one can certainly speak of a Dionysian frenzy, Philocleon creates no poetry. Nor can one maintain that his soul is in any sense "tender" or "virgin" (*abaton*). However, the text also suggests strongly that Philocleon dances with energy and skill. His contact with "Dionysus" (he had not gotten drunk for a long time), after a long lapse, has magically revitalized him.

As he had set his own house whirling (*eis**kekuklēken,*** emphasis mine), so he sets the Chorus of his colleagues whirling and slapping their bellies: *strobei: parabaine **kuklō** kai gastrison seauton* (1529). In this manner, dancing off the stage, the last words are given to, and are . . . the comic chorus (*khoron trugōdōn*) (1537). What has become of the wasps?

In the context of the city, they began as underpaid and exploited factotums of Cleon and his associates. By means of Bdelocleon's superior counterarguments (*antilegōn . . . kreittōn*) (1470), they became aware of their own victimization at Cleon's hands, and so had lost their pretext for punishing defendants in order to collect their pittance. Like Cleon, however, their liberation from a life of falsehood, deception, and injustice did not translate directly into its opposite. Perhaps the paradigm of a life like Bdelocleon's recommended itself on account of its luxury and superficial refinement. But Bdelocleon hardly presented an image of a good human life. Nor, of course, is he "supposed" to. *Wasps* is a comedy. There are no "role models." Every character, including the hapless victims of Philocleon's mistreatment, is held up for derision in some way. That all human beings are subject to ridicule in some way and at some time—this is the stuff of which the philosophical comedy of Aristophanes is made. Once again, this essentially human ridiculousness is the analogue of Socratic ignorance, the only human wisdom.[67]

Although the liberation from falsehood, deception, and injustice came nowhere near the inception of philosophical dialogue on the nature of the best life for a human being, the area vacated by former mistaken beliefs left a space open for the advent of Dionysus. This space allowed for the transformation of a chorus comprised of wasps looking to protect their scant privileges and to harm helpless defendants, into a union of celebrants whirling in a dance of joy. As for Philocleon, this most hard-hearted of the wasps transforms into the ablest, most expert, and playful dancer of all. In its final scene, the earlier image of human life is transfigured. Human life is neither a matter of rhetorical manipulation nor of self-indulgent luxury. Rather, human life shines forth as a divinely mad dance of collective joy. But this means that the entire comedy, from its very beginning, was always such a dance—only waiting to break forth in its express visible form.

Wasps concludes with Bdelocleon nowhere in sight, and with the chorus led offstage by Philocleon. It began with Bdelocleon asleep on the roof beside his two slaves. At its outset, Philocleon is "humanly mad," and has to be prevented from escaping his son's house. At its conclusion, he is "divinely mad," having been purged of *some* of his human madness by means of the *logoi* of his son. Bdelocleon, however, was *never* mad in either sense. One is tempted to say that, like his analogue Pheidippides in *Clouds,* he has not been pushed to the limit as much, and his humanity is simply not sufficiently interesting to be visited by madness. Unlike Pheidippides, however, Bdelocleon's care for his father shows itself clearly in his wish to relieve Philocleon of the lies and pains under which he had been laboring.

Logos and *dialogos,* understood as "argument" and "dialogue," are Bdelocleon's means for beginning to turn his father (and his father's colleagues) away from the influence of Cleon, even if they fell short of turning him away from his habit of being a judge. The Chorus correctly characterized Bdelocleon's arguments as *antilegōn,* rebuttals. Their force, like that of Socratic *elegkhoi,* is not merely negative but also *purgative.* What about the possibility of pure positivity in the realm of *logos*? Both the dialogues of Plato and the comedies of Aristophanes strongly suggest that such positivity is not to be had by human beings. In Plato's *Apology* and elsewhere, Socratic ignorance serves as the philosophical guarantee of this. In *Wasps,* the confident *logoi* issuing from the mouths of two competing dogs bear witness to its corresponding comic insight. Our assent seals the former. Our laughter seals the latter.

The ridiculous thoughtfulness of Aristophanes thus reminds us that we are cheese-hogging dogs when we forget our limits, that we are at our human best when we remain mindful of these limits—and that when we do remain mindful, we leave room for the great, joyful gift of madness to visit us.

Part 2

Erōs and Human Limits

Three

Assemblywomen

Erōs and Human Law

The closest textual connection between the comedies of Aristophanes and the dialogues of Plato occurs in the connection between *Assemblywomen* and large sections of *Republic* book 5. Socrates himself has indicated that book 5 is comic in nature, doing so in an oblique but ultimately unmistakable manner. Near the conclusion of book 4, he and Glaucon agreed to a definition of justice:

> Socrates: Isn't the cause of all this that, so far as ruling and being ruled are concerned, each of the parts in him minds its own business? (*Oukoun toutōn pantōn aition, hoti autou tōn en autō hekaston ta hautou prattei arkhēs te peri kai tou arkhesthai*)
>
> Glaucon: That and nothing else is the cause.
>
> Socrates: Are you still looking for justice to be something different from this power which produces such men and cities?
>
> Glaucon: No, by Zeus, I'm not. (443b1–6)

This account of justice applies "not with respect to a man's minding his external business, but with respect to what is within, with respect to what truly concerns him and his own" (443c9d1).

However, soon thereafter Socrates finds himself having recourse to this just-secured definition of justice in a very different context. At the conclusion of book 4, Socrates and Glaucon appeared ready to address the matter of distinguishing the different kinds of cities and their corresponding souls.

But book 5 opens with the "interruption" of the discourse on the cities (which will not resume until book 8). Adeimantus, speaking for all of his other colleagues including Glaucon, accuses Socrates of "taking it easy, and robbing us of a 'whole section' (*eidos holon*) of the *logos*" (449c2). That *eidos* concerns the community of women and children. While the guardians might well, as friends, share all things in common (see 416d3–417b9), this result can hardly obtain so easily (!) in the case of women and children.

The "three waves" follow: (1) men and women exercising naked together and preparing for military service together; (2) marriages "arranged" in order to ensure the best offspring; (3) the so-called (and all-too-quickly called) philosopher-king, whose rule is required if cities and human beings are ever to be free of their evils. Granting that the first wave would be seen as ridiculous (*geloios*) in light of current practices, Socrates enjoins his interlocutors not to "be afraid of all the jokes (*skōmmata*)—of whatever kinds—the wits (*kharientōn*) might make if such a change took place in gymnastic, in music and, not least, in the bearing of arms and the riding of horses" (452b6–c2). However, he then says, "we must make our way to the rough part of the law, begging [the wits] not to mind their own business but to be serious" (452c4–6).

Socratic seriousness is governed by the following set of "principles":

> But, I suppose, when it became clear to those who used these practices that to uncover all such things is better than to hide them,[1] then what is ridiculous to the eyes disappeared in the light of what's best as revealed in *logois*. And this showed that he is foolish (*mataios*) who believes that anything is ridiculous other than the bad (*to kakon*), and who tries to produce laughter looking to any sight as ridiculous other than the sight of the foolish (*aphronos*) and the bad; or again, he who looks seriously (*spoudazei*) to any standard of beauty he sets up other than the good. (452d3–e2)

It is the business of the wits, i.e., of the comic poets, to ridicule what is ridiculous. As I have often maintained, the laughter provoked by such ridicule is truth-disclosing laughter. That business, to a comic poet, is "what truly concerns him and his own." Since justice consists precisely in doing that which truly concerns a person and is that person's own, the comic poets such as Aristophanes would be *perpetrating an injustice* if they withheld their ridicule and were serious. From this playfully oblique Socratic interlude, the context for the "three waves" is clear. Human beings are given over to folly. If we were not, philosophy would not exist at all. Since folly is a feature of every one of us, it is simply *impossible* for *logoi* to make disappear what the eyes see, and to reserve our laughter only for the foolish and the bad. Similarly, it is impossible for us to regard only goodness as beautiful. It is not the place here to discuss how the visible and the intelligible are ultimately intertwined in the *Republic.*[2] For us partial fools, the treatment of Teiresias by Oedipus does not produce laughter, nor do we regard Alcibiades as ugly without qualification. What, then, can be made of the Socratic "principles" as detailed in the above citation? They deserve ridicule. They are *comic.* But the Aristophanic comic includes seriousness in its very provocation of laughter.

Given the specific contents of the second of the three waves, one can easily discern what appears to be an *agōn* in *logos* not only within the *Republic* and within *Assemblywomen,* but between the philosopher Plato and the comic poet Aristophanes. This crossing of the two, whether it turns out indeed to be an *agōn* or perhaps something more and/or something different, will surely bear close attention and could well yield philosophical results that exceed those yielded by *Clouds* and *Wasps,* given this close textual engagement.

LINES 1–168

Assemblywomen begins with its heroine, Praxagora (Woman Effective in Public),[3] offering a paean to the "radiant eye of the wheel-whirled lamp, most beautiful (*kallist'*) invention of skilled artisans" (1–2). The peculiar beauty of this lamp is connected with its bearing "the sun's radiant honors (*timas*) in your nozzles" (5). However, the reflected light of this praiseworthy lamp resides just as much in what it hides as in what it illuminates. The eye that draws its sight from it reveals and conceals both public matters and private ones. Praxagora has hatched a plot whereby the women of Athens will seize political power from the men, who have managed the city's affairs ineptly. The "radiant eye" knows of this plot, which is hidden entirely from the men who are its target. In private, the "radiant eye" alone can see the women's preparation for essaying "Aphrodite's maneuvers":

> You alone illuminate (*monos . . . lampeis*) the ineffable nooks
> between our thighs,
> When you singe away the hair that sprouts there;
> And you stand by us when stealthily we open pantries
> Full of bread and the liquor of Bacchus;
> And you're an accomplice who never blabs to the neighbors.
> So you'll be in our present plans (*bouleumata*) too . . . (12–18)

Praxagora's power then, both public and private, draws from a source that serves to illuminate and to cover up simultaneously. The ultimate source of her power, however, derives from her shrewd intelligence. She presents an image of herself that is at least somewhat unwholesome. Her conspiracy against the current political establishment depends upon secrecy and subterfuge. Not only the usual womanly adornments and niceties belong to her erotic repertoire, but also she suggests that they are employed in a libertine fashion. The "radiant eye" does not blab to the neighbors about the goings-on between her "walls." However, this canny and comic self-presentation to which both illumination and covering-up belong conceals a depth that must be noted. Praxagora possesses many of the traits belonging to a *philosopher.* Just as well, she has traits that make her a suitable *founder of cities.* In other words, she may ultimately have to be measured against that purportedly highest of Socratic standards, that of *philosopher-ruler.*

For one, Praxagora recognizes her own limits. She is well aware that women not only have no vote, but also are not even allowed in the public assembly where democratic decisions are made. On the private side, she also knows that her natural charms fall short of the divine Aphrodite's. But she also recognizes the wonderful possibilities within these limits. She is hardly resigned to the civic powerlessness to which her gender seems destined. Instead she enacts a twofold plan: to take over the rule of the city and to introduce wise rule that will end faction between citizens. And she is able to secure satisfying sexual ardor by enhancing her natural appearance and by augmenting the passion of her partner. While a comic heroine such as Praxagora certainly appears in a different guise than the one of the philosopher Socrates in a Platonic dialogue, both are characterized by their awareness of their own limits, and by an unflappable confidence and cheerful bearing in the face of—and perhaps even because of—this awareness.

Her plan to ascend to the rule of the city requires wholesale dishonesty: stealth, disguise, and theft. The conspiracy is strictly secret. The women procure false beards, and steal the clothing and boots of their husbands. This is done successfully, but not without difficulties. The women are a bit late. First Woman's[4] sailor husband kept her busy all night, "sailing me under the sheets" (39). Second Woman's husband ate too many anchovies on the previous evening and coughed the entire night. However, both have made important preparations. First Woman has grown "armpits bushier than underbrush" (60–61) and has oiled herself so she appears to be an "outdoor" man rather than an indoor, housebound woman. Second Woman discarded her razor "so that I'd get hairy all over and not look female at all" (66–67).

What can be said concerning all of this deception? Here, the intersection with Plato's *Republic* is especially resonant. First of all, certain kinds of lies were given a pass as early as *Republic* book 2: "Now, what about the lie in speeches (*en tois logois*)? When and for whom is it also useful, so as not to deserve hatred? Isn't it useful against enemies, and, as a preventive, like a drug, for those who are called friends (*tōn kaloumenōn philōn*) when from madness or from some folly they attempt to do something bad" (382c6–9).

The status of lies is elevated to a virtual *necessity*, however, when it comes to the building of cities. After declaring that "eminent rulers" are needed (*dei akrōn einai tōn arkhontōn*) (459b11) and adding that "it will be a necessity (*anagkē*) for them to use many drugs (*pharmakois pollois khrēsthai*)" (459c 2–3), Socrates identifies *lies* as these very drugs.

In response to Glaucon's inquiry as to the purpose of these lies, Socrates responds first in a general way: "It's likely that our rulers will have to risk (*kinduneuei*) a throng of lies and deceptions (*tō pseudei kai tē apatē*) for the benefit of the ruled. And, of course, we said that everything of this sort is useful as a form of remedy (*pharmakou*)" (459c8–d2). He follows this general answer with more specific remarks regarding the regulation of "marriages and procreations," which I will take up when this point in *Assemblywomen* is reached. For now, it is sufficient to note that on account of her ability to lie for the benefit of her fellow citizens and so to build Athens anew out of these lies, Praxagora may indeed also qualify as a founder of cities.

If a stretch can be made such that the women-conspirators are regarded as analogous to the guardians in the *Republic*, as I suggest here, then they must be constrained from the kinds of speeches and deeds that are unsuitable to their nature as the highest class in their city. Just as in the *Republic*, the plan is motivated entirely by the desire "to do something good for the city" (*hōst' agathon ti praxai tēn polin*) (108). The plan necessitates their arriving in full male costume at the assembly early and taking their places at the front. They are to speak to their "fellow citizens" in the manner of men. They must not *knit* in public, as Second Woman wishes to do and for which Praxagora scolds her (87–93). Nor should any woman climb over a crowd of people in order to get to the front and in so doing reveal her "Phormisius" who, as Henderson notes, was "a moderate democrat whose beard suggested female genitalia."[5]

When challenged by First Woman to explain "how a gathering (*xunousia*) of women with women's insight (*thēluphōn*) can address the public" (110–111), Praxagora replies conclusively and at once: "Very excellently, that's how": *polu men oun arista pou* (111). Her provocative argument in support of this conclusion: "They say that the young men who have been reamed (*spodountai*)[6]"—i.e., who have had the "below" position in homosexual encounters—"are the most 'wondrous' at speaking (*deinotatous einai legein*): by luck (*kata tukhēn*), we are suited for this" (112–114). The "logical" form of the argument is clear: since both *spodountai* men and women are "below" in sexual positions, and *spodountai* men are wondrous speakers, women will also share this "virtue." However, there may be an even coarser layer to the argument: those "on the bottom" are the ones who tend to cry out *deinotaton* in the sense of "most thunderously," "most loudly," perhaps "most dramatically" in this context. In this sense, the similar sexual "natures" of *spodountai* men and women grant them similar powers in public speaking.

One can discover a distant but discernible connection between this comic likeness in *Assemblywomen* and two related comparisons between the genders in Plato's *Republic.* At 454c1–5, Socrates dismisses the view that "the nature of the bald and the longhaired" is a difference in nature that is sufficient to bar one of these classes from performing an art, such as shoemaking. He likens such a difference to the one according to which "the female bears and the male mounts" (454d9–10), which has no relevance when considering the performance of some art (*tekhnēn*) or practice. The similarities between the genders concern the "distinction" (*diapheron*), the "excellence" (as Bloom translates) in such performance, whether this excellence belongs to a man or a woman.

Certainly, Socrates asserts the *general* superiority of men over women in the practice of certain arts and practices, but he grants that women may well surpass men in any of them:

> Therefore, my friend, there is no practice of a city's governors which belongs to woman because she's woman, or man because he's man; but the natures (*hai phuseis*) are scattered alike among both animals (*en amphoin toin zōoin*); and woman participates (*metekhei*) according to nature (*kata phusin*) in all practices, and man to all, but in all of them woman is weaker than man. (455d6–e2)

"A nature," here, refers to the capacity to perform a certain skill or practice. Most emphatically, "man" and "woman" are not "natures," but "animals" who participate in natures. While Glaucon agrees that "many women are better than many men in many things," and Socrates concurs, it does seem that Socrates believes that the best performer in any nature will be a man. A woman doctor will clearly be a better doctor than would a man shoemaker, but the best doctor and the best shoemaker will both be men.

However, Socrates' argument does not, strictly speaking, support this conclusion, even if the general premise is granted. Even if a large majority of women are better cooks than the large majority of men, it is still possible for the best cook to be a man. The same obtains in the cases of guardians and rulers. Given the possibility of some superiority for either gender *within* a nature, it follows that it is possible for a member of a minority of generally weaker guardians and less able rulers to be the best guardian and the best ruler of all. Socrates the philosopher will not call such a ruler by name, but only designate this leader by a term that will prove to be highly problematic: philosopher-king. Aristophanes the comic poet will call this leader by name: she is a woman, and her name is Praxagora.

Her cohorts do not, at first, inspire confidence. Immediately after Praxagora declares the good luck of their suitability for public speaking, First Woman replies, "I don't know: not having experience is dangerous (*deinon*)" (115). Garlanded and thirsty, she wishes to drink wine (*piein*) (133) before speaking, as if attending a symposium. After Praxagora chastises her, First Woman argues that there must be a great deal of wine consumed at the Assembly, since the men's decrees are "like the ravings of drunkards" (139). Praxagora not only tells her to sit down, but says, "You are good for nothing (*ouden gar ei*)" (144). With these three words, a division between *what is true* and *what is good for the city* begins to show itself. First Woman has spoken the truth about the deliberations of the Athenian assembly, and Praxagora certainly agrees with this analysis. However, First Woman's proposed public persona and behavior as a garlanded drunkard would defeat the entire political agenda—aimed at the good of the city—of Praxagora and of her women associates. As has already become apparent, lies are necessary for the building of cities. First Woman, while full of "virtue" for the occasion (i.e., hairy, oiled, and bearded) disqualifies herself by "truthfully" imitating the "effective" deliberations of the assemblymen.

Second Woman cannot restrain herself from swearing by goddesses instead of gods, and by addressing "ladies" instead of men. Praxagora calls her "loser" or "disastrous one" (*dustēne*) on account of these quite understandable slips of the tongue. However, like her predecessor, if Second Woman slipped this way in the actual public speech, the vision of a good city could not have even found utterance. Within the comic interplay of the quite human women, one discerns a deadly serious truth: political plotting against a well established regime requires great care, and allows very little room for error. Thus, Praxagora herself must take responsibility.

LINES 169–310C

In her rehearsal speech, Praxagora asks for the gods' blessing, denounces the city's proclivity for "always employing *ponērois* (wretched men) as leaders" (178), recalls the inconstancy of popular opinion, and claims that "you, the people, are the causes of these": *humeis gar est', ō dēme, toutōn aitioi* (205). Each draws his civic pay from public funds, but angles for private gain. This "man's" solution: turn over the governance of the city to the women, since "we already employ them as stewards and treasurers in our own houses": *kai gar en tais oikiais tautais epitropois kai tamiaisi khrōmetha* (211–212).

Bearded Praxagora explains that the "characters" (*tropous*)[7] of women are better than those of men, and enumerates the many aspects of this superiority. First and foremost is their honoring of ancient tradition and their steadfast resistance to innovation, as illustrated by the way they dye their wool. The dye stays fast and does not fade. By contrast, men would seek to meddle with some innovation (*ti kainon g' allo periērgazeto*) (220) even if the ancient custom functioned very well. In her *logos,* Praxagora effectively appeals to the constancy of women in all matters, opposing this quality to the inconstancy in men of which she earlier spoke. This constancy is manifest in cooking, in carrying burdens on their heads, in celebrating the women-only Thesmophoria,[8] in baking cookies, in driving their husbands crazy, in hiding their lovers in the house, in buying themselves extra treats, in loving their wine quite pure (*euzōron*), and by rejoicing in fucking (*binoumenai khairousin*) (228).

Each line at 221–229 ends with the same group of words: *hōsper kai pro tou:* "as they always have." In this way, the proclaimed constancy of character is rhetorically reinforced. So too is "his" admonition to the "men" not to beat around the bush or ask what their plans are, "but let's simply let them rule": *all' haplō tropō eōmen arkhein* (231–232). They would treat soldiers with much more care, they would use their greater "fundraising" skills, and as consummate cheaters themselves, they would never be cheated when in power. Happy lives shall follow upon the acceptance of this proposal.

The two other women are delighted and full of wonder. Second Woman asks, "Where, O poor dear, did you learn such beautiful speech?": *pothen, ō talaina, taut' emathes houtō kalōs;* (242). Praxagora's rhetorical proficiency came as a result of her hearing the orators when she lived with her husband on the Pnyx, the site of the assembly. First Woman's response, in which she elects Praxagora "general" or "commander" (*stratēgon*) for her own part, and in the names of the other women, bears some close scrutiny: "Then that was not for nothing, honey, that you were so wondrous (*deinē*) and wise (*sophē*)" (245). Here, First Woman employs the same word she used not long ago in a negative and fearful sense, *deinos,* now in a positive and courageous sense.

In the previous chapter, I read Bdelocleon's portrayal of his retort to the wasps as *deinēs* (*Wasps* 650), a word that could mean "wondrous," "marvelous," or perhaps even "terrifying." The Choral Ode of Sophocles' *Antigone* begins with the words: *polla ta deina kouden an- / thrōpou deinoteron pelei* (332–333). This has been translated variously. David Grene's translation, which has been widely used for undergraduates who are experiencing the tragedies for the first time, reads as follows: "Many are the wonders, none / is more wonderful than man."[9] The Harvard edition, translated by Hugh Lloyd-Jones, reads: "Many things are formidable, and none more formidable than man."[10] (Given the acknowledgement of the power of Hades over man as well as the justice that the gods uphold, it is hard to see how *man* merits a superlative here.) The three major lexical definitions as found in Liddell and Scott are "fearful, terrible," "marvelously strong, powerful," and "clever, skillful."[11] In more thoughtful translations, Hölderlin translates *deina* as *ungeheuer,* "monstrous," and Heidegger translates it as *unheimlich,* "uncanny,"[12] or "not at home."[13] For the most part, the "fearful" overtone in *deinos* dominates in the Platonic dialogues,[14] but this is not the meaning I will draw upon. Instead, attending to the breadth and depth that is thought in the poetic word, I will seek out the aspect in the dialogues that thinks the most wondrous and the most fearful together. If I had to render this most provocative word by a synonym, I could not. The best I can do is to translate Kant's *Erhaben* into English as "sublime," and regard it in the Kantian sense as "absolutely great."[15] The experience of the Kantian sublime is both (1) painful, because it outstrips our capacity for human conception and imagination, and (2) pleasurable, because it points the way to a measure and a dignity for human beings that transcends mere sensibility.[16] But this would hardly do for a translation. For the latter, the context must be consulted and the most likely choice made in accord with it.

However, it can well point to a Platonic theme that occurs in several dialogues, and may shed light on the relationship between comedy, tragedy, and philosophy. *Deinos* embraces the most wondrous and the most fearful at once. Allowing "sublime" to serve as a plausible analogue for *deinos,* then both extremes can be regarded as included when this word is thought. In the *Crito,* for example, an analogue of comic and tragic *deinos* can be located in Socrates' discussion of "the people"—more properly, "the many" (*hoi polloi*). Crito observes that *hoi polloi* would not believe that Socrates refused to escape when he could have, but would rather suppose that his friends held onto their money rather than use it to free him. He adds, "Your present situation makes it pretty clear *hoi polloi* can inflict not the least but the greatest evils (*tōn kakōn*) if one is slandered among them" (44d2–5). Socrates is entirely unimpressed: "Would that *hoi polloi* could inflict the greatest evils, for then they would be capable of the greatest good, and that would be beautiful (*kalōs*), but now they cannot do either. They can neither make a man wise (*phronimon*) nor foolish (*aphrona*), but they do things randomly (*tukhōsi*)" (44d6–10). Note that Socrates calls the copresence of "the greatest evil" and "the greatest good" by the name *beautiful.* There does not seem to be a strict distinction in Greek thought between beauty and sublimity as there is in modern thought. *Kalos* indicates something very much like "shiningly."[17]

In a previous discussion, I have pointed out how "the good itself," the ultimate object of all life and all study, lies beyond the scope of the *Republic,* and suggested that it may lie beyond the scope of direct human apprehension. In the *Philebus,* however, a glimpse of such apprehension is provided. While this glimpse cannot in any sense be called anything like "direct apprehension of the good," it certainly qualifies as a certain sighting of it. There, Socrates points out to Protarchus that "any compound, however made, which lacks measure (*metrou*) and proportion (*summetrou*), must necessarily destroy its components and first of all itself" (64d9–e1). It is not a true compound but a jumble, and a misfortune to its possessors. Since the good is the standard of all value, and the value of anything depends upon those marks of beauty called "measure" and "proportion": "the power of the good has taken refuge in the nature of the beautiful": *katapepheugen hēmin hē tou agathou dunamis eis tēn tou kalou phusin* (64e5–6).[18]

Praxagora is a comic instantiation of Platonic beauty, mixing the female and the male with that measure and proportion conducive to thought-provoking laughter. She continues to reveal how well-named she is by displaying other rhetorical skills she acquired by listening carefully while living in Pnyx. She has no doubt heard orators respond to abusive assemblymen, so she demonstrates how she would respond to current Athenian abusers. She would rebuff Cephalus by first calling him "crazy" (*paraphronein*) (249), and then "melancholy-mad"[19] (*melagkholan*) (251). She'll tell the rough politician called Neocleides the Squinter to "go squint up a dog's ass" (255). She'll "counter-screw" if "they try to screw" her, confident she "knows a few tricks" herself (256–258). She'll elbow any policeman who jumps her. Public orators, in order to be effective, must know how to handle hecklers. Praxagora knows this and has prepared accordingly and diligently.

Does Praxagora now think like a man? She does, if "thinking like a man" means using skillful rhetoric to persuade large numbers of people and fending off anyone who stands in the way of one's aims, using abusive language, and applying some force if these will serve the purpose. First Woman notes that she and her colleagues must remind themselves to put their hands up when they vote, because "we're so accustomed (*eithismenai*) to raising our legs" (265). Is First Woman thinking like a woman? Or rather, does the laughter provoked by this comic sequence not raise the question of what a man, and what a woman, *genuinely* is? What role does custom (*ethos*) play in shaping a man or a woman? Recalling the discussion of the *Republic* not long ago, does *phusis,* an ability to perform a certain skill or practice, trump *ethos*? In the Socratic comedy, matters that would look ridiculous if they were done as said—such as men and women exercising naked together—seem to raise difficult questions since their "natures" seem to differ, but "upon deliberation (*episkepsamenō*), it isn't at all hard" (455a7). However, a "sober" deliberation upon the Socratic comedy finds that with regard to men and women, *ethos* provides woefully inadequate resistance to *phusis.* Socrates declared earlier that only someone foolish would regard anything but the bad as ridiculous, and hold anything but the bad up for laughter. The one who holds a standard of beauty other than the good is also foolish (453d3–e2). The naked men will presumably not be aroused by the presence of the naked women, because the latter are "clothed in virtue instead of robes" (*aretēn anti himatiōn amphiesontai*) (457a6–7). Could deliberation produce a more ridiculous result?

The "deliberations" in Aristophanes' Athenian assembly are ridiculous in a somewhat different way. The women are clothed in male attire. Among other arguments, a woman masquerading as a man argues—persuasively to the men, it turns out—that women rejoice in fucking (*binoumenai khairousin*) (228), and that as master cheaters themselves, they could not be cheated when in power. The "deliberation" certainly occurs, but it is concealed from view. Here we find laughter-producing "truths" employed within a big lie that is told in the assembly for a putatively noble purpose, the good of the city. Praxagora's deliberations, aimed at the twin "goods" of the women rising to power and of the consequent recreation of Athens, concern the manipulation of *logos* within a situation that has already been made into something of a sham.

The concealment of the speaker's ultimate purpose belongs to the rhetorician's art. In the Platonic dialogues, it recalls the persuasive but fraudulent *logoi* of the "non-lovers" (*mē erōsin*) in the *Phaedrus,* whether by Lysias as recited by Phaedrus, or by its "shameful" competitor offered by Socrates. Matters become more complicated here. While Socratic deliberations in *Republic* books 2–5 reach the conclusion that many lies, of a certain kind at least, are necessary, Praxagorean "deliberations" simply take this for granted. Those imbued with the Socratic principle concerning the ability of *logos* to regard only the bad as worthy of laughter would, if they are taken as *serious,* have an inhumanly easy time keeping a straight face as First Woman declares the difficulty of concealing her gender: she may find herself "raising her legs" as is habitual, rather than her arms. Praxagora agrees and provides some mnemonic advice: "This is not an easy one: just remember that you vote by undraping your right arm and raising your hand" (266–267).

However, once again an accord obtains between Aristophanic comedy and Platonic philosophy. The city, as it now exists, requires major changes if it is to be a truly suitable place for human beings. In both the *Republic* and in *Assemblywomen* (as well as in the other Aristophanic comedies under consideration here), the image of a *house* (*oikos*) plays a major role. In *Assemblywomen,* the ability of the women to rule the affairs within the walls of their house gives evidence of their ability to govern the affairs of a much larger "house," their city. In the *Republic,* Socrates assigns austere houses suitable for guardians rather than luxurious houses that one might suppose should be awarded to the best and most capable citizens who undertake the most dangerous work. Here, "house" can be looked at in another way, as imaging the soul of an individual human being, each part of which has "its own business" to mind in the proper manner. In both the dialogue and the comedy, the building of the city in *logos* involves attention to the way human beings are "housed." At this early stage, we can see that both the Platonic and the Aristophanic housings involve order and restraint within, even as the former seems "serious" and the latter "ridiculous." There is *much* overlap between the serious and the ridiculous.

The Chorus of Man-Masquerading Women, behind the Chorus Leader, hurry to the assembly in order to get the seats up front. This is important for two reasons: those grouped together in front can make a more visible display of support, showing influence beyond their actual numbers;[20] and only the first 600 who attend will receive the three obol pay.[21] The oddly placed choral song lasts forty lines. (Most such parabases mark the entrance of the Chorus. This one is followed by its exit.) By its means, the spectators are informed of the current social and political situation. One portion of the song deserves special attention. Lines 295a–c read:

sautō prosekhōn hopōs
mēden parakhordieis
hōn dei s' apodeixai

A literal translation would read: "See to it you don't / strike a wrong note / concerning that which it is necessary for you to demonstrate."[22] Not long after, the Chorus commits precisely such a blunder, calling their cohort "womenfolk" (*philas*), instead of "menfolk" (*philous*) (299a–c). But what exactly is the blunder? The blunder, the false note, is *telling the truth*! Must truth and falsity become so readily exchangeable in the political arena in order for the good of the city to be served? Must they necessarily occur in such a monstrous mix in *any* political setting? These are the genuine questions raised through the thoughtful questioning in the Platonic dialogues, and by means of the laughter provoked in the Aristophanic comedies.

LINES 310C–475

Not long ago, I raised the issue concerning what it means to think like a man, casting it in the lofty language of *ethos* and *phusis.* Coming forward to instantiate this issue—*ecce homo!*—is one Blepyrus ("Peeper"), husband of Praxagora. He is wearing his wife's slip and slippers. He is old, thoroughly confused, and utterly uncomfortable. Having groped around fruitlessly in search of his own clothes, he offers the boorish metaphor: "the dung man has been knocking at my back door": *ho d' ēdē tēn thuran epeikhe krouōn ho kopreaios* (316–317). Stepping out of his house and facing the audience, the questions with which his "discourse" begins could not be more earthbound:

> What's going on? Where has my wife gone?
> It's getting near dawn now, and she does not appear.
> I've been lying awake for ages, needing to shit (*khezētiōn*),
> Seeking to take my shoes in the dark
> And my cloak. (311–315)

His questioning grows desperate: "Where oh where (*pou pou*) can someone shit in private?" (320). He cries out in lamentation over his stupidity at marrying at his advanced age, and suspects his absent wife of deceiving him. Then, anticipating some small measure of relief and calculating that at night no one would see him (except the spectators!), he squats —but is soon joined and seen by his neighbor.

Of course his neighbor's wife is also a conspirator, and has taken his neighbor's cloak and boots as well. Decorously, Blepyrus informs his neighbor that he is shitting outside because "I didn't want to shit on the comforter: just had it cleaned" (347), and describes his constipation as "some sort of choke pear's got my food blockaded inside" (354). He worries about his excretory function when he next eats, there being no room within, and asks the spectators whether there is an asshole expert among them knowledgeable about his condition (*kataprōktōn deinos esti tēn tekhnēn*) (364). Another crude metaphor concludes his complaint: a plea to Hileithya, goddess of childbirth (!), to bring relief so that he does not become "a comic dung-pot" (*skōramis kōmōdikē*) (369–371).

Can anything be said in favor of this entirely loutish man? Indeed it can. Regarding Blepyrus as a comic character and interpreting his pronouncements in accord with the peculiar amusement-park-mirroring that so often takes place between the dialogues of Plato and the comedies of Aristophanes, Blepyrus is the comic image of a *Socratic philosopher,* the paradigm for which is given in the *Apology:* he is entirely full of dung, and (but) he knows it. By contrast with his wife Praxagora, who attempts to combine the uneasily joined traits of both philosopher and ruler, Blepyrus' concerns go no further than the purification from his current state—a purification that may promise only more of the same. Once more like Socrates, Blepyrus is "greedy for images," although the images Blepyrus has here presented may seem quite distant from those depicting the piloting of ships, the sun, the divided line, the cave, and the myth of Er.

Like so many of Aristophanes' comic figures, Blepyrus shows signs of a full humanity. He has the normal dignity of a respectable citizen. He seeks to defecate outside only because he believes that he will escape detection. When Chremes enters, sees him squatting, and asks whether he is defecating, Blepyrus has sufficient self-esteem to deny it with a "white lie" in his own behalf (and to tell a second one claiming that he grabbed the slip he was wearing by mistake). Chremes reports that a crowd of pale-faced men took over the Assembly and finished its business before dawn, not only altering the governance of Athens (but more importantly to the men) depriving them of their three-obol pay. Parodying Achilles' elegy for the dead Patroclus in Aeschylus' *Myrmidons* (frag. 138),[23] Blepyrus sings: "Antilochus, raise not the dirge for those three obols / but for me who yet live: for all I have is gone" (391–392).

After Chremes relates a poor man's plea to the Assembly for money and free provisions, he tells Blepyrus about the speech of "a pale, well-presented (*euprepēs*) young man" who "sprang to his feet and addressed the people, arguing (*legein*) in favor of it being necessary (*khrē*) to hand the city over to the women" (427–430). The "crowd" in front agreed heartily (*eu legoi*) (431). Those in the rear however, who came from the country, made deep rumbles (*aneborboruxan*) (433), indicating strong disagreement. This is another reference, somewhat more oblique, to the kind of intestinal rumbling that occurs before defecation. Blepyrus affirms his kinship with their disapproving response as he "lowers" the location of a function placed somewhat higher in the Platonic dialogues: the deep rumblings come "because they are using their intellect, by God": *noun gar eikhon, nē Dia* (434).

Blepyrus then learns that this good-looking, articulate speaker has denounced him as a villain (*panourgon*) (436), a thief (*kleptēn*) (437), and a slanderer (*sukophantēn*) (438), as are most of the men gathered there. Blepyrus agrees! He also agrees with the speaker that that women are "bursting with brains," and trustworthy with secrets—unlike men who leak Council's deliberations all the time. He confesses that, unlike women, who do not cheat even when no witnesses to an agreement are present, men cheat even when there *are* witnesses. He learns that the Assembly, having tried everything else to rid Athens of its ills, voted to turn the city's governance over to the women.

Before considering Blepyrus' attempt to absorb this news, his affirmation of Praxagora's accusations deserves close attention. Likening Blepyrus to the Socratic philosopher in the *Republic,* it should be noted that the philosophic nature has "no taste for falsehood; that is, they are completely unwilling to admit what's false but hate it, while cherishing the truth" (485d2–3). The truth about Blepyrus consists of his collection of odious and dishonest traits. It is significant that Praxagora does not list *lying* among them. This is because however else he may conduct himself, here is a man who cherishes truth.

Slowly, the benefits of the new political arrangement sink into his soul. Since the women will handle all of the city's affairs, he will be relieved of previously onerous responsibilities, such as going to court, caring for dependants, even laboring to wake himself in the morning. Chremes reassures him: "By God, that's all the women's concern now; you can stop groaning and stay at home farting all day" (464). However, this arrangement is not without a drawback. Blepyrus astutely notes that with the women in control, even the old men like him will have to "screw them" (*kinein heautas*) (468) on command. The penalty for failure is severe: "They won't make us breakfast!" But Blepyrus' remark in the midst of this foolishness could not be less foolish: "When forced, it's most terrible of all": *to pros bian deinotaton* (471).

In the *Wasps* chapter above, Philocleon kidnapped Dardanis the flute girl. She was almost certainly a slave. It was at least plausible to suppose that her role included the provision of sexual pleasures to the men at the symposium. While father and son engaged in heated argument, Dardanis escaped at the very first opportunity. If her humanity was of no account to the men, it was certainly dear to her. In *Assemblywomen,* we find another subtly powerful affirmation of women's humanity, here in the voice of the ridiculous but truthful Blepyrus: "When forced, it's most terrible of all": *to pros bian deinotaton*. Of course, this provision of Praxagora's "city in *logos*" is especially ludicrous coming from an old man. However, the measureless horror of the rape of women by men is no joke at all. The laughter provoked by this line differs from that of beholding Blepyrus in his wife's clothing. It is a much darker laughter disclosing, one would hope, an insight denouncing an aspect of Greek culture that allows for the most terrible dehumanization of many women and so degrades it. The simultaneous ridiculous/thoughtfulness of Aristophanes reaches its bright/dark consummation in Blepyrus' utterly stunning remark.

LINES 476–562

These lines open with the command by the Chorus Leader to her cohorts to march circumspectly, lest one of the "roguish men" (*panourgoi*) (481) inspects their "shape" (*skhēma*) (483) from the rear, thereby discovering their true identities. Such a discovery would place them "in disgrace before all their husbands" (*hēmin d' an aiskhunēn pheroi pasaisi para tois andrasin*) (484–486), and would lead to catastrophe. They change back into their customary dress "in the shade, by the wall of the house" (*epi skias elthousa pros to teikhnion*) (496). They meet the triumphant Praxagora, who announces the "good fortune of their business" (*eutukhōs ta pragmat'*) (504–505), and directs the Chorus Leader to establish order among the women while she returns to her own house.

There is much here that deserves study. First of all, the adjective "roguish" (Henderson has "no-good") is applied not merely to a few or to some but, among men, to *hoi polloi* (481). When the matter concerns the study of the *skhēma* of women, the majority of men are in some sense, by nature, *panourgoi.* Unlike Plato's male guardians in *logos* who will putatively be able to look upon their naked female cohorts as clothed in virtue instead of robes, the "real" men who inhabit Praxagora's city are able to notice a woman's swaying hips even when concealed beneath specifically male garments. Further, why are the women so afraid of detection? If discovered, their plight would become unimaginably worse. Once again, the rulers in the Socratic city in *logos* must tell many lies, and engage many co-conspirators, yet *conceal* all of this—lest the "ruled" for whose sake these lies are putatively told become enraged upon their discovery and turn upon their rulers with the viciousness they have been trained to use upon enemies.

Finally, the women must change back "to the way you were" (*palin metaskeuaze sautēn authis hēper ēstha*) (499a–b) in the shade, by the house wall. Concealment once again belongs to the very nature of the political process, as I have endeavored to demonstrate all along. However, it belongs to the private realm as well. In this realm, a difference in nature between men and women also seems to be affirmed. Men are pictured as inept fools and cheaters, placing their own personal interests first, far ahead of those of the city. Women are depicted as competent and honorable, accustomed to subordinate their own interests first to the good of their households, and now to the good of the city. The deals made between women do not require contracts,[24] while the men cheat even when contracts have been drawn up between them.

But having participated in this great deception, can the women *truly* return "to the way they were"? Or is it the case, as Socrates argues in *Republic* book 2, that "to lie and to have lied in the soul about the things that are . . . and to hold a lie there is what everyone would least accept; and that everyone hates a lie in that place most of all" (382b1–5)? Surely such a lie as this one cannot be likened "to the truth as best we can," and so made "useful" (*khrēsimon*) (382d3). Given that astonishing lies are required for the founding of a *politeia* and for sustaining it, and that these lies are not without deleterious effect in the individual soul, what conclusions can be drawn? The first is that for genuine seekers of truth, the political arena is not a promising place to look. If it is to be found there at all, it will be mixed in with all kinds of lies and deceptions, some of which are necessary and some of which are not. Furthermore, lies to oneself—lies "that everyone hates . . . in [the soul] most of all"—are indeed shameful, and require some kind of hiding such as "changing clothing" in the shadows next to a wall, where no one can see. In the comedy here, this involves the shedding of a costume and of false behaviors, for which Praxagora praises the women as "most manly" (*andreiotatai*) (519).

The Chorus Leader places herself and her cohorts at the disposal of Praxagora, of whom she says, "I know that I've never encountered a woman more impressive than you." The word Henderson translates as "most impressive" is the multifaceted *deinotera.* In the previous context, its meaning was its most negative—horrible beyond measure. Here, several meanings are overlaid: most clever, most daring, most dangerous. Taken together, they constitute qualities of leadership that inspire and embolden others to follow. Praxagora will employ the women as counselors "in running the office to which I've been elected" (*hina tēs arkhēs, hēn arti kekheirotonēmai, xumbouloisin pasais humin khrēsōmai*) (517–518), because of their aforementioned manliness.

Here again, the thought-provoking laughter of Aristophanic comedy at once contrasts with and echoes the Platonic take on male/female natures. Treating the difference between the genders as relatively insignificant when deciding who is best suited to perform a particular art, the *Republic* argued that male and female alike could perform the same art. While Aristophanes places the practice of ruling clearly on the side of the male, this peculiar "nature" can be acquired by women. While Socrates has a great deal to say about the arts belonging to the three classes of citizens in his city in *logos,* he has nothing precise to say about the gender of the rulers! We may, perhaps, assume that the rulers and/or the founders are male, as I do. However, as I concluded earlier, there does not seem to be anything belonging to the ruling/founding art as art that is *specifically* male. In any case, the comic-poetic competence of Praxagora provides a wonderful image through which the many foibles of *actual* male rule can be exposed to the ridicule that they deserve.

The dialogue between Blepyrus and Praxagora exhibits far more than Praxagora's more nimble mind. Most notably, it suggests the helplessly ridiculous appearance presented by the simply truthful human being when brought up against the politically clever. Much as Socrates notes that the one who has sought truth and dwelled in its nearness will look like a fool when dragged before the orators in the political arena and in the law courts, Blepyrus—the philosopher's comic analogue—is easily manipulated by his *deinotaton* wife. She wore his boots and stomped like he does in order to fool any would-be thief of his cloak who might have suspected that a weak woman was wearing it. In response to his lament that her actions cost him his assembly pay, she responds with the lie that she was out performing her midwife's art and received a payment greater than her husband would have received from the Assembly, since the child she delivered was a boy.[25] When he reports to her that the Assembly has turned the city over to the women, she plays dumb. The final comic/truth-affirming moment in their exchange occurs after Praxagora, as if in surprise, rejoices that "aggressive people will be in no position to treat the city shamefully in any way, or to testify or trump up charges," and Blepyrus responds: *mēdamōs pros tōn theōn touti poiēsēs mēd' aphelē mou ton bion* (562–563). Henderson translates, again correctly, "Good heavens, don't do that, don't take away my livelihood!" I offer an alternative: "No way, by God, don't wipe out my life!"[26] Blepyrus' is *truly* an ugly, disgraceful (*aiskhron*) life, and he affirms it proudly.

There is yet another element in this dialogue that points in another direction. Praxagora's political cleverness, her ability to lie about the most important matters, is surely on parade here. However, so too is her fidelity to her husband. While their *dialogos* lacks the elegance and sophistication of a modern comedy of manners, the Dionysian stage is hardly the place for these qualities. Blepyrus suspects that his wife has been visiting one or more paramours (though she hardly seemed dressed for a tryst). Praxagora challenges him to "check it out" by smelling perfume on her head. With typical delicacy, Blepyrus reacts, "What? Can't a woman get fucked (*bineitai*) even without perfume?" His wife answers, "Not I, sad to say" (525–526). Sommerstein explains the prominent role of perfume in Greek sexual arousal, and persuasively suggests that in the absence of perfume Blepyrus cannot perform.[27] But her words suggest that the much younger and charismatic Praxagora has no lovers, for younger men would not require this stimulation. Thus, Praxagora exhibits the "philosophical" side of her philosopher-ruler character. She holds true to the marriage vow to her husband, of whom she may be fonder than she lets on.

LINES 563–652

A neighbor, impressed by what he has overheard, comes out of his house and urges Blepyrus to allow his wife to lay out her plan. She promises an end to mugging, envy, poverty, wrangling, dunning, etc., in other words to many of those items that would be listed in the *Republic* under the heading "evils (*kakōn*) for the cities [and] . . . for human kind" (473d6). "Unless the philosophers rule as kings or those now called kings and chiefs genuinely and adequately philosophize, and political power and philosophy fall together (*xumpesē*), while the many natures now making their way from either apart from the other are necessarily excluded can there be rest from these evils" (473c11–d5).

Socrates never uses the word philosopher-king, and there is strong reason for this. At *Republic* 485c3–4, Socrates says the following about those having a philosophic nature: they have "no taste for falsehood; that is, they are completely unwilling to admit what's false but hate it, while cherishing the truth." And after a bit of play culminating in Glaucon's admission that there is "no way" the same nature could be both a lover of wisdom and a lover of falsehood, Socrates says (with apparent redundancy), "therefore the man who is really a lover of learning must strive as intensely as possible for every kind of truth" (485d2–3).

As has been shown, this emphasis upon the philosopher's unswerving orientation toward truth and corresponding hatred of falsehood serves to distinguish him absolutely from the political ruler, to whom falsehood is clearly necessary. The ruler must use many drugs (459c2–3), among them "a throng of lies and deceptions for the benefit of the ruled" which have utilitarian value "as a form of remedy" (*en pharmakou eidei*) (459c8–d1). The most dramatic lie of all with respect to the city has already been told: the noble lie, which arose "of need" (*en deonti*) (414b9), and which told the guardians and rest of the city that the education and rearing that they had actually undergone had itself been a lie. Thus, a philosopher-king is impossible, less possible even than a clever and strong-minded young wife-of-a-crude-old-fool coming to rule Athens and eliminating all of its evils. The philosopher who is also king, and the king or chief who also "genuinely and sufficiently" (*gnēsiōs te kai hikanōs*) philosophizes, are images belonging to the philosopher's comedy. The Neighbor in *Assemblywomen* offers a conditional similar in form, if not in scale, to its spectacular analogue in the philosopher's comedy in *Republic* book 5, cited above. "That"—i.e., the end of the aforementioned evils—"would be great, by Poseidon, if she's not lying (*pseusetai*)" (568).[28] The poet's comedy will allow this conditional to play out in a very different manner than it does in its philosophical counterpart.

In the case of *Assemblywomen* especially, but in the other comedies as well, the comic poet operates according to a different standard. The standard for the comic poet, as well as for the tragedian, is set by the demands of the Dionysian festival. To treat this much too quickly, the festival is a sacred place during which human beings can behold themselves in their essential humanity. Tragedies exhibit the appropriately human limits by showing their heroes, taken from the Greek mythological tradition, shattering against the limits they would transgress. By contrast, as I have endeavored to show, comedies disclose these limits by having their heroes, taken from common life but stripped of the veneer of respectability, treating these limits as if they did not exist.

What, then, is the difference between the comedy of the poets and that of the philosopher? Aristophanic comedy and Aristophanes are in service to *Dionysus,* god of wine, drunkenness, natural excess. This comedy's proper space is on the stage of the Dionysiad. Socratic comedy and Socrates are in service to *Apollo,* god of clarity, form, and order. Accordingly, Apollonian (here Socratic) comedy takes a lofty form of playfulness, exposing ridiculous aspects by means of the subtle play of ideas—e.g., the good city, the nature of human beings—against other ideas and other realities that reveal absurdities concealed within this play of ideas. Dionysian comedy revels playfully in the coarser realities of human life, exposing through laughter (at least in Aristophanic comedy) the ideas that are concealed in political, social, and sexual realities—with much subtlety as well. As I have attempted to demonstrate throughout, the philosophical outcomes of Socratic and Aristophanic comedy are so often akin to one another that this kinship can be no surprise, and what the dialogues disclose through thought-provoking *logos* and what the comedies disclose through thought-provoking laughter inform one another and enhance one another.[29]

The Choral song and the tag line from the Chorus Leader provide an excellent illustration. Praxagora, confident that even her husband will be unable to speak against her proposal, is urged by the Chorus to be both "shrewd (*phrena*) and philosophical (*philosophon*)" (571). But the careful reader/listener might wonder: is it possible to be shrewd and philosophical simultaneously? The *Republic* seems to show forcefully that it is *not* possible. In *Assemblywomen,* the *comic* heroine incorporates them both. The search for truth, belonging to the philosophic nature, requires that one seek the truth and only the truth, forgoing political shrewdness; political shrewdness requires the employment of many lies for the benefit of the ruled.

The Chorus next urges Praxagora to use both qualities to "fight for your comrades" (*philaisin*) (572), i.e., the women. Then it asserts something different, namely that the fight is not just for the women but for the "city's people as a whole" (*politēn / dēmon*) (574–575). The following proposal by the Chorus members is equally convoluted: Praxagora is instructed to present "some sort of wise scheme" (*ti sophou tinos exeurēmatos*) (577). However, she is to include nothing that has ever been done before, because "they hate to consider (*theōntai*) the same old stuff over and over again" (579–580). This wise "scheme" or "strategy" must include every detail of civic organization, hence must include those fundamental matters such as property, marriage, children, etc. However, as including nothing whatsoever (*mēte . . . mēt'*) (578) of what had been proposed before, these matters cannot be considered at all. Finally, the Chorus Leader contravenes everything her Chorus has urged. Suddenly, wisdom does not seem so important. Another quality supervenes: "But no delay, it is necessary to put your thought into play now: *speed* is what spectators most favor": *hōs to* ***takhunein*** *kharitōn metekhei pleiston para toisi theatais* (581–582, emphasis mine).

After insisting that no one object (*anteipē*) or interrupt (*hupokrousē*) until she has finished her presentation, Praxagora begins: "I propose that everyone owns everything in common (*koinōnein*)" (590). Absolute economic equality will be the rule, and there will be "one and the same common standard of life for all" (594). The ridiculous mini-dialogue between Praxagora and Blepyrus that follows may yield a glimpse beyond the political discourse:

> Blepyrus: How would it be the same for everyone?
> Praxagora: If we were eating shit, you'd want the first bite.
> Blepyrus: We'll have the shit in common, too?
> Praxagora: My God, you cut me off by interrupting (*hupokrousas*) . . . (594–596)

First of all, the hilarious response of Blepyrus discloses that the "all" in "all things are held in common" cannot be absolutely inclusive. As was said in *Republic* book 5, all belongs to the public and common domain with the exception of the body (464d8–9). Secondly, Blepyrus' response can be interpreted as ridicule of his wife's proposal, i.e., read as, "You're full of shit." Finally, the word for "interrupt," *hupokrouō,* can also have the salacious meaning of "bang below."[30] Rereading the passage with this word, Praxagora's retort might be, "Stop fucking around." Thus, in this context the exchange can be seen as playful bantering between affectionate spouses, a comic analogue—another amusement-park-mirror distortion—of the love between Odysseus and Penelope, or between Hector and Andromache.

Though the Neighbor is concerned about the economics of property, Blepyrus is interested in a different species of the subject: "If a man sees a girl, desires her and wishes to poke her cunt (*skalathurai*[31]), he'll be able to take her price from this common fund and have all that's commonly wanted, when he's slept with her (*xugkatadarthōn*)" (611–613). But Praxagora seems to sweeten the proposal further, by making the women common property of the men to sleep with free of charge, making children if they like.

Blepyrus supposes that he has a shrewd objection, framed as a question: "Then won't everyone head for the ripest young woman[32] and seek to bang her?": *pōs oun ou pantes iasin epi tēn hōraiotatēn autōn kai zētēsousin epeidein* (615–616). As usual, Praxagora can anticipate her husband's "intellectual predilections" and responds that "the homely and bob-nosed women will sit right next to 'the classy ones' (*tas semnas*), and if a man wants the latter he'll have to bang (*hupokrousei* [once again]) the ugly one first" (617–618). In this way, the requirement for equality in all things will be achieved in "the male drama." Men, young and old alike, who would otherwise have no chance at a "ripe young thing" will not only face better odds, but also have guaranteed access. Similarly women, old and young, who would otherwise be deprived of sexual pleasure will enjoy a similar guarantee.[33]

However, the word that Henderson translates as "classy" has overtones in Greek that echo far beyond our "classy." *Tas semnas* also means "the holy ones," the "revered ones." How can one connect the notion of a "classy young woman," or even more excessively a "ripe young thing," with holiness and reverence? I suggest strongly that Aristophanic comedy here discloses the Greek-Platonic sense of beauty as a divine gift by reducing it to just another commodity—here a sexual one—in the political economy. (This is analogous to the reduction of Zeus' thunder to "farting" from the soup served at the Panathenaea.) Further, insofar as "the power of the good has taken refuge in the nature of the beautiful" (*Philebus* 64e5–6), goodness, too, has been comically relocated from "beyond being" to a mere earthbound ancillary component in the satisfaction of human lust.

The most obviously germane philosophical material consists in Blepyrus' reduction of citizens to human beings who seek only to satisfy their lusts for comfort and for sexual satisfaction. How can such a view of human beings even arise? It can arise only if one abstracts from their more fundamental needs as human beings *in a city.* (This is the crucial sense of Aristotle's "The human being is, *by nature* [*kata phusin*], a political animal.") There are no guardians, nor any discussion of military structure in Praxagora's city. Consequently, there is no mention whatsoever of education in her city. As will soon be shown, no citizen will even have to work. The only sacrifices concern some unpleasantness surrounding the sexual servicing of the ugly and the old. Even those women who are divinely graced and revered, *tas semnas,* are regarded as if they were no more than flowers in season and ripe for the plucking. Blepyrus represents the "human clay" with which the wise Praxagora must shape her city.

The poet's city thus acknowledges both more of human nature than does the philosopher's, and less. Where the Socratic comedy abstracts from the individual bodily *erōs* of the human being, proceeding as if this necessary "first rung" on the *Symposium*'s "ladder of love" did not exist, the Aristophanic comedy abstracts from the remainder of the ascending rungs, proceeding as if—among other things—neither philosophy nor poetry could take place, not to mention virtually all non-sexual civilized relations. The love of one body is the necessary condition for transcendence in the *Symposium.* In the Socratic comedy in the *Republic,* this order is reversed: first there occurs transcendence (subordinating individual desire and identifying one's own good with the good of the city), and only later—when men and women are past childbearing—is free sexual mixing permitted. In *Assemblywomen,* transcendence is signaled only by its absence. Feasting and sex are the only issues for human beings. If one attempted to discern an account of virtue in *Assemblywomen,* this account would consist of the equal access of each citizen to animal self-satisfaction.

Plato's *Philebus* provides another provocative case in which individual *erōs* seems to be absent from consideration. Concerning which "possessions" best serve human life, the axiological order (roughly speaking) is: (1) measure and moderation, (2) beauty and proportion, (3) *nous* and good sense (*phronēsis*), (4) the arts and sciences, and (5) the harmless and pain-free pleasures associated with knowledge and, in certain cases, perception. Earlier, *erōs* is listed by Socrates amidst other similar qualities: "anger, fear, yearning, mourning, *erōs,* jealousy, envy, and the like" as being "pains of the soul and the soul only" (*Philebus* 47e1–4) The contrast with the *daimon Erōs* as characterized in Socrates' recollection of Diotima's instruction in the *Symposium* could hardly be more dramatic.

If the *Symposium* ceased at the conclusion of Socrates'/Diotima's *logos,* which ended with an approach to pure, disembodied, unsullied beauty, it would seem as if *erōs* in its lowly, human form as a kind of ache in the soul had been transcended completely. Of course the dialogue is far from over at that point. The entrance of the drunken, young, beautiful Alcibiades seems to disrupt both the kind of speeches given and the nature of the gathering. However, Alcibiades finds unequivocal welcome among those gathered. The earlier agreement that no wine would be consumed gives way immediately to Alcibiades' proffering of large quantities of wine to be consumed quickly and eagerly by each of those present. *Logoi* to be presented in praise of *Erōs* are left behind by Alcibiades, who chooses to praise Socrates instead. Within this praise, the comically painful individual longing of Alcibiades for Socrates' favors, the younger for the older, comes forth as its center.

Just as one can distinguish the Socratic comedy from the Aristophanic comedy as Apollonian is distinguished from Dionysian, one can distinguish the pre-Alcibiades symposium from the post-Alcibiades symposium in terms of the same Apollonian/Dionysian distinction. While no wine was consumed, the gathering could only be regarded as an Apollonian collection of *logoi.* The gathering does not become a symposium properly speaking, a *sum-posion,* until wine is consumed in honor of Dionysus, the god whose festival provided its occasion. Read closely, the axiology that occurs near the conclusion of the *Philebus* raises questions as well as provides a guide: "but first the eternal nature has chosen measure, moderation, fitness, and all which is to be considered similar to these": *alla prōton men pē peri metron kai to metrion kai kairion kai panta hoposa khrħ toiauta nomizein, tēn aidion hērēsthai phusin* (*Philebus* 66a6–9). "Measure and moderation" are granted by the "eternal nature," not by human *tekhnē.* After its denunciation of pleasure as the greatest good, the dialogue does not end with an exhortation to measure, but with a non-specific reference by Protarchus to further matters he wishes to discuss with Socrates. I suggest that this so-called "later" dialogue, at least as read in the context here, is aporetic in its own peculiar way: not only is the question, how indeed is measure to be achieved in the face of the "ache" of bodily *erōs*? But also, of what can measure consist, given the necessary presence of the Dionysian in life? Thus, if the Socratic and the Aristophanic comedies could somehow be "integrated" into one another, or "balanced" together, the elusive measure might "come to light." But they cannot. They are akin, but they must be separate.[34]

Hence, one can find nothing remotely resembling such specific practical problems in the *Republic*, as those that Blepyrus notes in *Assemblywomen*. When told that older men like him would have to "go with" the ugly ones first, he complains that "our cocks won't have anything left when we get" to the beautiful, sacred ones Praxagora promised earlier. His loving wife retorts first, that no one will want to sleep with him anyway and second, that he has a sexual potency problem as well. Unprovoked by this rejoinder (and further suggesting the underlying good nature of their banter), Blepyrus' theoretical acumen leads him to note that while she makes sense of the female drama, since "no woman's hole will go unplugged" (623–624), he fears that the ugly men will suffer while the women will "pursue the beautiful ones" (*epi tous de kalous badiountai*) (625). But Praxagora's egalitarianism is thoroughgoing: every woman will have to sleep with an ugly man before enjoying herself with an attractive one.

Thus, Aristophanes has presented a second comedy of *erōs* within the larger erotic play of *Assemblywomen*. Praxagora's egalitarianism has fractured human desire into something that scarcely resembles *erōs* at all. Recalling Glaucon's apt reminder at *Republic* 458d5–6 that erotic necessities are more stinging (*drimuterai*) than geometrical ones in persuading most people, Praxagora seeks to displace much of this sting with her rule. The bodily *erōs* in human beings that is naturally oriented toward bodily beauty is not only redirected and deflected but countermanded as well. Absurdly, desire is oriented in both genders toward the undesirable. The results of this will resound in the later parts of the play. For now, it suffices to note that the "slight adjustment" required for the equal satisfaction of erotic desire for all citizens is a "fine-tuning" that wreaks havoc with its avowed purpose. Erotic "necessities," regarded as the outcome of the natural pull of human desire, are replaced with a choice between unwanted sexual performances by those in their prime on one side, and utter abstinence on the other.

In this light, the interchange on the ignorance of who one's specific parent or child might be, takes on a kindred hue to its treatment in the *Republic*. There, this mutual and thorough ignorance served to bind the city more closely together, as the bonds between citizens would also be regarded as bonds of biological kinship. Here this same ignorance would reduce the common practice of sons beating their fathers. In the past, others did not care when such a beating occurred, but under the new order these same others would be ready to intervene, fearing that their own father was receiving a beating (at someone else's hand).[35] Thus, the same supposed bonds of kinship would further peace among the citizens, if indeed for entirely and comically different reasons.

LINES 650–727

The ever-inquisitive Blepyrus wonders who will farm the land. The slaves will, answers Praxagora. This differs from the practice in Athens of having citizens manage the farm while slaves worked it (though in Sparta slaves took charge of farming), but there may be another Platonic affinity, though with the *Laws* rather than the *Republic.*[36] Praxagora answers her husband's concerns one by one. On the male side, there will be no lawsuits, no debts, no fights, no thefts, no muggings. The provision for all of the needs to each from the common store would render these either meaningless or obviously counterproductive. Even the need for overcoats will be provided for by the weaving skill of the women. All that remains for the men is "to get slicked up and head for dinner when the shadow stick's ten feet" (651), i.e., late in the afternoon.[37] Thus, what appears to be the most pleasurable life of all is promised to the men, consisting of work-free days of late sleep and relaxation and of exquisite sexual satisfaction, so long as they first perform their one and only disagreeable task.

However, there are several complications that once again deserve closer scrutiny. Perhaps even more radically than in the *Republic,* Praxagora's remaking of the city will bring an even more emphatic end to the private realm. As she previously decreed in the matter of sexual access, even one's body will not, strictly speaking, be one's own—at least Socrates' city in *logos* preserved the privacy of the individual body (citizens will possess "nothing private but the body, while the rest is in common" [*Republic* 464d8–9]). This ruling woman's city will not merely build houses for certain classes of citizens, but will knock out the walls between the existing ones of all houses:[38]

Blepyrus: What way of life (*diaitan*) will you make (*poiēseis*)?

Praxagora: Common for all (*koinēn pasin*). I will make the city into one household (*mian oikēsin*), breaking through the partitions to make one dwelling, so that everyone can walk into everyone's space. (673–675)

Unlike in Socrates' city in *logos* in the *Republic,* there is no division of labor since there is no labor, and no class hierarchy because every citizen is equal in status and in privileges to every other. With such an arrangement, what can be the result of likening the city to an individual soul, as took place in the *Republic*?

It is indeed a task for one who sees sharply. Equality, as we have seen, means only equal satisfaction of pathological desires. The human soul can therefore be read off as closely analogous to the desiring part of the soul in the *Republic.* Can spirit (*thumos*) be located in Praxagora's city? In the *Republic,* spirit could align itself either with calculation (*logismos*) or desire (*epithumia*), with Socrates' seeing that it became an ally of calculation *against* desire. If spirit *can* be regarded as a separate quality in Praxagora's city, it would be allied with the purpose of all human activity in the city, desire's satisfaction. And what about calculation? This quality is a function not of class but of gender—the women have it all.

Thus, one of several absurd conclusions can obtain. The human soul, as read off from the Praxagorean city, can have the same three parts as the Socratic soul, except that desire is highest, spirit (if it is present) is its ally, and calculation is lowest and the servant of the other two. Or if calculation is indeed highest since it is the necessary condition for the proper functioning of the other two, the human soul is fundamentally female, and when spirit is allied with it the city functions best. The soul, then, is a function of the kind of body within which it is housed. Accordingly, when males are in charge, misrule, disorder, and folly plague the city, since their bodies house no *logismos.* There is no direct analogy, then, to a soul that is proper to all human beings.

Another alternative is the following: there are no guardians in the Praxagorean city[39] (given that the only task for men is to show up properly oiled and dressed at dinner), and only its founder possesses the calculative art properly speaking. The other women serve as something like Platonic auxiliaries. The men are even lower than artisans. A human soul modeled on these elements would be woefully misshapen—could this be a painfully, comically accurate picture of the human soul in its imperfection? Could this be a comic analogue of what Socrates said concerning how we see the soul as maimed, in the myth of Er, like the sea god Glaucus, who "resembles any beast rather than what he was by nature, so, too we see the soul in such a condition because of countless evils" (*Republic* 611d5–8)?

Praxagora's vision preeminently includes feasts, beginning with one that same day, at which all of the men will leave sated, drunk, and garlanded. As they traverse the street, each will be lured inside one of the women's quarters with the promise of a very attractive woman waiting inside for him. But first, he must sleep with an unappealing woman. As for the inferior men who are normally rejected by the fair in favor of their handsome and desirable counterparts, they may affirm their new status by saying to the latter, "Hey you, where do you think you're off to? You're going to get nothing anyway: the law says that the snub-nosed (*simois*) and the ugly get first fuck (*proterois binein*), while you grab the petals of your double-hung fig branch and jerk off in the doorway" (705–709). With this, Praxagora displays both sides of her philosopher/ruler nature. The philosopher stands "on principle." Given her egalitarian political philosophy, all of the rules support her idealistic view. The politician knows the nature of her subjects and can move them rhetorically; she can "speak their language." Here, she combines rigorous adherence to her *logos* and thorough knowledge of how the men and women in her city actually speak. That is why her husband expresses such enthusiastic pride in his subordinate affiliation with this great ruler. They leave together after he asks her if he may "tag along at your side, and share the spotlight, with people saying 'Behold (*thaumazete*), that's none other than the lady commander's husband!'" (725–727).

There is yet another, perhaps more uncomfortable parallel with the *Republic* involving the matter of non-citizens. I am reluctant to offer an answer. However, I will surely raise the question in all of the discomfort that I experience. In the *Republic,* Greeks who are conquered in warfare will not be enslaved but will receive gentle treatment, while the barbarians (the others) are to be given no quarter. In *Assemblywomen,* Praxagora rules that slave women can no longer wear makeup (that might lure the hearts of the male citizens), can only sleep with other slaves, and must have "their pussies trimmed like a woolen barn jacket" (724).

The best way to regard the Apollonian and Dionysian comedies on the issue of citizen and slave (or other) is not at all clear to me. Historically, there is some material on Greek slavery that suggests that at one extreme some slaves had a great deal of autonomy and even held positions of responsibility, while at the other life could hardly be more dangerous and more miserable. Of course basic civic rights were denied, and no one would freely choose such status. However, perhaps one can discover a different lens through which to consider the matter of slavery and its implied "otherness" and inferiority, perhaps an implicit critique by the poet, the philosopher, or both. I cannot discover either textual or interpretive evidence for such a critique, though my early twenty-first-century eyes long to find one. It seems to me that both philosophically and dramatically, slaves are *other.* In this sense, Hegel seems entirely correct: in the advance of the concept of freedom, the Greeks grasped human freedom in the (implicit) proposition "some are free." It remained for modern thought to conceive truly that and how "humanity is free, and that freedom of spirit is the essence of humanity's nature."[40]

However, this return to Plato and Aristophanes allows us to raise again a difficult question. This question perhaps reflects back upon the impossibility of the philosophical nature joining with the ruling nature. It belongs to the credit and glory of philosophy that it has shown how, morally speaking, there is no "we and they." We are bound by a common humanity, however one understands this, and any atavistic appeals that would dispute this—to slavery preeminently, but also to race, gender, sexual orientation, economic status, etc.—are quite simply mistaken and corrupt. A long journey was required to attain this truth, but the journey could not have been more worthwhile.

It does not take long at all—in fact, it seems built into human nature—to declare "us" as distinct from "them." Whether we speak of the constantly turbulent geopolitical arena in which various nations and ethnic groups collide violently, or of much lesser matters such as "us faculty" and "those administrators," "continental philosophy" and "analytic philosophy," or even to such matters as "us vegetarians" and "those carnivores," identity requires—or at least seems very much to require—that a person, group, nation, or "philosophy" is *not some other* person, group, nation, or "philosophy." Returning to the treatment of the inferior other in *Assemblywomen* and in the *Republic,* I can only suggest an implicit recognition of a pure humanity, but of a different sort than one that we might conceive at present. With some misgivings (but not many), pure humanity for Aristophanes and Plato consists of a universal desire for power in conflict with the desire for good. The barbarians are not Greek, so no dialogue with them is possible. They are simply *other* in that sense, but they could destroy you utterly if given a chance. The slave girls have the same power of sexual allure as do the Greek women, and they could attract the Greek men and so weaken the city if given a chance. They must therefore be "disempowered," whether by taking their lives and seizing their land, or by seizing their make-up and humiliating their privacy. Pure humanity, the humanity that is common to us all, finds itself always in tension with impure humanity. We find an ongoing *agōn* of goodness and power.

LINES 728–876

This protracted exchange between Neighbor and Man (*ANĒR*) has surprising Platonic echoes. Before exploring them, I shall comment on what might seem to be a trivial matter of translation. Henderson renders *ANĒR* as "Selfish Man"; Sommerstein has "Dissident." The context certainly seems to support either reading, given that this character is both self-centered and rule-flouting. However, I prefer to keep to a minimalist reading in accord with the text. "Neighbor" is, specifically, a neighbor of ruler

Praxagora. His geographical nearness to her also signals his proximity and respect for her proclamations. "Man" is, quite simply and specifically, a man—a more or less ordinary member of *hoi polloi.* I can hardly think of many people turning in all of their property at the command of a political ruler, least of all to a ruler who has not been in office for even one full day. To call such a man "selfish" or "dissident" is either redundant or rhetorical. Words such as "circumspect" could serve just as well. He is a man, a human being, very much like the vast majority of us. Once again, *ecce homo!*

Their comically heated exchange images the more elegant conversation in *Republic* book 2, between Glaucon and Adeimantus on one side and Socrates on the other. Socrates is the neighbor of justice, which he values both for itself and for its benefits. He allows himself to be ruled, just as "Neighbor" does. But Socrates subjects himself to what is best as shown through *logos.* Glaucon and Adeimantus might each be called "Man +." They seek the benefits of justice but fear and wish to avoid what *hoi polloi* regards as its dangers. They are willing to have Socrates convince them that they have nothing to fear and everything to gain—hardly a small, and perhaps even an impossible task. They belong to the city but, drawn to the person of Socrates, try to find a way to be liberated from its customary claims. Thus, they can become players in the philosopher's comedy.

"Man" has neither the vision nor the desire to attempt a different way of life. He knows that rulers lie and/or that their measures often misfire. Rather than throw in his lot with some new scheme of whatever provenance, he protects himself. "Me turn in my stuff? I'd be a miserable (*kakodaimōn*) excuse for a man and of little *nous* (intelligence). First of all I'll have to test and study (*skepsomai*) the situation a great deal" (746–749). His prudential self-interest resembles that of the person in the *Republic* who appears to be just but is not, and would benefit from this appearance. Lacking any sense of transcendence but fully anchored to the city and knowledgeable about his fellow human beings, "Man" will never be a philosopher, but that is hardly his ambition. Unlike "Neighbor," he would much rather protect his status as "nobody's fool." He displays this characteristic later on in this section by attempting to sneak into and share in the symposium without having surrendered his goods.

Therefore "Man" is stunned, incredulous, when he sees "Neighbor" bringing his possessions to the marketplace to surrender them to the state, in accord with the law of the land. He hurls a number of epithets at him for his innocent folly: "miserable one" (*kakodaimōn*) (760); "wretch" (*dustēne*) (763); "stupid" (*anoētos*) (764); "the biggest fool beyond all conception" (*ēlithiōtatos . . . hapaxapantōn*) (765). As Glaucon proclaimed in the voice of *hoi polloi* in *Republic* book 2, "The man who is able to do [injustice] and *is truly a man* (*hōs alēthōs andra*) would never set down a compact with anyone not to do injustice and not to suffer it" (359b1–3). "Man," according to the measure of *hoi polloi,* is indeed a true man.

He will "protect himself" (*phulaxomai*) (769). He is "distrustful" (*apistōn*) (774), and is convinced that "the others will be distrustful also (*apistēsousi gar*)" (775). *Giving* "is not in our heritage (*patrion*)" (777). *Taking* is another matter. Taking without giving would be best of all. This is clearly shown in the posture of the gods, who have their hands out and their palms up in their statues. This, too, has resonances in *Republic* book 2, where Adeimantus, once again in the voice of *hoi polloi,* indicates that the gods can be "bribed" with sacrifices (364b2–365a2).

The distrustfulness of "Man" conflicts radically with the trust of "Neighbor," but not with the distrust of the philosopher. Both "Man" and "Philosopher" share distrust. Their difference consists of its orientation. Whereas "Man" distrusts *logoi* and trusts only those habits and practices that can best secure his safety and advantage, the philosopher *distrusts* these, calling them into question. The philosopher's trust is oriented toward what Socrates in the *Phaedo* called the healthiest (or strongest) *logos*: "Then I lay down (*hupothemenos*) in each case the *logos* I judge to be healthiest (*errōmenestaton*), and whatever seems to me (*moi dokē*) to agree (*sumphōnein*) with it, I set down (*tithēmi*) as true" (100a3–a8).

The "healthiest *logoi*" consist of the ones that affirm the *eidē* of which he has always spoken: "the beautiful itself according to itself, and the good and the great and all the rest" (*Phaedo* 100b1–8). The interpretation of the so-called Platonic "Forms" is, of course, one of the most provocative matters in the Platonic dialogues, and this is hardly the occasion for an extensive discussion of it. According to my reading, the most decisive account occurs in the passage in *Republic* book 5 (475b–476d). To summarize: (1) People who can see an *eidos* all by itself—e.g., beauty all by itself—are "rare indeed," possibly non-existent. In any case, these people are not called "awake" (nor are they, of course, "asleep"). (2) Those who see beautiful *things* but who cannot acknowledge the *eidos* of beauty are "asleep," as if dreaming. (3) Those who can apprehend *both,* and can distinguish the *eidos* (beauty) from what participates in it (beautiful things), are "awake." "Awake" here signifies awareness of the kind of seeing that belongs to all human apprehension. It might be characterized as the condition of beholding the glimpse of being that belongs to all appearing, and secures the truth of the *logoi* concerning that appearing.

The discovery of truth, then, never ascends to certainty. Note that "whatever *seems to me* (*moi dokē*) to agree (*sumphōnein*) with it, *I set down* (*tithēmi*) as true" (*Phaedo* 100a3–a8—emphases mine). This "setting down" is far from arbitrary. Only those *logoi* are posited as true that are best able to withstand the contest of *logoi,* or that are clearly most in accord with the *logoi* concerning the *eidē.* If better *logoi* should come forth in the future, then the earlier ascription of truth would be revised. (Socrates had shown this earlier in the *Phaedo,* in his renunciation of the "natural science" that he earlier believed would provide the pathway to wisdom.)

The distrust of *logos* embodied by "Man" in *Assemblywomen* is called "the greatest evil" in the *Phaedo.* After asserting misology as the greatest danger to the human soul and after urging his hearers not to distrust *logos* even in the face of a great many inadequate arguments, Socrates says of his own attempts to argue for the soul's immortality:

> If what I say happens to be true [and the soul is indeed immortal], then it is admirable (*kalōs*) to be persuaded by it; and if there is nothing for me after death, at any rate I shall not be unpleasant to my friends by my lamentations in these last moments. And this ignorance of mine will not last—that would be an evil—but would soon end. (*Phaedo* 91b2–9)

There is no worry over the outcome of the *logoi,* since nothing but good can come from Socrates' occupation in search of the best argument for immortality. Nothing but good, however, could come to him were he occupied with the search for the best *logos* on *any* subject. Even a bad *logos* does no harm, once it is refuted. Either he discovers a good *logos* and it is admirable that he is persuaded by it, or it falls short and he can be brought before his ignorance. In the course of his search for such a *logos* on immortality, it becomes clear that its occasioning subject—death, specifically his own—seems to produce no more fear in Socrates than any other. He is either unafraid of death, or he does not impose his fear on others. But the issue for the interlocutors is precisely this fear, with the issues of immortality and the quality of *logoi* offered for it regarded as possible means of overcoming it.

In the *Apology,* Socrates speaks of a redirection of fear from fear of death to fear of doing injustice. Death's nature and consequences are unknown, and it is disgraceful to fear what one does not know. But it is known that to do injustice is disgraceful. Thus one should never fear death, but should only fear doing injustice (28b3–9). Fear itself is not disgraceful. It is one of the human things, part of the challenge of our humanity. Socrates' call for its redirection is a powerful one. The ease of assenting to his *logos* conceals the great difficulty of its acceptance in deed. So the genuine problem is not the "logic" of the *logoi.* The challenge is to be governed by trust in the best *logos,* rather than by any other measure—and such other measures virtually always have a governing component of fear.

By contrast, as we have seen, "Man" distrusts *logoi* and trusts only that which will offer him safety and advantage. In this sense, he resembles most of Socrates' interlocutors. On the other hand, "Neighbor" trusts *logoi* without subjecting them to the examination required to establish their truth. In a peculiar way then, he deserves this rebuke from "Man":

Man:	Do you think that a sensible person (*sōphrona*) should do all that he is told?
Neighbor:	Most of all!
Man:	You mean an imbecile (*abelteron*) should! (767–768)

If one were to lift these characters from their comic context for a moment and "examine" their souls in accord with the Platonic measure, "Man" is clearly worse off than "Neighbor" because "Man" is a misologist and so suffers the greatest evil. The possible and even likely folly of "Neighbor" may be "bad," but this kind of badness is shared by all human beings and is remediable, at least in principle. The overcoming of misology is at once the most urgent and most difficult of tasks. In the *Phaedo, **music*** is hit upon as that means to redirect trust from that trust tied to fear of the pains of the body and of death to trust in *logos.*

After offering his second argument for the immortality of the soul in the *Phaedo,* Socrates chides Simmias for the latter's childishness in supposing that the soul will disperse after death, and especially "in a high wind and not in calm weather" (77e1–2). Simmias concedes that there is "a child within which has such fears" (77e5), and entreats Socrates to help in persuading it "not to fear death as if it were a she-monster (*mormolukeia*)" (77e6–7). Socrates' answer: "You must *chant* (*epadein*) every day, until you charm the fear away" (77e9–10). Then, after Simmias calls Socrates a "good singer" (*agathon epōdon*) (78a1) of such charms, and bemoans the incipient loss of his friend, Socrates counsels his interlocutors to search vigorously and everywhere for such an epode: "There is nothing of greater necessity for which you could spend your money" (78a5–6). Thus, one who is capable of such singing—proper to the music of Homer—is the one who is most necessary of all. Socrates, whose services are had for free, is one such singer. Part of the song of Socrates is that this same song is most valuable of all. In this light, the Socrates who practices music on the prompting of a dream is the one whose *logoi* are sufficient to charm away the fear of death. But the two arguments for the immortality of the soul, while good enough for Socrates who shows no such fear, are insufficient for Simmias and Cebes.

I suggest strongly that Aristophanes is an inspired writer of songs that can also charm away this irrational fear. The Aristophanic charm consists of the power of his inimitable comedies to provoke laughter at, and *with,* the most fundamental and vexing matters confronting our humanity. A key "measure" of the Socratic song occurs in *Republic* book 10: "nor are any of the human things worthy of great seriousness": *ti tōn anthrōpinōn axion on megalēs spoudēs* (604c1). Aristophanic comedy exemplifies this "measure" not only insofar as it subjects the human things to laughter, but also that folded within this laughter is seriousness—not *great* seriousness, since great seriousness would exceed what is called for, but seriousness appropriate to the human situation. In this way, the reported friendship between the two singers, philosophical and comic, points beyond the personal and even beyond the kinship of their subject matter. Just as Socrates chants *logoi* to his interlocutors, Aristophanes—through his actors—chants poetic creations (*poiēmata*) for those gathered at the Dionysiad. Where the *logoi* of Socrates attempt to reorient trust in a direct manner, by means of "sung argument," the *poiēmata* of Aristophanes do so indirectly, by presenting misology through the hilarious but perhaps uncomfortable absurdity of his creation called "Man," and later through the most ridiculously gruesome death-wish of one beautiful young Epigenes.

Once again, "Man" is "nobody's fool" by the measure of the city. He is one of *hoi polloi*'s most astute representatives and commentators. Just as Socrates spoke of the "random manner" (*tukhōsi*) of *hoi polloi* in the *Crito* (44d10), who "easily put men to death and would bring them to life if they could, without thinking" (48c5–6), "Man" knows this well. His fellow citizens are quick to vote on something, but then ignore the result. He reminds "Neighbor" about various actions taken in the past that either failed or were rescinded. One concerned salt; another instituted a tax that fell far short (811–829). "Man" can even be credited with a view of gender equality. When "Neighbor" reminds him that their past malfunctions occurred on the men's watch but that women are now in charge, this makes no difference at all to "Man," who replies: "And I'll keep an eye on them, so help me Poseidon, so they don't piss all over (*katourēsōsi*) me" (831–832).

While "Neighbor" departs for the common store with all of his possessions in spite of such *logoi,* "Man" exercises "prudence" according to the measure of *hoi polloi.* From the same premise, assumed to be true by both Socrates and "Man" as well as by their creators, Socrates draws the opposite conclusion: this very inconstancy invalidates the measure of *hoi polloi.* For a good human life, only the healthiest, strongest *logos* can serve as a guide, even—especially—in the absence of certainty. One splendid way of accomplishing the transition from the former conclusion to the latter is to personify the former and hold it up to playful ridicule in song.

LINES 877–975B

An *agōn* of *logoi* erupts between a woman called First Old Woman (*GRAUS A*) and Young Woman (*NEANIS*). What the two share, at the very least, is a strong capacity for coarse language and a willingness to make use of this talent. They also share an aching sexual desire that does not even ascend to the first rung of Diotima's ladder of *Erōs.* This first rung at least requires the presence of a beautiful body. Aristophanes' women seem eager to accept *anyone,* so long as he is young and so can satisfy their craving.

Who can these nameless women be? The knowledge available to us of the lives of women in classical Athens makes it difficult, perhaps impossible to say. Sommerstein offers a plausible account: they must be citizens and not *hetaireia* (courtesans), since all commercial sex has been outlawed. The old women are likely widows, and the young women did not reside in a household headed by a man, but represent "a substantial submerged class of citizen women, of whom speeches and inscriptions tell us little," who have to "make their own living as best as they can."[41] One could simply call them "single women." However, I am not persuaded by Sommerstein's account, though of course it is impossible to be confident. First Old Woman swears like a sailor, not unlike Praxagora. There is little historical warrant for supposing that grown women were quite so blunt and so specific in expressing the sexual side of their nature. There is even less warrant for supposing that young girls would do so, given the sheltered, housebound upbringing they received which took place apart from men. This upbringing was preparation for them to be virginal brides in arranged marriages to men of means, and to live out their years subjugated to their husbands and as second-class citizens, with less education than the *hetaireia* with whom their husbands were able to consort.

So the question is: where did they learn to swear so abusively, and to speak in so foul-mouthed a manner? The women of classical Athens did not speak in this way, but to their credit, *Aristophanes'* women did. They are inspired comic characters, serving to expose the measure and limits of appropriate speech by exceeding these limits raucously and hilariously. After First Old Woman sneaks forward to her window and calls upon the Muses to give her lips a sweet and voluptuous song, Young Woman catches on to her and berates her with the epithet, *ō sapra:* "O rotten one" (884).[42] First Old Woman responds by presenting *something* to her interlocutor (perhaps her backside, perhaps her middle finger, perhaps a dildo)[43] and singing a six-line song that does not seem Muse-inspired. Young Woman picks up its length and meter in response, and First Old Woman brings the three-part musical dialogue to a conclusion.

First Old Woman's initial "musical argument" consists of the following: to have a good time, one should sleep with the old woman, both because she is "wise" (*sophon*) (894) in sexual matters unlike the young, and because a young woman is far more likely than an old one to abandon a lover for someone else (892–897). Young Woman sings of the softness of her thighs and blossoms of her firm breasts, as contrasted with the "old hag's" unsuccessful attempt to make herself attractive—but she, the First Old Woman, is rather "Death's darling" (*tō Thanatō melēma*) (905).[44] First Old Woman concludes this charming duet by wishing that her antagonist's "twat falls off" (*ekpesoi sou to trēma*) (906), and praying that the man whom she takes into her arms to kiss turns into a snake.[45]

Once again, close attention to what may seem like vulgar banter played merely for laughs yields insights of philosophical import. The "musical argument" of First Old Woman in her first six-line song may indeed be a sound one. She is both more sexually experienced and less likely to be unfaithful to a younger lover, while a young woman is indeed more likely to leave for another. But where human *erōs* is concerned, sound arguments are useless, however musical they are. The Young Woman's response makes no argument at all. Her song merely calls attention to her physical attributes. Nothing else is required. First Old Woman's final tirade is a concession to Young Woman's superior physical loveliness, and to its power to inspire an enormously passionate reaction from young men.

No *logos* that First Old Woman can provide, whether in song or in prose, can compete with the beauty of youth. She knows this well, because once upon a time she was a young woman with the same seductive powers as her antagonist. Young Woman knows that on account of her youthful beauty, no *logos* from her is necessary. It would not even occur to her to offer one. If all of this were left to nature, First Old Woman would not have dressed and primped for a sexual encounter, and Young Woman would not be attempting to outfox her competitor for sexual access to a young man. According to nature, *erōs* trumps *logos.* But in Praxagora's city, *erōs* is made subject to that *logos* of equality according to which the needs and desires of every citizen are fully met.

An analogous regulation in Plato's *Laws* is even stricter than the ones that occur in the *Republic* and in *Assemblywomen.* All sexual relations other than ones undertaken for procreation are to be forbidden by law (*Laws* 838e4–7)! But a slippage from this standard occurs immediately. Acknowledging the difficulty of attaining it, the Athenian Stranger makes appeals beyond the law to the sacred (*kathierōsis*), and finally to song. Even after suggesting that one of these recourses could bring *erōs* under management, there is further retreat. The Stranger concedes its unlikelihood almost at once, and quickly retreats to the more modest goal of restraining some of the impulses some of the time in some of the people, expressing this far less ambitious goal as a *wish*. But even the latter proves too ambitious. Divine dispensation is required! He concedes in his last passage that all of his proposals "may be in the manner of myths now spoken as prayers" (*tauta dē kathaper isōs en muthō ta nun legomen' estin eukhai*) (841c6), though one or two of his proposals might be enforced "if the god wishes" (*ei theos etheloi*) (841d1).

In the remainder of this section of *Assemblywomen,* the futility even of "myths now spoken as prayers" receives comic truth. First Old Woman and Young Woman jockey to be first in line for the sexual attention of a young heartthrob named Epigenes. For his part, Praxagora's law is on his mind only as an obstacle to the satisfaction of his lust:

> Ah my fine wrought golden
> Prize, bud of Aphrodite,
> honeybee of the Muses, nurseling
> of the Graces, personification of Pleasure,
> open up and welcome me.
> It's you I'm hurting for! (973–975b)

Note that here, far from being limited by law and *logos, erōs*—at least as aching sexual desire—gives rise to *logos,* indeed gives rise to a peculiar kind of poetry that is sincere and manipulative at once. Epigenes aches for sexual consummation as he sings of Goddesses, Muses, and Graces, just as the Young Woman had earlier begged "*Erōs* / please make this boy / come to my very own bed" (958–959b). Recalling the discussion of *erōs* in the *Symposium,* it has begotten a kind of madness. This "comic-divine" madness, however, never reaches even the most minimal levels of transcendence. Should Epigenes achieve the consummation for which he and Young Woman yearn, one finds it difficult to imagine further songs of prayer to divinities from him soon afterward. Once again, *ecce homo.*

LINES 976–1111

The following famous passage from the *Symposium* will serve to set up the comments on this section.

> All of us are pregnant, Socrates, in body and in soul, and as soon as we come to a certain age, we naturally desire to give birth. Now no one can possibly give birth in anything ugly; only in something beautiful. That's because when a man and a woman come together in order to give birth,

> that's a godly affair. Pregnancy, reproduction—this is an immortal thing for a mortal animal to do, and it cannot occur in anything that is out of harmony, but ugliness is out of harmony with all that is godly. Beauty, however, is in harmony with the divine . . . That's why, whenever pregnant animals or persons draw near to beauty, they become gentle and joyfully disposed . . . but near ugliness they are sullen (*skuthrōpon*) and draw back in pain. (206c1–d6)[46]

This section of *Assemblywomen* features the anguish of Epigenes. The First Old Woman has outmaneuvered the Young Woman, and seeks her sexual pleasure from him, as the law requires. A recalcitrant Epigenes resists,[47] only to find himself in the clutches of two other Old Women with similar desires. All three invoke Praxagora's law, and Epigenes treats all three with revulsion. The last two drag him off after his mock-tragic lament. There should be no surprise at the erotic desires of the older people. Looking at the matter of age and sexuality in the *Republic,* Socrates declares in his Apollonian comedy that men and women beyond the age of procreation will be free "of course . . . to have sexual intercourse (*suggignesthai*) with whoever they wish," so long as the incest taboo is observed. While the comic complication concerns the impossibility of determining who is a member of one's "natural" family, and the calculation offered at *Republic* 461d2–e3 virtually assures that any *natural* incest taboo will be broken, the possibility of copulations with both older and younger partners by both sexes is at least worthy of consideration.

This is so because humans are erotic beings even after youth is long gone. And human beings who "draw near to beauty . . . become gentle and joyfully disposed . . . but near ugliness they are sullen and draw back in pain." In *Assemblywomen,* the issue of *erōs* and time is disclosed in this thoughtfully ridiculous section. It is clear that the fate of the old women awaits Young Woman, just as Epigenes will one day likely be the butt of his wife's jests concerning his prowess, as is Blepyrus. But two related matters are equally clear: (1) time is forgotten by both old and young when the prospect of an erotic encounter draws near, and (2) youth and beauty in the object of desire virtually always wins the day.[48] In Diotima's *logos,* procreation serves as the means by which mortals attain a measure of immortality. However, thralldom in the beautiful provides blissful oblivion to the waxing and the waning in the order of becoming.

To the uninhibited, delighted laughter of young and old alike, octogenarian comedienne Moms Mabley would intone from the stage of the Apollo Theater in Harlem, "No, honey, I don't like no old men, uh-uh. No, no old men. I'd rather pay a young man's way from here to California than to tell an old man the distance!"[49] In *Die Zauberflöte,* Mozart's Pa-

pageno is horrified by the prospect of marriage to the young and beautiful Papagena when she is disguised as a shrewish elderly wench. Poet Friedrich Hölderlin, in his ode *Sokrates und Alcibiades,* has Socrates explain his attraction to Alcibiades: *Und es neigen die Weisen / Oft am Ende zu Schönem sich:* "and the wise incline themselves / often at the end to the beautiful." Youth and beauty are twinned in these otherwise quite disparate but paradigmatic examples.

However, the twinning of physical beauty and youth appears to be disrupted in both Plato's *Theaetetus* and in Xenophon's *Symposium.* In the former, Theodorus explains to Socrates that Theaetetus, while surely worthy (*axion*), is "not beautiful at all (*ouk esti kalos*), but rather like you, snub-nosed (*simotēta*), with eyes that stick out, though these features are not so pronounced with him" (143e5–9). These qualities would entitle the two men to "first fuck" in Praxagora's city, but their erotic orientation differs. This orientation culminates in Socrates' praise of Theaetetus' willingness and ability to answer the most searching questions thoughtfully: "Why you are beautiful, Theaetetus, and not, as Theodorus said, ugly; for he who speaks beautifully is beautiful and good" (185e2–4). Here, beauty and worthy *logos* are twinned. Further, the form taken by Socrates' praise indicates that he, too, is beautiful!

A comedy of Socratic beauty takes place in Xenophon's *Symposium.* There, Socrates wins an *agōn* on beauty with the breathtaking young Critobolus, the most beautiful youth of all. He leads the youth playfully astray, manipulating an agreement to a characterization of beauty as belonging to things that are "well made for the functions for which we attain them, or if they are naturally well-constituted to serve our needs"[50] (bk. 5, 4). Critobolus is constrained to admit in *logos* that Socrates' famous features, which enable him to see both to the side and straight ahead, to smell odors issuing from all sides, to bite off more food and to kiss with more lip, make him more beautiful than the beautiful young boy (bk. 5, 4–10). Socrates' victory is complete, until . . .

Socrates insists on shining a light on Critobolus' face before the vote on the contest of beauty, almost as if to remind them of what the boy looked like! The unanimous vote in the boy's favor occurs in light of the Socratic gesture. What can be concluded from this tangled web of beauty, youth, and *logos*? I do not see that it can be untangled. The opinions of mathematician Theodorus (in *Theaetetus*), composer Mozart (and his librettist), poet Hölderlin, and comedienne Mabley are no mere random ramblings of *hoi polloi,* but natural and worthy homages to the beauty of youth. Similarly, the Socratic encomium to Theaetetus is no mere comforting platitude from an ugly man to an ugly boy, but an affirmation of the bond of *erōs* to goodness as disclosed through *logos.* To a human being, beauty manifests itself shiningly in both manners.

But why does youth seem always to win the day, even among those regarded as the most thoughtful? Why, to ask a question that may be ridiculous on its face, did Hölderlin not write an ode entitled *Socrates and Theaetetus*? I suggest with great hesitation, but with some measure of confidence, that even the most thoughtful are drawn to youth for its presentation of what shines forth most shiningly of all. In Hölderlin's ode, the question: "Why do you pay homage to this boy most of all? Don't you know anyone greater?" is answered with: *Wer das Tiefste gedacht, liebt das Lebendigste:* "He who has most deeply thought, loves what is most alive."[51] In an all too simple formulation, youthful beauty appears as optimal life.

In the Platonic *Symposium,* Alcibiades rails against and simultaneously praises Socrates for the latter's combination of attraction and resistance to his youthful beauty, and for his efforts to turn his soul toward a life governed by *logos,* a virtue-loving life. In *Assemblywomen,* we find no such ambivalence. The victory of youthful beauty is assumed, as is the defeat of ugliness. The legislative *logos* of Praxagora provides no counterweight whatsoever to the pull of human *erōs* toward youthful beauty. Nor, in *Symposium,* does the recollected speech of Diotima prevent the symposiasts' welcome to the young and beautiful Alcibiades, or the reorientation of the symposium after his arrival. The old women (and old men) populating Praxagora's city who lust after the young honor *Erōs* just as surely as—if not more surely than—the wine-eschewing speakers of Plato's dialogue. The laughter they provoke in us is in recognition of the optimal life that shines forth from youthful beauty.

Of course youthful beauty is itself erotically disposed toward youthful beauty and not toward old age at all. After First Old Woman tells Epigenes that he'll buy her a wedding garland, he responds that it will be a waxen one—designed for funerals—implying that she will "disintegrate pretty quickly" (1036) after their first sexual encounter. The Young Woman rescues him, for which he politely promises her a "big, juicy token of my gratitude": *megalēn apodōsō kai pakheian soi kharin* (1048). But a Second Old Woman enters, and drags Epigenes off in the name of the law: "It's not me but the law that drags you away": *all' ouk egō, all' ho nomos helkei s'* (1055–1056). He calls her by the name of a she-monster, "Empusa, covered with one big blood-blister," and threatens to defecate on the spot if she doesn't permit him to use a bathroom. Before this matter is satisfactorily resolved, a Third Old Woman enters who inspires poetry from Epigenes that contrasts with his earlier song of *erōs* to the Young Woman:

> . . . O Heracles
> O Pan, O Corybantes, O Dioscuri
> here's another horror, and much more revolting (*polu toutou to kakon exōlesteron*) than the last.
> Please, someone, tell me what in the world it is?
> A monkey plastered with make-up?
> An old woman (*graus*) arisen from the underworld? (1068–1074)

The gods he invokes here are nothing like Aphrodite, Muses, or the Graces. Heracles was a hero who was granted a young wife. Pan loved nymphs. The Corybantes guarded Dionysus. The Dioscuri were sons of Zeus, friendly to men, who granted epiphanies in moments of crisis.[52] As the Second and Third Old Women drag him away, he asks, "But how can I manage to man two boats with a single oar?" "Beautifully, after you've wolfed down a potful of love bulbs (*bolbōn*[53])" (1091–1092), answers the Second Old Woman. Plied with aphrodisiacs and required by law to comply, Epigenes hilariously employs the language of a tragic hero: *oimoi kakodaimōn: eggus ēdē tēs thuras helkomenos eim'*: "What a miserable fate! I'm dragged to the threshold [of Hades]" (1093).

His mock-tragic song to the spectators combines the ridiculous with what can accurately be called the most-unseemly-grotesque. He is "thrice-ill-fated" (*ō triskakodaimōn*) if he has "to fuck (*binein*) an old bag all night and all day" (1099–1100), and then must repeat the act with another. Zeus has so damned him. Should this *kakodaimōn* occur, he proposes a burial in which he is sandwiched between the two women, atop one just as he has "penetrated the channel" (*hostis toioutois thēriois suneirxomai*) (1104) and beneath the other, who shall be mired in cement and covered with pitch; she will stand in as his funeral urn. *Assemblywomen* 1098–1112 seems to bear out Strauss' observation according to which "it is obvious that malice is a necessary ingredient of the Aristophanic comedy."[54]

Beyond the satire on tragic speeches and the spectacle of a young man dragged off against his will by two older women, why does such malice provoke laughter here? Why did the audience of the Apollo Theater howl with glee as Moms Mabley described the shortcomings (in every sense) of the old men she had known? Again, I answer with a mixture of puzzlement and confidence. I have been arguing all along that Aristophanic comedy, as opposed to its less worthy instances, provides *thought-provoking* laughter. I suggest that in these lines, thought is provoked by an image of the fate to which we are all assigned—death and, most often, decay preceding death.

The spectacle of old women dressed seductively for sexual encounters to which they are legally entitled suggests, in its quite jarring and oddly charming effort to recover the attractions of their youth, an acknowledgement of the fate that soon awaits them. The howls of Epigenes similarly reflect death-awareness. The close proximity with the old women commanded by Praxagora's law, supposedly designed to assure equal sexual pleasure to all, has the effect of bringing one and all before what Heidegger has called "the possibility of the absolute impossibility-of-Dasein."[55] The comic presentation of the monstrously hilarious death Epigenes wishes for himself reveals the profound sense in which Praxagora has indeed provided "one and the same common standard of life for all."

In order to read the details of the text as closely as possible, I shall treat the comedy as if it were a piece of realism (it would be the worst realistic play ever written). Epigenes wishes sexual congress with the Young Woman. This wish is reciprocated. But the law states that he must first consummate a sexual encounter with an old woman. He gambles that he can escape his legal obligation to First Old Woman, loses his bet, and is dragged off by two other old women. If indeed Zeus has damned him and his wish is carried out, he will be buried between these women just as he enters the first. As Socrates might ask, *ti legei:* what does this mean, or say? Epigenes does not claim that he is incapable of performing either with the First Old Woman or with the other two. He merely finds the prospect unappetizing. Thus, this section of *Assemblywomen* means that his aversion to the older women is stronger than his attraction to the Young Woman.

This conclusion adds something further to the claim in Socrates' recollection of Diotima's *logos* that near beauty, humans desire to procreate, but near ugliness, people and animals are sullen, draw back in pain, and "hold onto what they have inside them" (206d5–7). Returning to *Assemblywomen* as comedy, no one wishes to have a child, either of the soul or of the body. Everyone wishes carnal pleasure. The ridiculous thoughtfulness of Aristophanes provides the following addition: Epigenes' desire for Young Woman is not at all a part of a calculus of pleasure, or of any calculus at all. It is entirely a function of thralldom in the beautiful, thralldom that lies outside any exchange economy or negotiation. Similarly, his revulsion in the face of the ugly cannot be measured in this way, but absolutely stunts and buries his desire. *Erōs* not only trumps *logos,* but shows itself as originarily "un-engaged" from *logos* altogether. This is an enhancement of the famous "ladder of love," according to which *erōs* need not ascend beyond the love of beautiful bodies. It also enhances the characterization of *erōs* in the *Phaedrus* as madness bestowed by the gods, unaccountable by any human measure. *Erōs* cannot be captured by *logos* precisely because *erōs* gives rise to *logos* in the first place.

Uncomfortable as it is to say, beauty draws forth optimal life, ugliness suggests decay and death. The old, ugly women are drawn to the young, handsome man. The young, handsome man withdraws from the old, ugly women. All—young and old, beautiful, ugly, and "average" (a characterization of my own physical appearance made in class by one of my students, who is herself a beautiful young woman)—are drawn to, and pay homage to, the beautiful in all of its ways of appearing.

LINES 1112–CONCLUSION

Praxagora's inebriated maidservant, a new character, emerges to usher in the conclusion of *Assemblywomen.* More accurately, however, *Dionysus* brings the comedy to its conclusion, just as the god did in *Wasps.* After praising the blessed *dēmos,* rejoicing in the happiness of the earth, pronouncing her mistress "most blessed of all," and honoring Zeus for the fragrance of her fine perfumes, she reserves her most extensive and most fulsome encomium for wine:

> But far surpassing all these fragrances
> Are those nice little bottles of Thracian wine:
> They stay in your head a long time,
> When those others have completely evaporated.
> So far they're the best, yes by far, O Gods.
> Pour it neat and it will make you merry (*euphranei*) the whole night,
> if you pick the one with the best bouquet. (1119–1124)

As in other Aristophanic comedies, one can find inconsistencies in the final section with what preceded. In *Peace,* for example, Trugaios returns to earth with his youthful new bride Theoria, although at the start of the play he already had a wife and child. Here, Blepyrus enters without his wife, but with a girl on each arm, although he and his wife had exited together shortly before. The reason, I suggest, is not oversight on the part of the playwright, but rather celebration of the transformative power of the life-affirming festival. Praxagora's maidservant informs the spectators that none other than *Praxagora* has instructed her to escort Blepyrus and the two girls to the feast.

The maidservant and Blepyrus extend the invitation beyond the stage. From the former: "any of you spectators who favor us, / and any of you judges who are not looking elsewhere, / come along with us: we'll supply everything" (1141–1143). Then Blepyrus entreats Praxagora's maidservant to "invite all of them, leaving no one out" (1145). The Chorus Leader at the head of the procession, the maidservant, Blepyrus, and his two female companions depart for the feast, with all of them descending into the orchestra. Blepyrus' invitation to one and all to rejoice in their earthly nature recollects the original spirit of the Dionysian festival, which has been characterized by Nietzsche as the abandonment of the boundaries between human being and human being that had been placed by their individuation, and a return of all in all to the unity of primal earthbound nature.

The Chorus Leader offers some words of advice to the judges, appealing first to "the wise" (*tois sophois*) to remember the wise (*tōn sophōn*) parts and "judge in my favor" (1155). She makes a similar appeal to those who took pleasure in the ridiculous parts. Finally, she asks for the vote of everyone (1156–1160). But her concluding words deserve special attention, as they echo matters that have arisen around *judging* in the prior two plays.

In *Clouds,* the Chorus Leader denounces the judges for their lack of discrimination in awarding it third prize in its first production. In *Wasps,* the character of Philocleon embodied the distinction between being a judge in the true sense and the act of judging that may indeed contradict it. In their comical context, both plays address the possible and often actual disconnect between nominal and real judging. In *Assemblywomen,* on the pretext of concern that the play has had to be performed first among the comedies, the Chorus Leader first tells the judges how to judge, then insults them further. She instructs thusly: "Above all it is necessary not to break your oath, but to judge all of the choruses rightly": *alla panta tauta khrē memnēmenous mē piorkein, alla krinein tous khorous orthōs aei.* Immediately thereafter, she demands that they "not act like evil courtesans (*kakais hetairais*), who only remember their latest companions" (1159–1163).

First of all, such disparaging language can hardly endear the judges to *Assemblywomen.*[56] But there is a striking parallel between the Chorus Leader's song and the *logos* of Socrates in the *Apology.* In his opening statement, Socrates goes so far as to refuse to address the judges with any form of the word "to judge," but instructs them that it is the virtue of the judge to judge in accord with justice, just as it is the virtue of the orator to speak the truth. He addresses those gathered as *ō andres Athēnaioi,* "men of Athens." They will have to prove themselves worthy of the name "judges." This, too, is hardly a strategically effective means. Later, after declaring that he would not seek the pity of the distressed family members, he further risks alienation from those who hold his life in his hands by suggesting that many of his would-be judges availed themselves of this unworthy means, and thus may become angry at his refusal to do so. Rather, he claims that to beg the judges for sympathy in any way would be impious, for such entreaties are designed to deform the judge's proper measure of judgment: "It is necessary not to encourage you in the habit of breaking your oaths": *khrē oute hēmas ethizein humas epiorkein outh' humas ethizesthai* (*Apology* 35c5–6).

Once again, we are presented with a back and forth reflecting of Aristophanic comedy and Platonic dialogue. The Chorus Leader in the former ridiculously courts the favor of the festival judges by a mixture of insult and sanctimony, imploring them to keep their oaths (implicitly) in the manner of married people, rather than like "professional women" whose "promise" is good only to her most recent male companion. Socrates challenges those assembled to pay attention only to the evidence concerning what is just and what is unjust, acting in the manner of the man who liberates the first of the cave dwellers, dragging him painfully away, against his will, from his earlier false habitation. For *Assemblywomen,* only a prize is at stake. For the *Apology,* the life of Socrates is at stake.

However, Socrates certainly does not interpret his situation in that manner. He considers it shameful to cherish life for its own sake. Only justice gives life value; an unjust life is not worth living. The "slander and jealousy of the many" (*hē tōn pollōn diabolē te kai phthonos*) (28a8–9) merits no respect. They have put good men to death in the past and will surely do so in the future. As shown earlier in the brief discussion of the *Crito,* the many deserve no consideration, for they cannot make a man wise or foolish, but act randomly. I suggest that the Aristophanic mixture of challenge and ridicule where a prize hangs in the balance is yet another amusement-park-mirror image in which the genuine requirement of judging is revealed precisely through the laughter that such an image provokes.

Looking prosaically at this song within a song, it is accurate to observe that a play, speech, or poem that goes first in a competition may be at some disadvantage with some judges. It is also accurate to note that there is something at once self-serving and degrading to remind one's judges of this, just as it is a dreadful tactic to suggest that some of the judges may not be paying proper attention. Suggesting that the judges vote for your play before the others have been seen and heard is inane. However, it remains true that each play "should always be judged rightly" (*alla krinein . . . orthōs*) (1160). Though the context of the Socratic and Aristophanic challenges to their audiences could hardly be more different, they reveal the same fundamental truth: judging rightly involves no more and no less than judging in accord with the evidence presented and evaluated in *logos,* setting aside all else.

Assemblywomen concludes with Blepyrus and the two girls dancing themselves toward a feast without precedent, a wholly new recipe concocted for Praxagora's city:

> *lopadotemakhoselakhogaleo-*
> *kranioleipsanodriminupotrimmato-*
> *silphioliparomelitokatakekhumeno-*
> *kikhlepikossuphophattoperistera-*
> *lektruonoptopiphallidokigklope-*
> *leiolagōosiraiobaphētraga-*
> *lopterugōn* (1169–77)

Following Henderson's translation but leaving out the connectives, this longest word in the Greek language reads:

> Limpetssaltfishsharksteakdogfish
> mulletsoddfishsavorypicklesauce
> thrushesblackbirdsvariouspigeons
> roosterspanroastedwagtailslarks
> chunksofharemarinatedinmulledwine
> alldrizzledwithhoneysilphium
> vinegaroilandspicesgalore.[57]

This assemblage features what can delicately be called a massive synthesis of Greek treats. The absence of beef and pork does not surprise, for these are generally reserved for sacrifice. A twofold comic sense attaches to this Aristophanic creation: (1) just as the Dionysian involves an end to individuation as made manifest in the collectivity of the chorus' coming forth to present the finale, the mixing together of the disparate foods into a single dish denominated by a single word does so as well; and (2) everyone can find *something* to enjoy in this marvelous mix,[58] therefore sustaining Praxagora's vision of one and the same standard of life for all. The chorus dances spiritedly as it sings a song of victory and dances off to another feast, the feast of victory.[59]

However, the remainder of the lines following the astonishing food, and the brief penultimate remark of Blepyrus, raises a question that perhaps reflects back to Praxagora's plan at its inception, and with it to the nature of the political itself. Immediately after the content of the marvelous meal has been detailed as above, the chorus addresses Blepyrus somewhat strangely:

> Chorus: Now that you've heard what awaits you
> grab your plate quickly,
> then raise the dust
> but take some porridge for dinner.
> Blepyrus: But ***they are stuffing it in*** (*alla* ***laimattousi*** *pou*).
> (Emphasis mine.)

Again, I may be stretching a point, but I cannot help wondering whether this final scene does not contain a jest upon the entire audience of spectators and readers. I wonder, that is, whether Praxagora's proposal of equality for all does not function as a mask for at least the *de facto* priority of women over men. The two girls accompanying Blepyrus are devouring the feast of food. But Blepyrus, the maidservant's "master, I mean my mistress' husband" (*despotēn, ton andr', hopou 'sti tēs emēs kektēmenēs*) (1125–1126), receives no offer of the marvelous mix of delicacies. Rather, he is directed to eat mere porridge (*lekithos*) instead. To stretch this point yet further, the word for porridge (*lekithos*) has a sound not unlike the word for speech (*logos*). In addition to being shoved toward a dull meal, Blepyrus may well be receiving the message that he should "eat his words," that he should just shut up. In other words, the women really *are* in charge, and have begun to reinstate a contempt for men just as acute as the contempt that the women had suffered previously.

What Platonic echoes are there, if any? First of all, like the Platonic city presented in the *Republic,* the Aristophanic city cannot be built, even in *logos.* No architect can overcome the erotic nature of human beings, male or female, understood individually or collectively. It further follows that neither an aristocratic nor an egalitarian city can be built in *logos.* Human *erōs* will always disrupt the most careful plans undertaken with the best of motives. However, this makes no case whatsoever against *erōs.* It not only indicates the impossibility of subjecting *erōs* to human law and control, but celebrates its life-giving and life-affirming power, a power that no political organization can direct entirely. One can say that political organization exists on the negative side for the protection of its citizens from both external attack and from internal strife, and from the positive side that it exists for the sake of furthering the good of its citizens and the community. When, for example, contemporary readers look at *Republic* book 5 and at *Assemblywomen,* they often see these works through a modern lens. No doubt, this modern lens has been crafted at least in part from materials provided by the *Republic.* However, as John Sallis has pointed out in *Platonic Legacies,* what has *not* been read and handed down has its own peculiar significance, and upon receiving just attention reveals dimensions that have remained hidden from view. By pairing *Republic* book 5 and *Assemblywomen,* we come to sense a depth lying beneath politics and political philosophy. *Erōs*—not of human origin and outside human mastery, but giving wholeness and worth as nothing else can—hovers beneath and around us everywhere. Laws of marriage attempt to manage it, with a great deal less than total success. Treaties between nations make similar attempts, with similar results.

In the introduction, I cited Schiller as the philosopher who ascribed the greatest disclosive power to comedy, even though his contemporary and admirer Hegel also regarded it highly. For Schiller, as we saw, the tragic poet must "make a leap" while the comic poet must already "be at home." While tragedy has a more significant point, namely the disclosure of the appropriately human limits, comedy "proceeds to a more significant purpose and it would, were it to attain it, render tragedy superfluous and impossible."[60] But since he found Aristophanes "absolutely reprehensible" for his ridicule, his crudeness, and above all for his undignified treatment of the lower class (thus remaining a true Kantian), there is little doubt that if indeed he had read it, *Assemblywomen* would have appalled him. Much more recently, Leo Strauss wrote, "It is not sufficient to say that the *Assembly of Women* is the ugliest comedy; it is *the* ugly comedy,"[61] citing the torturing of the young man by the ones he calls "hags" as particularly odious.

I could not disagree more. First of all, in Aristophanes virtually *everyone* is held up to ridicule, even Praxagora who is presented, toward the end, as a procuress of girls for her questionably potent husband. Further, *Assemblywomen* is a *comedy* and not at all a realistic play. Hegel speaks wisely when he maintains that Aristophanic comedy does not merely represent, but *is* "the laughing bliss (*Seligkeit*) of the Olympian gods."[62] The nonsense on the stage of *Assemblywomen* resembles nothing so much as the play of the Olympians, in which one finds much plotting, much anger, much pain, *erōs* rampant—but nothing of any real consequence to the immortal participants. Insofar as calculation, pleasure, pain, and *erōs* are of great consequence to human beings, Praxagora's city provides a vicarious image of an impossible erotic life in which, through our laughter, we celebrate our own *erōs* as it inhabits our own mortal lives.

Four

Lysistrata

Erōs and Transcendence

In this chapter, I propose an interpretation of this most popular of Aristophanes' comedies that moves in a different direction than is usual. The abundance and the virtuosity of sexual punning, innuendo, and actual imagery that permeates virtually every scene of the comedy provides contemporary audiences with straightforward access and enjoyment. With its underlying feminist themes,[1] its make-love-not-war sentiments, its more serious concerns with the terrible costs of war and with matters of competent governance generally, *Lysistrata* is an especially timely play for us.

These matters require little commentary and those that do, such as the historical and linguistic matters, have been ably treated elsewhere.[2] A reading of *Lysistrata* through a different lens, in order to discern its philosophical yield, gives the play another and deeper side. While this deeper side is unmistakably present in its text, *Lysistrata*'s own hilarity and good cheer has seemed to overwhelm it in the literature.

In *Assemblywomen, erōs* made itself manifest as the direct desire for sexual satisfaction—little or nothing more. Further, the city of Athens was presented first of all as a city of selfish, bungling men; then as a reorganized city under the principle of equality; finally once again as a city of self-seeking individuals for whom the new laws instituted by Praxagora are either means or obstacles to self-gratification. In terms of Plato's *Symposium, erōs* never ascends beyond the love of beautiful bodies. More precisely, it never even ascends to this lowest rung, for in the *Symposium* this initial rung unfolds into beautiful *logoi* (210a8), none of which are remotely present in the erotic discourses of *Assemblywomen.*

By contrast, *erōs* serves transcendent purposes in *Lysistrata.* The physical beauty and sexual charms of the wives are withheld from their husbands, a withholding that aims at the great political goal of ending warfare, and at the great private goal of familial happiness. The men are depicted as politically inept, but this ineptitude has far more dangerous consequences than those in *Assemblywomen.* Their folly leads to deep human misery on all fronts. At the same time, they are granted moral nobility: they are scrupulously faithful to their wives. While away from home, they do not avail themselves of *hetaireia* to satisfy their sexual frustrations, nor do they "employ their hand" (*dephesthai*) for relief. The women are initially depicted as silly and superficial, but they too share in the moral nobility of their husbands, whom they love just as truly and just as ardently as they are loved. The superficial difference consists of their complaints concerning the unavailability of those technological products useful for easing their sexual frustration in their husbands' absence.

Erōs, then, serves not merely as sexual desire for one beautiful body, but as the seal of a sacred promise. As the comedy unfolds directly into the public, the private, and the universal realms, I shall endeavor to direct attention to these subtler and more philosophical dimensions.

LINES 1–145

The play opens with its heroine Lysistrata bemoaning the propensity of her gender to frivolity. First among her examples is "a revel for Bacchus" (*Bakkheion*). This is a most peculiar example, since the comedy is being performed at a Bacchic (Dionysian) festival, which at the very least is an outgrowth of the Bacchanalian revels of the past, and might well be regarded virtually identical to them. There is neither shame nor negativity attached to rejoicing in one's erotic nature. When Lysistrata expresses her annoyance with the women for being late to the "serious" meeting she called, decrying the view held by "the men that we're capable of any sort of mischief" (*para men tois andrasin nenomismetha einai panourgoi*) (11–12), her friend Kalonike agrees at once: "By God, we are!" (12).

The word *panourgos* at its most negative pole points to wickedness, and at its most positive it points to cunning. Henderson's "mischief," which can point both to criminal activity and to playfulness, captures these two poles in a single word. Lysistrata regards the feminine propensity to *panourgoi* as entirely frivolous, at least in the current context. Her friend, who just might have a greater appreciation of both the wholeness and the actuality of womanly experience, celebrates the feminine capacity for *pan-*

ourgia. Lysistrata stands alone among the plays of Aristophanes insofar as it takes its name neither from its chorus nor from a communal matter, but from an individual character. However, the *character* Lysistrata is unlike her counterpart Praxagora in *Assemblywomen:* however one might regard Blepyrus, he is certainly both present and crucial to the action of the play. Just as crucially in my view, nowhere do we find a distinct identity for the husband of Lysistrata.[3] One wonders whether, on the few occasions she speaks of her husband, he serves merely as a rhetorical figure with no real existence.

This may explain her dour mood at the outset of the play. It may also explain her misunderstanding of the women's tardiness to the meeting. Kalonike must remind her of the many tiring household tasks that the women have to perform. Lysistrata, who appears to judge political things as far weightier than personal ones, retorts, "there are other matters more constructive (*prourgiaitera*) than all of that" (20–21).

What follows this exchange is a series of what might appear to be nothing more than phallic puns. Kalonike wonders whether the agenda of Lysistrata's meeting is "something big" (*pēlikon ti*) (23)? Lysistrata replies with one word: *mega.* Is it also thick, Kalonike wonders (*mōn kai pakhu*) (23)? "Big and thick, by God" (*nē ton Dia kai Pakhu*) (24), Lysistrata answers. The wonderfully *panourgos* Kalonike asks, "Then why are we not all here?" to which a testy Lysistrata replies, "That's not how I meant it! If it were, we'd all have gathered quickly" (24–25).

Looking away from the merely comic aspect and toward its philosophical depth (in perhaps another comical manner), a "big" question suggests itself: what is magnitude? What does it mean to call something "big"? Big and thick? Abstracted from other properties, "big" and "thick" refer indifferently to the dimensionality of objects in mathematical terms. In metaphorical usage, "big" and "thick" might refer to matters of surpassing importance and complexity. In the second sailing (*deuteros plous*) of Plato's *Phaedo,* Socrates chooses to divest this matter of its intellectual formidability by proceeding "simply, artlessly, and perhaps naively": *haplōs kai atekhnōs kai isōs euēthōs* (100d3–4). Hypothesizing the *eidē* such as the beautiful itself, the good itself, and the large itself, he will posit these and nothing else as the causes of beauty, goodness, and largeness in things respectively.[4]

Largeness or "the large" (*ta megala*) is spoken of as "the form of the cause" (*tēs aitias to eidos*) (100b3–4) of anything's "being large, largeness or the larger as the cause of anything being larger (*kai ta meizō meizō*), and littler things are littler by smallness (*kai smikrotēti ta elattō elattō*)" (100e5–6). Socrates claims to be unable to understand the kinds of causes in natural science that he learned of earlier, in particular material causes and noetic causes. He ignores any causal ascriptions other than these hypothesized eidetic ones. Why? Not only do such causes seem truest, but they also provide *safety.* "Safety" in this context has a most peculiar ring to it, a comic ring. It is comic first of all because Socrates is to meet his death later that day and feels entirely safe, while his interlocutors Simmias and Cebes do not feel safe at all, and require continuous reassurance that their souls are indeed immortal. Further, Socrates' argument for the soul's immortality—which he constructs in analogy with the ones on beauty, goodness, and largeness—is one of his weaker ones, hinging as it does on the problematic ascription of an eidetic nature to *life.*

Opposing "forms" (*eidē*) repel one another: a body that is sick admits nothing in it of health, and vice versa, hence the soul—alive by its very nature—cannot entertain death. The soul is alive, therefore it is deathless by nature. I maintain that this is not only an unconvincing argument, but a comic one as well, insofar as it rests entirely upon the earlier and hypothetical positing of the *eidē* as cited in a previous chapter:

> Then laying down (*hupothemenos*) in each case the *logos* I judge (*krinō*) to be healthiest (*errōmenestaton*), and whatever seems to me (*moi dokē*) to agree (*sumphōnein*) with it, I set down (*tithēmi*) as true, and what does not as not true. (*Phaedo* 100a3–8)

Thus, even if the eidetic argument is regarded as sound (which it is not) it cannot be entirely convincing, as it presupposes a series of positings and "semblances."

However, I believe that this ragged argument is sufficient to provide safety for the soul of Socrates, who seems entirely unconcerned with the immortality of his own soul even on the day he is to die. In my view, the immortality of the soul was never a serious issue for him.[5] Rather, the quality of his life on earth occupied his entire attention. As noted in a previous chapter, fear of death was the greatest evil for this life, and as what comes after death is unknown and it is disgraceful to fear what one does not know, fear of death is disgraceful—that is, it works against a good life. It is in service to this good life that Socrates launches this comic argument, and keeping this good life *safe* is his entire object.

The issue of magnitude contains analogous complexity in *Lysistrata.* Of course no discussion takes on *ta megala* as the cause either of a male erection or of a political matter being *mega.* However, Lysistrata's denunciation of her colleagues for their proclivity toward sexual joy at the expense of the good of the city overlooks unseen but detectable causes built into the comic scene between the two women. First, it overlooks the *erōs* of the women as bound up with the joy they take in their politically sanctioned marriages. Second, it overlooks the legal restrictions on female participation in matters of policy. Finally, as Kalonike already observed, it overlooks the time-consuming—and energy-consuming—duties of a wife.[6]

Further, in what way and in what context can a male sexual organ be called *mega*? In strictly eidetic terms, it has magnitude in the same way that any object does. Similarly, calling a male erection *mega* is lexically unenlightening in the extreme. If we were to speak in a serious eidetic way, to call a male erection *mega* tells us nothing, but to say that it is *meizōn* (larger) than a limp penis by virtue of its participation in *ta meizon* (the larger) gives at least somewhat more precision—but that is beside the point as well. Aristophanes is a *poet,* and at the outset of *Lysistrata* his poetry has fashioned a bond between *erōs* and largeness, magnitude. The kind of largeness that belongs to the male is the kind that is sought by the female. But this largeness, though it surely includes the sexual, is far from merely sexual. *Ta megala* gestures as well toward the possibility of a great civic life. For such a life, the women—disenfranchised, relegated to the private economy of the home, victimized in so many ways by the folly of their men—must seek their satisfaction by (temporarily) leaving their men achingly *mega.* Strangely and comically, the male erection is not principally at issue, but serves as an emblem for matters that are *meizō,* that differ not in degree, but in kind.[7]

In the comedy, Lysistrata's seriousness contrasts with Kalonike's playful sense of humor: Lysistrata's plan includes saving all of Greece, while Kalonike wouldn't mind if the Peloponnesians and the Boeotians (except for their delicious eels, a more oblique sexual reference) were rendered extinct. Thus the poet inverts the seriousness of actual political life, in which a sex strike is ridiculous and narrow political hatred of the other is commonplace. Kalonike is incredulous that she and her colleagues are even capable of conceiving a serious plan. She presents the apotheosis of womanhood as follows: "What can mere women do that is intelligent (*phronimon*) and brilliant (*lampron*)? We sit around the house looking pretty, wearing saffron dresses and make-up" (42–44). Lysistrata agrees at once, seizing upon the liberating possibility dwelling therein: salvation resides in "fancy little dresses, perfumes, slippers, rouge, and diaphanous undergarments" (46–49).

Can such matters as the sexually provocative adornments of women be regarded as "intelligent (*phronimon*) and brilliant (*lampron*)"? I would answer with a resounding "Yes!" to both. They are products of human intelligence, designed with the purpose of serving marital happiness. They celebrate shining female beauty in a most stimulating manner, i.e., by *partly concealing it,* by letting it shadow itself forward and making it more maddeningly enticing thereby. Thus, these garments empower generous erotic play to which concealment belongs by its very nature. In *Lysistrata,* it is never a matter merely of sexual ache, as it was in *Assemblywomen.* The matter in *Lysistrata* always concerns caring, loving ritual, and mutual pleasure. Thus, once it becomes clear to Kalonike that the cessation of all violence between men is her friend's goal, she also comes to agree: "By God, [the women] should have taken wing and flown here by now" (55).

Lysistrata's Athenian colleague Myrrhine joins the two, and is met with silence and disapprobation from her friends for her tardiness in the face of pressing business (*pragmatos*). But when Myrrhine asks after its pressing importance (*parousaisin*), she is told that it would be better to wait until the women from other parts of Greece get there.

Appropriate time is another theme of *Lysistrata.* There is a right moment for action, and right stretches during which to withhold action. No strictly numerical determinations are possible in such matters. Rather, their determination remains an ongoing challenge and a necessary component of our human condition. The comedy takes place in a region removed from the actual political universe that we inhabit, and so allows us to consider that universe and to enjoy the way poetry can make it manifest to us.

As the women arrive, erotic play between them begins. The fair-skinned Athenian women teasingly gush over the tanned Spartan Lampito. Lampito's rigorous gymnastic program enables her to touch her heels to her buttocks in a jump, and has given her skin a splendidly vital appearance. Lysistrata: "How vivid your beauty! What rosy cheeks, what firmness of physique! You could throttle a bull!" (79–81). Kalonike first observes, "What a beautiful set of tits you have," then begins to play with them until Lampito protests, "You're feeling me up (*hupopsalassete*) like a beast for sacrifice!" (83–84). Myrrhine notes that like Boeotia, the Boeotian woman has "a lush bottomland," and Kalonike agrees, adding that her bush is "most elegantly (*kompsotata*) pruned" (86–88). The Corinthian woman has *kh'haia* —"substance" (Henderson) or "noble lines" (Sommerstein)—both front and back, suggesting that the Corinthian woman is both well bred and quite large.

Here, the Athenian women playfully measure their visiting counterparts solely in terms of the way their sexuality shines forth to the eye. Their common womanhood transcends their regional specificity. The sexual allure they hold for their respective men proves to be the source of their strength. It transforms their specifically female vulnerability into something powerful and noble. As I shall endeavor to show in what follows, the parentage of *Erōs* as presented in Diotima's words to Socrates in the *Symposium* resonates throughout *Lysistrata. Poros* (Resource) became drunk on nectar at the celebration of the birth of Aphrodite, and *Penia* (Poverty), lacking resource, is nevertheless far from resourceless: she "schemes (*epibouleuousa*) to produce a child by Resource, and she lay with him and thereby conceived *Erōs*" (*Symposium* 203b7–c1).

Even at this early stage, the resonances can be heard. In war, *erōs* is a leading casualty. For its rebirth, the women—who have no direct power over public political or economic policy—are not entirely without resource. They might, however, scheme and find an indirect way to effect their ultimate goal, peace, and with it the restoration of familial life and the joy that peace brings. I suggest that there is an analogue between the drunkenness of Resource in the *Symposium*, which renders him vulnerable to a most worthy plot envisaged by Poverty, and the sexual pain of the Greek men in *Lysistrata*. The goal of both is clearly the same: the advent of Love.

Just as Poverty had to await the right moment to seduce Resource, so Lysistrata's announcement of her plan required preparation of the ground. Just as in the *Symposium,* the flesh is the site of the initial erotic bond in *Lysistrata:* here, in marriage, it sustains this bond even as the other dimensions belonging to human love grow deeper. It is marriage's "necessary condition." Lysistrata first engages the gathering of women by questioning them about the absence of their husbands, who are their children's fathers, during wartime. Lysistrata is the only one who makes an explicitly sexual remark, lamenting the absence of lovers and regretting the unavailability even of small dildos that might have provided some relief. Henderson has Kalonike speak this passage, but Sommerstein gives it to Lysistrata. Since I find no compelling textual evidence of a husband for Lysistrata, it seems to me that Lysistrata is the more likely speaker. Still further, by tilting the discussion clearly toward sexual matters, it prepares the way for her goal, to end the war, and for her proposal, which will provide the means.

Holding out the possibility of ending the war, Lysistrata's "dialogue" with them has led to the women's enthusiastic concurrence with her plan in advance of its proposal. Their language is replete with excess. Kalonike would pawn the dress she is wearing and drink up the money she received for it. Myrrhine would go further: she would slice herself in two and donate half. Lampito, the only woman whose remarks indicate a still higher vision, adds, "And I would climb to the summit of [the tallest mountain,] Taygetus, if I could see peace (*eiranan*) from there" (117–118). What is to be made of this excess? It is yet another instance of *erōs* overflowing *logos,* bringing joy forth, disclosing measure precisely by transgressing it.

Again, the issue of *right moment* arises. But is there ever a right moment to tell a robustly erotic married woman to forego sexual pleasure? There may be no moment when one would hear an immediate "yes," but that does not mean that a right moment does not exist. There is a way and a time to bring up unpleasant aspects belonging to matters of importance, and an allowance of time for their wisdom to sink in. The comedy allows us to understand this painful aspect of the human condition through the laughter it provokes. Lysistrata delivers the news straight and hard: "All right, we must abstain from the prick": *aphektea toinun estin hēmin tou peous* (124).

The women begin to abandon her. The paradigmatic response comes from her friend Kalonike: "Anything else you want, anything at all! I'm even ready to walk through fire; rather that than the prick. There's nothing like it, my dear Lysistrata" (133–135). Only Lampito has the "largeness" to see beyond the view of her colleagues, who would rather see the war continue than to forgo sexual gratification for any length of time. Agreeing with the horrified women that "it's difficult for females to sleep alone without the hard-on (*aneu psōlas*)," she continues, "but no matter, I agree: we need peace" (144–145). Lysistrata's accolade is this: "you're the only real woman here": *su kai monē toutōn gunē* (145).

Note that this accolade affirms two qualities of women who deserve that name in the genuine sense: they are authentically erotic beings, and they are authentically intellectual beings. The hilarious excess of the women's negative response to Lysistrata's plan of abstinence recalls their equally excessive affirmative response to her initial suggestion that the women might be able to end the war. No exemption from this two-sided excess exists for Lampito. However, her genuine womanhood consists of an *erōs* that ascends from the sexual to the universal-intellectual, from love of the *psōlē* to love of *eirēnē*. Her vision is sufficient to encompass both in a single glance, her *logos* is supple enough to express both in a single sentence. This simple, wise sentence spoken by the tanned, gymnastically sculpted, large-breasted comical Spartan woman brings *erōs* to *logos* as well as any of the interlocutors in Plato's *Symposium*.

Thus, one of the smallest *logoi* in this first section is the largest—the one with the "most" magnitude.

LINES 146–253

In terms of plot coherence, this section provides a vexing puzzle. The men are at war. Their wives have not seen them in quite some time. Nevertheless, Lysistrata argues that her plan for peace will work because the men will *see* their women presenting themselves in their most lascivious garments, but the women will keep their distance:

> If we . . . walked past them wearing only our diaphanous undergarment
> with our pubes plucked in a neat triangle, and the men got hard and
> hankered to ball us, but we didn't go near them and kept away,
> they'd sue for peace, and quickly, you can count on that! (149–154)

How can the men be (1) away at war, and (2) available to their wives for sexual teasing in their home neighborhood at the same time? Henderson theorizes plausibly, "Henceforth we are to imagine the husbands to be at home, and we have the impression that wives being unavailable to husbands are turning the tables on husbands who have been unavailable to their wives. Comic poets can have their cake and eat it, too."[8]

Henderson's view is preferable to my own on all sober grounds. But *Lysistrata* is not a sober play. Driven by *erōs* in celebration of Dionysus, I suggest—begging the reader's pardon—the region in which *Lysistrata* takes place is not governed by linear time or geometrical space. Spatz views *Lysistrata* as primarily a diversion from the agonizing consequences of the Peloponnesian War for Athens, providing a comforting fantasy for an Athenian audience that feels the oncoming victory of Sparta.[9] I say that this diversion from contemporary political reality can be regarded both positively in itself, and in another way: *Lysistrata* the play and Lysistrata the character are world-creators. The ultimate characteristic of the world they create, brought into being through the gift of Aristophanes, is peace-bringing *erōs* triumphant over all.

Just as in our actual world, there are practical problems in this imagined world that must be addressed. Some problems might be common to both. In particular, husbands whose wives have taken special measures to arouse them have reason to expect erotic consummation. When this expectation is not met, they might well interpret the wives' behavior as mockery, and grow enraged. They might drag them into the bedroom by force and beat them (160–162). What, then? Lysistrata advises: "You must submit in an especially bad way": *parekhein khrē kaka kakōs* (163). She points out that men get no pleasure from such forced couplings, and that other ways remain for wives to make their husband's lives miserable: "No husband can have a happy life (*euphranthēsetai*) if his wife does not join in with him (*xumpherē*)" (165–166).

This comment reveals several elements that call for attention. First, Lysistrata's ability to detach herself from the dynamics of marital life further suggests that she may be husbandless. In addition, it echoes some of the non-laughable sections with which the previous two chapters dealt, namely those concerned with the rape of women. Here, this theme arises differently, in the context of marriage and lingerie: not only are the wives pained, but their husbands experience pain also, however asymmetrically. In the erotic bond of husband and wife, reciprocity is the joy-bringing means of its security. The withholding of *erōs* receives its entire inspiration from *erōs*.

The women's oath of abstinence is a wholly sincere yet wholly comic celebration of Dionysus, for the sake of the festival that bears his name. Intoxication and release from inhibition are two primary qualities of the Dionysian. The oath of the women, which is taken on a large wine jug, however, calls for the opposite: total rational control over their sexual impulses. Lysistrata has each of them swear, among other things, to let no man of any kind "approach me with a hard-on" (*hostis pros eme proseisin estukōs lege*) (214). The women promise to present themselves to their husbands at their most alluring at all times, yet never to surrender willingly to their husbands, and if forced never to move their hips, never to raise their legs, never to crouch down "like a lioness on a cheesegrater" (231–232). Let excellent wine grace the lips of the celibate! Let mere water disappoint the indulgent.

The women of Greece, those in their sexual prime, declare . . . chaste sexual warfare?

LINES 254–386

Another task awaits the older women, who declare their own gender war. The Chorus of Women (*KHOROS GUNAIKŌN*) storm and occupy the Acropolis, the center of Athenian public life. This section opens with the response of the men's Chorus Leader and the Chorus of Old Men (*KHOROS GERONTŌN*). Like Strepsiades, Blepyrus, and Philocleon, these men cut a figure that could hardly be less formidable. The Chorus Leader urges his men forward, even though their shoulders ache from carrying olivewood. The Chorus responds with a lament that their counterparts, who they call collectively "women, the manifestly evil nuisance we've nurtured in our homes" (*gunaikas, has eboskomen kat' oikon emphanes kakon*) (260), now control the sacred image of Athena on the Acropolis and have locked the citadel gates. The locking of the citadel gates by the older women reflects the withholding of sexual congress by the younger women. This "denial of entry" to the men in both the private and the public realms, from the women's point of view, serves as a necessary and temporary obstacle to their joyous welcome. The women, characterized by the men as wrongly nurtured and now vicious, are rather the true nurturers.

The superior physical strength of the Chorus of Women in *Lysistrata* is analogous to their superior intellectual strength in *Assemblywomen,* which had no such major choral role but which addressed itself to matters of wisdom and cleverness. We are presented with another scene of men laboring against the weaknesses attendant upon aging, and of laughable comments issuing from their mouths as they attempt to carry their heavy torches up the hill to the Acropolis. The goal, as declared by their Chorus Leader:

> As quickly as possible (*takhista*), let's hurry to the city . . .
> So we can lay these logs in a circle around the women who
> Have instigated or abetted this business.
> Let's erect a single pyre and incinerate them with our own hands,
> All of them, on a single decree (*psēphou*) . . . (266–270)

In the first line of the epirrhema that follows, Aristophanes' art shines with a special brightness. This line is certain to bring forth an enormous laugh from spectators and at least a broad smile from readers. The aging Chorus of Men, whose "hurry as quickly as possible" is not very fast at all, whose members are huffing and puffing from effort and are as far as can be from arousing fear or respect in anyone, sing: "By Demeter, they won't laugh at me while I'm alive!" (272). However, like the Chorus of Wasps in the play bearing their name, the old men were indeed once physically powerful, proving their strength on military battlefields in their youth. The Chorus and its Leader affirm this proudly.

Unlike *Wasps,* which attributed the weakness and poverty of the old men to their exploitation by demagogues, *Lysistrata* suggests that the weakness of the men—here depicted in relation to the strength of the women—is attributable to the toll of warfare. The poetic synthesis of crude, even cruel ridicule coupled with subtle sensitivity recalls the combination of excess and measure that Socrates, in the *Phaedrus* and the *Ion,* called divine madness. The old men are presented as objects of derision and of respect simultaneously. Their ferocious words are belied by their weary bones, but they *were* once fierce, their bodies *were* once young and strong. The laughter at their plight is rough and gentle at once, as is their treatment by the women.

More than any of the comedies discussed in the previous chapters, *Lysistrata* presents a thoughtful critique of the honor-loving (*philotimos*) soul, as it is called in *Republic* book 8. The outrage of the men stems from their being bested by women, whom they regard as inferior both in physical prowess and at deliberation. Rather than crediting the women for their courage and brains, they hold themselves responsible for not using their powers to make them more properly submissive. As the comedy unfolds so too does this theme, which echoes the *Republic*'s relegation of the timocratic soul to a status below that of the best soul.

The plot by the men to "smoke the women out" backfires hilariously. The women are not incinerated in a circular pyre of logs. Rather, the smoke blinds the men carrying the logs that are so heavy they must be put down long before they can use them to batter the gates. In addition, the rising smoke allows the Leader of the Women's Chorus to discover the nearby presence of the men who would set their fires, and to urge the women forward even faster. The women respond at once and most enthusiastically: "Fly, fly, Nikodike" (*petou petou, Nikodikē*) (321), before "the old men who mean death" (*hupo te gerontōn olethrōn*) (325) arrive. "Nikodike," the name of the Athenian temple that faces the entrance to the Acropolis on the right, literally means "victory of justice."

Water is the "weapon" of the women. It proves to be more than sufficient for its task. In the terms presented in Plato's *Timaeus,* fire and water are homogeneous in their underlying structures in that their common, underlying, invisible tetrahedral form is comprised of isosceles triangles. While water is not as mobile as fire, it is more complex, comprised of twelve such triangles to fire's four. Though perhaps not as spectacular as fire, water serves as fire's triumphant adversary. Athena is the goddess of victory as well as the goddess of wisdom. Carrying large pitchers of water as they race to the Acropolis, the Grecian women honor both dominions of their goddess.

The two Choruses meet and their respective Leaders exchange words. With deep comic pain, the superior intellectual and military power of the women asserts itself. The Women's Chorus Leader calls her opponents "especially wretched men" (*andres ponōponēroi*) (350). Her male counterpart can only respond helplessly, as he surveys the large number of women assembled for battle, for whom the men are unprepared. The two Leaders then warn one another: the Men's Leader threatens a "one-two" punch and asks whether the Women's Leader has anything "terrifying" (*deinon*) (366) in return. "I'll rip out your lungs and your guts with my fangs" (367) is her prompt, gentle reply. After a series of similarly gracious exchanges, the Men's Leader exclaims, "Did you hear her audacity (*thrasous*)?" (378). "I am free" (*eleuthera gar eimi*), is her simple and immediate response.

The Women's Chorus Leader is a "mere" poetic creation. In the context of Greek society, the preceding three words spoken by this poetic character might be seen by us, and perhaps by the Greek audience as well, as a laugh line. After all, Greek women were not free "as a matter of fact." Even the freedom here declared by the Women's Chorus Leader consists primarily of the imagined liberation from their political and cultural constraints. However, I suggest that these three simple words resound far beyond their immediate context. They resound even beyond Hegel's observation that Aristophanes brought to the stage a freedom we would not dream of were it not historically authenticated. They are the subsoil of every human soul, articulated technically by the voice of an actor with a woman's mask, and artistically by a nameless character in a Dionysian comedy.

Hegel viewed freedom's first coming to consciousness among the Greeks as a major world-historical development. However, insofar as they kept slaves and insofar as this freedom was "only accidental," full consciousness of freedom had to await "the Germanic peoples, through Christianity."[10] Further, despite his acknowledgement and appreciation of the necessity of art in the self-unfolding of spirit (*Geist*), especially of Greek art, Hegel could declare art as dead in the modern, rational era:

> [A]rt, considered in its highest vocation, is and remains for us a thing of the past. Thereby it has lost for us genuine truth and life, and has rather been transferred into our *ideas* instead of maintaining its earlier necessity in reality and occupying its higher place. What is aroused in us by works of art is not just immediate enjoyment but our judgment also, since we subject to our intellectual consideration (i) the content of art, and (ii) the work of art's means of presentation, and the appropriateness or inappropriateness of both to one another.[11]

This is not the place to discuss Hegel's philosophy of history nor his philosophy of art. However, given his own crediting of the importance of Aristophanes, I cannot help but suspect that *eleuthera gar eimi*—"I am free" —stands yet *ahead* of us, a gift to every human being in every language everywhere.

On a somewhat more earthbound plane, the Women's Leader douses the Men's Leader's torch together with its bearer, and explains to her befuddled adversary that she did this to him "so you'll bloom again": *hopōs anablastaneis* (384). The depth of her jest, which might seem like sheer mockery, is that she is telling the truth: the actuating motive behind her belligerence consists of her desire to end the blight of warfare so that the men, relieved of the dreadfulness of warfare, can celebrate life together with their women.

LINES 387–493

The Magistrate (or Commissioner—*PROBOULOS*) enters, with the intention of arresting the women. Historically, the Magistrate was installed as something of a check to the democracy, which often behaved unwisely.[12] However, in a dramatic sense Aristophanes' Magistrate proves himself even more foolish than the men who need his assistance. He has no idea why the women rebel, nor does he show the slightest curiosity. His first *logos,* which begins and ends with an "analysis" of their actions without seeking a single bit of information, deserves special attention: "So the women's insolence (*truphē*) has flared up again" (387), an insolence that he attributes to their "licentiousness" (*akolastasmata*)[13] (398). The Men's Chorus Leader responds in kind, twice attributing hubris to the women, and accusing them in particular of having committed "every outrage (*hai talla th' hubrikasi*), even doused us with those pitchers, so we get to shake water out of our clothes as if we peed in them" (400–402).

Hubris, as discussed earlier, entails more than mere extreme behavior and impropriety. It involves transgressing the appropriately human limits. The Women's Chorus has surely transgressed the culturally normative feminine limits. However, in raising the serious questions concerning the affairs not only of politics but of what most properly belongs to human life, they operate precisely in service to those limits they are accused of violating. The exchanges of *logoi* between the Men's and Women's Choruses bears little resemblance outwardly to a Platonic dialogue. But the uproarious interplay of the hapless men and the well-disciplined women aims at human wisdom just as surely as the conversation between Socrates and Theaetetus in the dialogue bearing the latter's name.

The Magistrate directs his slaves to jimmy open the locked Acropolis gates with crowbars when Lysistrata emerges, telling the Magistrate sharply, "Why do you need crowbars? It's not crowbars you need, but intellect (*nou*) and sense (or heart—*phrenōn*)" (431–432). She is proven right when the Magistrate calls her "you disgusting one" (*ō miara su*), and orders an archer (Henderson translates *toxotēs* as "policeman") to capture her and bind her hands fast. While Lysistrata threatens to make both the first archer and a second one go home crying should they dare to touch her at all (and they do not), more noteworthy still is her expression of contempt. If he should touch her with his fingertip, "public servant that he is" (*dēmosios ōn*) (436), she will launch a hurtful, successful, and humiliating counterattack.

The warlike posture of the Athenians does not signal strength. Rather it betrays a double weakness. First, the authority of the official's command generates no deference from the women, just as the ill-conceived warfare of the men engenders no admiration from them. Further, the men's foolishness on all sides—their failure to exercise both their *nous* and their *phrenes*—outrages the human essence that they had been granted. That the Magistrate is cowed and trashed by the three Old Women who enter from the gate, while the archers disappear in fright, signals a comic restoration of appropriate measure. If he should lay a hand on Lysistrata, says the first, "I'll beat the shit out of you": *epikhesei patoumenos* (439–440). The second promises the Magistrate a black eye. The third pledges to rip his hair out "till you groan and wail": *stenokōkutous* (448).[14] Once again, their language lacks the decorousness found in the Platonic dialogues. However, the sentiment that human wisdom deserves an eloquent defense is identical, and the words of the women are expertly tailored to the needs of their "interlocutors."

Although the overwhelmed Magistrate has enough remaining bravado to summon his Scythian colleagues to attack (though he does not enter the fray himself), the attackers are easily routed by their female counterparts. Lysistrata's *logos* of command in the midst of the battle reveals the noteworthy kinship of this comic scene to some Platonic themes. After she urges her troops on to military victory, commanding them not only to hit and smash their adversaries, but also to "revile them shamelessly" (*ou loidorēset', ouk anaiskhuntēsete*) (460)—Henderson has, "call them names, the nastier the better"—she suddenly gives another and very dissimilar order. Having achieved total military success both in deed and in word (one can imagine Homeric taunts from the mouths of the winners), she commands the women: "Stop, withdraw, do not strip the bodies": *pausasth', epanakhōreite, mē skuleuete* (461).

The latter command calls to mind the discussion in *Republic* book 5 of the appropriate treatment of Greek soldiers defeated by the soldiers of Socrates' Greek city in *logos:* while barbarians are regarded as enemies and given no quarter, Greeks act toward one another more gently, with an eye and an obligation to heal rather than exacerbate the wounds caused by "faction" (*stasis*). The harshest penalty to be visited upon their temporarily alienated countrymen consists of depriving them of one year's harvest. Enslavement does not deserve the slightest consideration. Socrates rejects the name "war" (*polemos*) for Greek versus Greek battles, since all Greeks are "lovers of Greeks" (*philellēnes*) (470e8), and are considered by one another "as kin" (*hōs oikeious*) (471a1—literally, "from the same house"). When death on the battlefield occurs in such a contest, the victorious "Greek soldiers must, therefore, leave off stripping corpses and preventing their recovery" (469e4–5).

Given the long history of intra-Greek warfare, not to mention the political turmoil in the aftermath of the Peloponnesian War, one must wonder how Socrates can entertain such an idealized view. However, I note once again that Socrates sets out the discussions in *Republic* book 5 as *comic* at the outset,[15] and note further he never seriously held to such a view.[16] At one point, he seems to deny or at least retreat from such an answer: "For the sake of a pattern (*paradeigmatos*) . . . that we were seeking," the *likeness* justice by itself and the perfectly just man, and their opposites (472c4–8). Since "the nature of acting (*prakhthēnai*) [attains] less truth than the nature of speaking (*lexeōs*)" (473a1–2), we must be content (*agapētos*) with the approximation that is closest to what has been said (473a5–b2).

But what follows (1) has not been said, (2) is presented in what we today would call conditional form and so is *not* asserted, and (3) constitutes Socrates' comic masterpiece, the so-called "philosopher-king," which is mentioned for the first time in the *Republic* in book 5. As was demonstrated earlier,[17] the philosophical nature and the nature of the ruler contradict one another, and so cannot possibly coincide in one person. Thus, since the philosophical and kingly natures do not come together (thereby affirming the antecedent of the conditional—unless = "if not"), the consequent, that there is "no rest from ills in the cities" is also affirmed.

In this context, Lysistrata's command to her troops to stop, to withdraw, and to leave the men with their possessions mirrors the philosophical comedy. Just as the Socratic comedy conceals the unavoidable darkness that lies at the heart of the political things by means of artful camouflage in *logos,* the poetic comedy discloses that darkness by means of the artistic imagery according to which this darkness can be overcome instantaneously. The Magistrate's archer-soldiers run away screaming, and the Magistrate can only lament that their rout is *kakon.*

The Men's Chorus Leader reproves the Magistrate for "engaging such beasts in words": *eis logon tois thēriois xunapteis* (468). The Men's Chorus calls the women "monsters" (*knōdalois*) (477), a term normally applied to very large animals, and calls for an investigation into this *pathos* that found the women occupying a great mythical king's "citadel / and the great crag of the Acropolis, / a restricted, holy place" (480–483). In a swift about-face from his advice to shun an engagement in *logos* with Lysistrata and her cohorts, the Men's Chorus Leader now demands that the Magistrate force precisely such a confrontation: "Now question her and don't give in and cross-examine everything she presents (*kai prosphere pantas elegkhous*); / it's disgraceful (*aiskhron*) to let this sort of behavior go unchallenged" (484–485). The next section will begin with the proposed engagement in *logos.*

There is much to consider in these last exchanges. Beasts (*thērion*), large and monstrous animals (*knōdalon*)—what are the men thinking? In one sense, of course, their soldiers have been ignominiously defeated by a roaring horde of angry women. Dehumanizing them is psychologically less painful than conceding the superior human performance of their opponents, especially given the expectation of their physical cowardice and weakness. However, the women are physically smaller than the men, have weapons that are less lethal than those of the men, and are bound by custom to defer to the men. In that sense, by enlarging their magnitude and discharging it in action far beyond what both nature (*phusis*) and custom (*nomos*) granted them, they have surely outgrown those two sources that supposedly determine both individual and social existence.[18]

Monsters they are—wonderful monsters whose monstrousness discloses human irrationality and folly, and seeks to rescue Greece from the consequences of both. Further, they show their monstrousness, their outsized natures, by *pulling back* instead of destroying their antagonists when they could. This restraint is even more breathtaking than the attack. It bespeaks a power that exceeds merely human control.

Finally, how is the aforementioned about-face of the Chorus Leader to be understood? Why is he suddenly so eager for an engagement in *logos*? Is it merely the threat from Lysistrata, who claims that she'd prefer to be "sitting modestly at home like a maiden" (473) but who will find "a wasp inside" if anyone harasses her (475)? Could it be the entreaty of the Men's Chorus? Is it because, in the absence of force, only talk remains? Or does a nobler impulse, buried beneath their outer folly, govern the sudden desire for an engagement in *logos*?

LINES 486–613

The Magistrate's *elegkhos* of Lysistrata begins and ends with the same success as the *agōn* launched by the Men's Chorus against the challenging Chorus of Women. In addition to the overarching *elegkhos,* of which the Magistrate is hopelessly incapable, two other Platonic echoes occur in these lines. First, Lysistrata provides many of her answers in images, a practice in which Socrates engages frequently and "greedily" (*Republic* 488a2). The turning points of the *Republic* are marked by images: the noble lie, the ship and the contest to rule it, the sun, divided line, and cave, the underworld as reported by Er at the dialogue's end. Second, Lysistrata's images one and all echo the likeness drawn in Republic book 2 between justice in an individual soul and justice in a city. In her images, she locates management (*tamieusete*) (494) rather than justice as the issue, and affirms a likeness between private (i.e., family) management of affairs and their public management. Henderson observes that since many manufacturing tasks were performed in the home, "Lysistrata's assimilation of domestic to political management . . . was not as far-fetched as it would be in our own culture. On the other hand, the spectators of *Lysistrata* will have found the idea of women managing public funds much more farfetched than we do."[19]

Looking at this matter through another, more philosophical lens, the result appears very different. What, after all, does an answer provide when it is given in an image? Of course, not all images can supply adequate answers. However, not all questions can be answered directly, non-imagistically. In the introduction to John Sallis' *Being and Logos: Reading the Platonic Dialogues,* he addresses what he calls "a certain opacity" belonging to crucial regions of human inquiry. How and why we came to be on the earth, what awaits us after our death, what belongs to a life well-lived—these and other most important questions do not yield up their answers readily, straightforwardly, or completely. However, we can experience them as questions and encounter them vicariously when an image is presented to us that captures both the light and the darkness belonging to them.

In Aristophanic comedy in general and in *Lysistrata* in particular, we experience a twofold image making. The framing of the comedy in which the women of Greece unite to end war and so to save their state constitutes the larger image. The "images within the image" here consist of Lysistrata's specific identification of skillful home management with wise statecraft, with which this section reaches its close.

However, just as the Platonic images exceed their mere presentation and call for a thought-provoking, vicarious participation of the reader, Aristophanic images similarly expand far beyond their manifest content and invite the readers' or spectators' engagement. The matter of management, and of whether a parallel indeed obtains between home economics and statecraft, is surely worthy of philosophical attention. But this is neither the principal issue of this section, nor of the poem. As we shall see, the principal aim of the women concerns *saving Greece itself.* Beyond even the matters treated in this section, Aristophanes' inspired image-making leads to those most fundamental matters concerning human finitude and the pursuit of the good life within its limits.

From the extended exchange that takes place in lines 486–505 between Lysistrata and the Magistrate in which *logoi* and threats are intermixed—with a warning to the Magistrate from First Old Woman at its end—the women will manage the public funds, wasted on war by the men, employing the same intelligence that they employ in the management of their households.

> Magistrate: These are war funds!
> Lysistrata: But war is not necessary in the first place. (*all' ouden dei prōton polemein*) (496–497)

Further, Lysistrata insists that the women will protect the men and save them from themselves, whether they wish to be saved or not, to which the Magistrate responds with hilarious outrage: "Horrifically you speak": *deinon ge legeis* (499). Lysistrata answers his challenge to discuss her understanding of war and peace.

Her first set of *logoi* present a seriocomic metamorphosis of husband/wife relations. She holds her silence, she reports, out of verbal and physical fear of her husband's wrath. (514 is the only line in which Lysistrata claims to speak to a *hanēr,* "husband.") Whether her "husband" is a rhetorical figure standing for all Greek husbands or is indeed actual, she suddenly finds the courage to confront him with words such as *ponēroteron* ("very wretched") (517), and when their decision-making becomes even more wretched, *anoētōs* ("senseless") (518). She admits to calling him, *ō kakodaimon* (Henderson has "sorry fool") involved in bad deliberations

(521–522). After provoking another *deinon* from the Magistrate upon offering him "good advice" that will put the men on the right track (527–529), Lysistrata humiliates the Magistrate by handing him her sewing basket and, with her Chorus and its Leader, proclaims the birth of a bright and peaceful new day.

Is any such scenario a real possibility, even granting that nothing can be done exactly as it is said (*Republic* 473a1–3)? Of course not. Even the most inept political figures never rise to the degree of haplessness achieved by the Magistrate; nor are rebellious political groups so effective against the established order, or so unequivocally committed to peace. However, the easily attained outlook indicating the cost of war suggests war's painfully ridiculous necessity. Some twenty-four centuries later Kant, in his treatise arguing for the rational hope for perpetual peace, will invoke an image drawn from ancient Greece. Male Phrygians would grow so enraptured by their goddess Cybele and by their desire to identify with her that they would sever their genitals at the end of her celebratory dance. Quoting Hume (who quotes Cicero), Kant offers the following as a reflection upon the folly of warfare: *sero sapiunt Phryges:* the Phrygians are wise too late. Kant's rational hope consists of the eventual recognition of this unsatisfactory, self-mutilating practice.

The comedy presents a vision of such a state of being as if the destructive and self-destructive impulses that lead to war can be corrected by the relatively simple means of fresh management, and that peace and happiness will reign upon its application. Lysistrata tells the magistrate that the women cannot only solve the "complicated international mess," but they can do so "with consummate ease" (*phaulōs panu*) (565–566). Taking the sewing basket back from the magistrate, she speaks in the image of weaving. Removing the ball of yarn from within it, she implicitly likens the yarn to the current condition of discord among the cities. Then she proposes that if allowed, the women will use their spindles to "wind up the war," by winding out the tangled strands and sending emissaries in every direction. Lacking much ability in the realm of image and metaphor, the Magistrate notes the uselessness of weaving materials in warfare, and calls his adversary by the name she called the men earlier, *anoētoi.*

Next, she likens unrefined and recently shorn sheep's wool to the current condition of the cities. Just as the wool requires purification from sheep dung, riff-raff, and thorns, the city must be purified of those who take government positions for their own ends. ("Card them out and pluck off their heads" [578].) Card the wool into "a sewing basket of unity and goodwill, mixing in everyone" (579–580), including resident aliens, friends, debtors to the public treasury, joining all into one big bobbin, out of which to weave a new and great cloak for "the people": *tō dēmō* (586).

Is such an image appropriate to the condition of cities? In one sense, the answer must be negative. The current condition of the cities has little in common with recently shorn wool. The condition of the wool is entirely a natural one, and its cleansing and its use for clothing is wholly the result of human effort and contrivance. Cities, of course, do not grow like sheep, nor can their imperfections be disposed of so easily. Unraveling and reorienting complex political realities is nothing like unraveling strands from knotted wool. Plucking the head from a human being is more difficult both existentially and morally than carding the dung from sheep's wool, if indeed this analogy is not too tortured from the outset: people of heterogeneous origins do not mix so readily, and the declaration of "unity and goodwill" arising in such a mixture seems hopelessly naïve. Isn't Lysistrata wiser than this?

However, just like the key word in Socrates' declaration—that *unless* philosophy and political power fall together in one person, the cities will never be relieved of their ills, the key word that belongs to this image-making is *if:* "that's how we'll wind up this war, *if* somehow we're allowed" (569). As in *Republic* book 5, what would be called the "truth value" of the antecedent affects the truth-value of the entire conditional. As was shown in the *Republic,* the antecedent "philosophy and political power *do not* come together" is true; thus by *modus ponens* the consequent, "the cities will never be relieved of their ills" is also true. In *Lysistrata,* a major difference obtains. The antecedent—"if we are somehow allowed" to refashion the current conditions in the manner of weavers handling yarn—is *false.* Therefore, the conclusion—namely that war will end and joy will reign—cannot logically be ruled out. Unlike the confluence of the philosophical and ruling natures, which contradict one another,[20] there is no such contradiction between the art of weaving and the art of statecraft, however distant the analogy may seem. Hope for peace remains possible.[21]

The Magistrate's contemptuous response incenses Lysistrata, inciting her to reveal the powerful forces driving her:

> Magistrate: Isn't it awful how these women go on like this with their sticks, and like that with their bobbins, when they share none of the war's burdens?
>
> Lysistrata: *What, O monster!* (*pagkatarate*) (588—emphasis mine)

She details the double pain of giving birth to sons and sending them to war, the pleasures of their primes denied them while their husbands are off fighting, and the plight of maidens denied the pleasures of marriage because war has diminished the presence and the supply of marriageable men.[22] These sources of pain, except of course for the pain of childbirth, would disappear should war cease to be. The women greet the Magistrate's suggestion, namely that the aforementioned frustration of the maidens could be relieved by "any man who could still get a hard-on," with a mock death sentence and burial—at which the Magistrate hurries off, giving up even his pretense of dignity.

Between the manifold collected anger directed by the women at the wasted lives, both male and female, occasioned by war; at the political corruption and blind ambition that so often brings it about; at the stupidity of so much political deliberation; and, I would add (though it cannot be a factor in a comedy such as this one), at the difficulty of making wise political decisions even under the best of circumstances—between this anger and the vision of a peace filled with untroubled sexual and familiar joy, and of harmony between all human beings, yawns an abyss. Even the image that introduces this vision is not without its dark side: the troublemakers, who are perhaps all too easily identified, are beheaded. (And does the Magistrate, appalling though he may be, deserve decapitation?) The vision of peace may remain a logically possible one, but darkness lies in the image from which it arises, both with respect to the impurities that must be removed and to the anger that directly informs it as its opposite.

What, then, might be drawn from this image in consideration of the foregoing? The image of an erotically ecstatic future free of fear can both rejoice the human heart and inform the human mind, even in the face of its virtually certain impossibility.

LINES 614–705

This section brings matters back to the aforementioned darkness. The *agōn* between the Choruses and their Leaders displays this darkness primarily through its small-mindedness: the arguments are rooted in angry recollections of past wrongs, they proceed stupidly, and they do not even attempt to reach a sensible conclusion on either side. To a contemporary non-classicist reader, the abundance of references specific to the time and place of *Lysistrata* is daunting. Henderson[23] and Sommerstein[24] both provide excellent guides to this material, as well as to the prosodic peculiarity of the section. For purposes of this interpretation, it is enough to study the *agōn* with respect to its philosophical yield alone.

What can be the philosophical yield of an *agōn* of *logoi* that is characterized by such small-mindedness? At the very least, it shows that even and perhaps especially in matters of great importance, we humans are capable of immense stupidity. The general position of the men approaches tautology: because they are men, they deserve whatever should come to them simply by virtue of the status of their manhood, whether this concerns the right to make policy, the right to silence women, or the right to collect their three obols' jury pay. The position of the women similarly rests upon the stature they have enjoyed as women: they were raised aristocratically, served the Panathenaea in various honorable capacities through their girlhood, observed the developments in the city at all times, and so are well-suited to give good advice that the city is bound to honor. The difference: men fight in wars, while women give birth to the men who fight and die in wars. If the women's argument has any advantage, it rests upon the obtuseness of the men and upon their incompetent stewardship of the city. The stewardship of the women has not been tested in actuality. Only their talent at *logos* and their passion to reverse the ills brought about by war have been demonstrated in the comedy.

Along with the pettiness that exists in inverse proportion to the heat generated by the *agōn* in *logos,* another kind of heat emerges. Sweat grows on both the men and the women, who gradually shed garments that would inhibit their readiness for battle. Near the outset of this section, the men remove their outer jackets. The women soon follow, after their Leader urges *ō philai graes* (her "beloved old women") to remove their outer garments as their first gesture toward combat. Goading them, the women remind the men of past failures while insulting them, calling them "miserable geezers" (*dustēnois gerousin*) (652). One finds it difficult to locate the underlying compassion animating the rebellion of the women here. However, this difficulty does not contradict the compassion, as we shall see.

The men call the women's behavior "extreme hubris," and declare that any "man with balls must stand up to this" (659, 661). At this point, the men are called upon by their Leader to remove a second garment in readiness, for the reason that "a man's got to smell like a man from the beginning" (662–663). Sommerstein has aptly captured the comic scene: "The men will thus be left 'theatrically naked,' i.e., wearing only the leotard and tights (with phallus attached) worn by all comic performers under their character costumes."[25] The forceful words of the Men's Chorus, juxtaposed with their flopping phalluses dangling from their tan leotard, could hardly provide a more outrageously ludicrous sight. Once more, *ecce homo.*[26]

And once more, this is *us.*

The Women strip off their shirts in response, "because we've got to smell like women mad enough to bite" (687–690). Aristophanes presents an image of humanity that is both revealing and recognizable on many levels. It is "revealing" in a literal sense, in that the men and women stand before each other unclothed, devoid of the most basic trappings of civilization. The most evident level is the laughter-provoking spectacle of naked old men and naked old women confronting one another, "ready for battle" (the scare quotes I employ are themselves odd, as the phrase often suggests incipient sexual congress rather than literal military action).

On still another level, the theatrical leotard signifying nakedness raises the question: what constitutes appropriately human self-presentation? Here, it seems to me that the characteristic distinction between *phusis* ("nature") and *nomos* ("culture, custom") provides little guidance, and misleads more than it helps. Although human beings are obviously born naked, to call nakedness our *natural* state equivocates upon the word. At the very least, "natural" comes to mean both "occurring through physical processes" and "usual" or "normal." One could certainly speak of a decline in precision or perhaps a slippage, whereby a word that once and perhaps properly referred to physical processes alone has, through common disuse, come to refer to every regularly occurring phenomenon regardless of its origin.

The propriety of clothing in public for humans is so basic as to transcend any *phusis/nomos* distinction. Briefly consider these two questions: (1) Is it natural for women to appear clothed in public? (2) Is it natural for men to appear naked in the *agora*? It is easy to say that the correct answers depend upon what is meant by "natural." More to the point, however, the latter determination sheds no light whatsoever upon that most problematic notion, *human nature.* I strongly suggest that with respect to us humans, the *phusis/nomos* distinction is at most a second-order one, an offshoot of the *erotic* dimension of human life. This comic image, presenting human nudity in a most unerotic manner, brings human *erōs* forth for enjoyment and thought as no tragic image to my knowledge ever has . . . or *can. Erōs* determines how, where, and whether humans are dressed in times of peace. When *erōs* is replaced by *polemos,* other concerns—freedom of movement, for example—supersede. But the erotic human body always underlies.

Therein lies the deepest depth of *Lysistrata.* Once the layers of human practice are stripped away, the *erotic human body* shows itself as their fundament. Lysistrata's campaign, with peace conceived as the condition for widespread familial, private sexual bliss, attempts to call the men back to this most basic human condition. According to this view, warfare is *erōs* destructively redirected. The entire education of the guardians in Plato's *Republic* can be accurately called an attempt to excise *erōs* from these youths. This education is also *comic,* since it "abstracts from that which cannot, properly speaking, be abstracted from."[27] As Socrates notes in passing but quite significantly nevertheless, once this odd education has achieved the identification of each citizen's good with the good of the city, "nothing is private but the body."[28]

What can be said about the matter of *smell*? The adversaries regard their gender-specific body odor as a happy byproduct of their disrobing for battle. The trumpeting of their smells as distinctive identifying marks could not be more ridiculous, given that the men and women stand virtually naked before one another's eyes. However, upon further reflection the juxtaposition of the warrior's visual nakedness with their olfactory scent proves both provocative and revealing.

In an essay entitled "Hades: Heraclitus, Fragment B 98," John Sallis painstakingly interprets Heraclitus' *hai psukhai osmōntai kath' Haidēn* (often translated, "souls smell in Hades").[29] Instead of reading *Hades* directly, either as the realm of the dead, as the god who holds sway in that realm, or both at once, he reads *Haidēn* in a way he there calls "phenomenally." As the mythical realm of death lies beyond any discernment, beyond any openness to sight or hearing, Sallis reads *Hades* as *concealment.* Insofar as the sense of smell provides the least material for teaching and learning of all the senses, and insofar as Hades is the realm of concealment, *hai psukhai osmōntai kath' Haidēn* can be translated as "Souls, employing the sense of smell, are engaged in the movement of concealment. Or, still more expandedly: The soul's employment of the sense of smell exemplifies and makes phenomenally manifest the soul's engagement in the movement of concealment, in the withdrawal of things into self-closure and indistinction."[30]

How does this bear upon the smelly men and women confronting one another on the comic stage? Far from revealing their true natures both to themselves and to their adversaries, the malodorous opponents put forth what is least constitutive of their humanity, as well as what is furthest from what is best in them. However, the sense of smell does have a proper place in our nature. It can provide harmless enjoyment in itself.[31] It can enhance sexual stimulation. But is smelling like a man *being* a man? Does smelling like a woman mean *being* a woman? Further, does being either a man or a woman constitute the true nature of being human? Finally, it is laughably foolish to place any great significance upon one's gender-specific smell or any smell. But the laughably foolish does belong to the true nature of being human, as the soul of Aristophanes, in its own movement of revealing and concealing, shows forth so splendidly.

LINES 706–780

As the old women disrobe in readiness for battle, their younger comrades begin to falter. Their "erotic human bodies" lust for sexual congress with their husbands. Their lust arises not out of the prospect of bliss within the context of peace and prosperity, but out of simple *need.* Political campaigns, whether martial or peaceful, are marked by human agency. Their requirements are dictated by their means and their goals. Similarly, individual moral drives for excellence demand certain measures as well. But the erotic human body has its own imperatives.

Lysistrata opens the scene by lamenting in stentorian and tragic terms, speaking of "the deeds of ignoble (*kakōn*) women and the female heart (*phrēn*) / do make me dispirited to and fro" (708–709), and declaring that the truth she has learned "is disgraceful (*aiskhron*) to speak of and grievous to remain silent" (713). Implored by the Women's Leader "not to hide" the dread news, Lysistrata answers in a quite different manner: "We need to fuck, to tell it as briefly as possible!": *binētiōmen, hē brakhiston tou logou* (715). I suggest strongly that while Lysistrata's sudden reversion from the loftiest language to the most vulgar certainly produces laughter, according to Aristophanes' ridiculous thoughtfulness her language is seamless. His comic logic requires the intimate joining of that which soars to the heights of human *logos* with that which pulls from the depths.

At the outset of this scene, the depths pull powerfully. The women are running in all directions in search of their husbands. Nor is this need one-sided, in case there could be the slightest doubt. In *Lysistrata,* the erotic human body is no free-floating nexus of sexuality, detached from its familial and political context. The women have no intention of pursuing sexual satisfaction apart from their marriages. The rebellion of the women is not a revolution that would tear down the basic pillars of Greek society. To the contrary, it is an attempt to reform certain aspects of their society so that it fulfills the needs of its citizens, so that it brings its citizens the joy that their nature holds open to them as a possibility. Their erotic bodies, far from being *alogia,* remain bound by the words of promise they had uttered, just as do the erotic human bodies of the men. Without the unbreakable marital bond, there is no comedy. With the unbreakable marital bond, there is both comedy and much human nobility in even those scenes that show human beings at their most vulnerable, and looking their most foolish. In human beings, the depths and the heights are joined—although there's plenty of pressure upon the joint. In the laughter it provokes, Aristophanic comedy shows and celebrates this pressure that makes us who we are.

Four different wives concoct four different transparently bogus excuses in order to leave the Acropolis for their homes and their husband-occupied beds, but are stopped by Lysistrata. Her way of turning the women around from their need is worthy of attention. The erotic need of the women comes dangerously close to breaking their oath taken upon the sacred Dionysian wine-jug to withhold sex until their husbands achieve peace. This appears to be another instance of *erōs* trumping *logos.* Yet with words, with a *logos* she claims is an oracle, Lysistrata persuades the women to hold fast. Somewhat like the oracle that Philocleon claimed to hear in *Wasps,* this one has a peculiar ring to it. It predicts victory for the women, but only if they stick together (767–768). The oracle itself (770–777) refers to swallows who, if they leave the phallus alone, will receive Zeus' favor, but if they do not leave the phallus alone, there is "no bird more disgustingly horny" (*katapugōnesteron*) (776).

As observed in chapter 2, the Delphic oracle never made clear and specific prophecies. Its words were always ambiguous. As cited earlier, oracles were "a result of the ambiguity inherent in the god's signs and in the Greek perception that ambiguity is the idiom of prophesy, that there are limits to man's access to knowledge of the future: the god speaks ambiguously and man may misinterpret the messages."[32] Thus, the outraged exclamation of the Third Wife (who earlier feigned a suddenly ripe pregnancy by inserting a metal helmet under her garment) is entirely appropriate: *saphēs g' ho khrēsmos nē Di. ō pantes Theoi:* "A clear oracle, by Zeus! Oh gods!" (777).

As I read this passage, Lysistrata is well aware of two matters. She recognizes that the Third Wife is mocking her: oracles simply never specify indulging in or avoiding phalluses as conditions for success or failure, and the "sparrows" are much too thinly veiled stand-ins for the women. She also realizes that in the throes of their erotic pain, her charges almost certainly lack the equilibrium of mind to detect such "subtleties." Accordingly, she takes the Third Wife's words as an endorsement, persuading the women to bear up and to honor the oracle as the section ends.

What about this so-called oracle? First of all, it is an obvious fake. Oracles simply did not take the form of extended poems. Those that extended beyond mere giving or withholding of divine sanction for an action were either cryptic (e.g., "know yourself"), or else they were recited by a priest or priestess, usually in a trance, speaking in the person of the god.[33] What, then, explains its effectiveness? I suggest that the coarse reference to the gratification that awaits the women if they can hold out a little longer (*aposkhōntai te phalētōn*—"leaving the phallus alone" [771]), coupled with the similarly crude and disparaging designation they would earn if they do not (*katapugōnesteron*—"the ones most shamelessly lustful") "touched" the women precisely at the place that would rivet their attention. If they broke their sacred oath on the wine-jug and yielded to their sexual impulse, they would indeed be regarded—at least by Lysistrata, at least in terms of her political aims (for she acknowledges the facticity of the need with her, *Binētiōmen,* at 715)—as *katapugōnesteron.* This undeserved appellation dishonors them, and dishonors the genuine character of their erotic bond to their husbands. In one sense, then, Lysistrata's fake "oracle" can be correctly regarded as rhetorical manipulation. In another, however, it can be regarded as a way to call the women back to their best selves, as the human beings who seek to bring peace to their state.

LINES 782–827

The choral interlude, in an exchange of *muthoi,* appears to proclaim the mutual hatred (*misos*) of the old men and old women. After the *muthoi* of misogynist Melanion and misanthrope Timon, the Leaders "enter into dialogue" concerning their respective pubic hair. The Women's Leader mocks her male counterpart's "large amount of bush" (*lokhmēn pollēn*) (800); the Men's Leader affirms his hairiness proudly. The Men's Leader wards off the threat of a kick by telling his counterpart that she would be "flashing her twat" (*ton sakandron ekphaneis*) (824); the Women's Leader brags that unlike his, her pubic hair "is singed clean with the lamp"[34] (827–828).

If I might make another stretch, I locate a concealed but definite concord at the heart of this *agōn.* First and least, there is a precise symmetry between the number and placement of lines sung by the men and by the women. Further and more significantly, hatred (*misos*) between men and women in this Aristophanic context bears a complementary relationship to *erōs.* Not a single line in *Lysistrata* suggests the possibility of indifference or of mild, reasoned acceptance or rejection. Accordingly, the depth and intensity of the hatred mirrors the depth and intensity of the love. *Lysistrata* was created in service to Dionysus, where *erōs* exceeds all social boundaries for the sake of a vicarious vision of our humanity.[35]

This vision includes . . . pubic hair! Once again, a difference emerges, and once again, it is a complementary difference. Recalling Socrates' comic analogy in which he likened the difference in natures between men and women to the difference between hairy and bald-headed men, there is certainly a "hairy" commonality within unmistakable sexual difference.

LINES 830–1013

There are several lenses through which the famous Myrrhine-Kinesias scene can be viewed. *Lysistrata* is the most frequently performed of Aristophanes' plays because one of these lenses is accessible to adolescents and to the adolescent in us all, namely the sequential sexual teasing to which Myrrhine subjects Kinesias, causing the latter's increasing, desperate, and hilarious frustration. Another lens consists of the strict fidelity between Kinesias and Myrrhine that undergirds the hilarity and makes it something much nobler than humiliation through mere titillation.[36] Though Myrrhine controls the action and Kinesias helplessly hopes that she'll yield, their shared marital erotic bond honors them both. Recall that Myrrhine said, upon Lysistrata's first proposal of her plan, that she'd rather see the war go on than give up "the prick" (130). Here, she has given it up . . . in order to get "it" back with her husband attached, whole and sound. The final lens is the lens that effaces all lenses, namely *madness.*

Kinesias enters alone at first, sporting a large erection under his tunic. Lysistrata chides him, "Who goes there, poking up within our defense perimeter? . . . A man?" (847, 848); Kinesias, pointing to his erection, replies "Of course a man." After a bit of byplay in which Lysistrata inflames Kinesias' longing for his wife, she calls Myrrhine to the ramparts where her husband is waiting in exchange for all of his money. His brief soliloquy (865–869) resembles Lysistrata's earlier lofty rhetorical flight together with its culminating dissonance (708–715). Since Myrrhine has been gone, he has experienced "no loveliness at all" (*oudemian . . . kharin*) (865). Instead, to him all is "burdensome" (*akhthomai*), "desolate" (*erēma*) (867). Why? *Estuka gar:* "Because I have a hard-on!" (869).

Once again, although it is played out primarily in the sexual arena, Kinesias' erotic need transcends the sexual. Myrrhine's merciless teasing has its effect only on account of Kinesias' faithful love. Kinesias flounders helplessly in response only because his love for Myrrhine entails his readiness to show vulnerability before her. He declares that he's "in agony" (*epitetrimmenos*) (876); he calls her *ō daimonia* for not coming to him for the sake of their child, who he is using for bait. Her enticing look and her "prickliness" (*duskolainei*) (887) only serve to excite him all the more. Having left home to join Lysistrata's brigade, Myrrhine appears uninterested in her child or in the declining cleanliness of her home. To her husband's ultimate request to engage in what he delicately calls "Aphrodite's holy mysteries" (*ta tēs Aphroditēs hier' anorgiasta*) (898), she responds in the name of the god that she will not, "until you men agree to a settlement that will stop the war" (900–901). Kinesias concurs at once, but given his current distress he would agree to anything.

The unconsummated seduction of Kinesias (908–959) has often been excerpted[37] as it seems to be able to stand on its own as a universal emblem of several concerns, contemporary and/or universal: turning the table on male dominance, base sexual humor, familial decorum, civilized eroticism. By means of her gradually more enticing tease, her husband's already desperate need reaches almost unbearable intensity. Myrrhine protests that though she loves Kinesias, she would not be able to return to the Acropolis "pure" (*hagnē*) if she yielded to his wishes; he tells her quickly just to wash herself off in a nearby spring. She cannot, of course, indulge his wishes in the presence of the child; Kinesias promptly sends the child home. Nor can she permit her groaning husband, who is human "no matter what kind of man you are" (918) to lie on the bare ground as he wishes and to embrace his wife there at once. In separate trips, she brings a cot, then a mattress, then a pillow, then a blanket. ("It's not a blanket I want, I want a fuck!" [934], cries the man who referred to conjugal bliss as "Aphrodite's holy mysteries" a moment before.) After teasing him further with some perfume, Myrrhine runs off to the Acropolis, leaving her husband in the throes of frantic sexual need.

Thus decontextualized, the scene can certainly please an audience. How much richer, however, when read in the flow of the entire play! The Men's Leader, fresh from his encounter with the Women's Chorus in which his charges expressed their "principled misogyny," denounces Myrrhine as a "detestable, revolting shrew": *hē pambdelura kai pammusara* (969). Kinesias defends her immediately and unequivocally: "By God, she's loving and utterly sweet!" (970). However, when the Men's Leader persists in his denunciation, Kinesias joins in "Yes, vile, vile!" (972). The section closes with a prayer to "Zeus, Zeus," to sweep Myrrhine upward, then to twirl her around, then to "let her fall back down to earth, / to land smack dab / on the point of my hard-on!" (979–980).

Myrrhine has driven Kinesias mad in two senses. First, he loudly countermands the dictates of reason by ascribing two apparently contradictory predicates to his wife, doing so in the space of a very short time. "Loving and utterly sweet" (*philē kai pagglukera*) conceptually repels "vile, vile" (*miara, miara*). Their "conceptual unity" can only be asserted by a man out of his senses, a madman. However, in holding himself within the measure of his marriage vow,[38] and in keeping to his agreement to heal the body politic from the disease of war, his madness is at least analogous to the divine madness spoken of in Plato's *Phaedrus.* Another logic, more fundamental than that of reason, holds sway here.

What about Myrrhine? Although she desires her husband more strongly than ever, she subordinates her sexual need entirely to the aforementioned healing. Coldly measured calculation appears to guide her taunting, but this appearance hides the longing that provides its power. Myrrhine also performs in the throes of divine madness. And the scene itself? It has been produced out of the divine madness of the poet Aristophanes, whose ridiculous thoughtfulness opens up several windows upon our multifaceted and often contradictory humanity. A strange but suggestive connection can be made between this scene, which features a man aching with lust and howling out inconsistent *logoi* on his wife's character, and the Choral Ode of Sophocles' *Antigone,* where the human being is called *hupsipolis: apolis:* "above the city: having no city" (370). If anything, this comic portrayal is more radical. *Hupsipolis* arises when human beings honor the laws of men and gods. *Apolis* results when they do not. But comic figures share these opposed traits whatever they do—and our *erōs* guarantees that, at some time, we all do.

A Spartan Herald enters sporting his own erection, which must be quite impressive given Kinesias' greeting: "And what might you be? Are you human or a Conisalus?" (982). (A Conisalus is "a demon or divinity associated with ithyphallic dances."[39]) Here Kinesias, supposedly mad with lust, is ready to ascribe non-human attributes to a being whose degree of sexual arousal appears excessive. One can hear Kinesias' affirmation of his own humanity in his question to the Herald. The shame of the Herald, who attempts to hide his priapic state, affirms the Herald's humanity as well. Soon, the two men learn from each other that this painful condition afflicts all Athenian and Spartan men alike,[40] the former through Lysistrata's call to action (or inaction!), the latter to Lampito's. Their aching duress forges an alliance between them that no amount of rational negotiation could achieve. Kinesias urges the Herald to go back to Sparta and bring back a delegation of official peace negotiators, and he will do the same with the Athenians. "This cock of mine will be Exhibit A" (1012).

The sense dwelling powerfully beneath this nonsense echoes books 2–4 of Plato's *Republic,* where the interlocutors discuss the building of cities in terms of *need.* The justice discovered in the first city arises precisely from the need that the various artisans have of one another. The second city comes into being from the desire for luxuries, and with this desire the need for guardians arises in order to acquire and to protect the comforts that were missing from the "city of sows," as Glaucon called the first city. The final, purged city has dispensed with luxuries. This stripping down also answered a need, a need to preserve the city from within. The education of the guardians and auxiliaries needed to excise all individual desires from their souls and to identify their own good with the good of the city, so that they would not take everything for themselves and so destroy the city.

With no need, no city can be. (Without need, neither philosophy, nor comedy, nor tragedy can come into being.) The incompleteness of our human nature, our need for external resources to complement those that we somehow possess, provides cities with their original reason for being. (Thus, once again, Aristotle's "The human being is, by nature [*kata phusin*], a political animal.") From his *logos* in Plato's *Symposium,* where "the name *erōs* is given for the desire for wholeness" (192e10–a3)—since we are decidedly finite, made "partial" as a result of Zeus' slicing—to his creation of an Athenian warrior and a Spartan Herald joined together in common cause by virtue of immense erotic agony seeking equally immense relief, Aristophanes has always tied *erōs* to need.

Lysistrata suggests, by means of its inspired comic exchange here, that only the most profound need and adversity can produce pragmatic political settlements between adversaries in the public domain. The sensible calculations offered earlier by the women (or, no doubt, by anyone) hold no sway. Only when much damage has already occurred, and much pain has ensued, does reason enter. Only negativity grounds constructive action. In the private realm, however, the most profound need—the one instilled by the sting of *erōs*—can bring the most joyous realization. Its fulfillment can exceed what was initially imagined. Even when the pain of sexual frustration reaches an almost unbearable pitch, husband and wife honor the now-transcendent erotic bond between them.

LINES 1014–1112

For reasons that I shall explain in due course, I will sharply distinguish the beginning of this section (1014–1042) from its remainder, then discuss the philosophical consequence of this distinction. At its outset, the Men's Leader places women on the nether side of beasts and even fire for formidable ferocity. The Women's Leader responds with playful chiding: "So you understand that, and yet you're still fighting me, when it's possible, you rascal, to have our lasting friendship?" (1016–1017). After her counterpart responds with a declaration of his eternal misogyny, the Women's Leader attends to him with a gesture so thoughtful, so gracious, and so generous that one is tempted to speak excessively: it is the human good itself, seen on the comic stage through a shining image. She covers the Men's Leader's erect nakedness by placing his tunic back upon his body. Stunned by her greatness of heart, he immediately acknowledges the magnitude of her deed in the name of the God (1022), and admits that the anger that caused him to take it off earlier was *ponēros,* wretched, low-minded.

With the Men's Leader appropriately covered, the Women's Leader observes momentously, "Now you look like a man again, and not so ridiculous." Looking like a man means being clothed in public. The merely animal aspect remains present but concealed. In this respect, clothing signifies a respect for *erōs* that is fundamental to a genuine human life. Disrobing belongs only in the private realm, where the sexual instincts converge with those of the being whose distinguishing mark, as Nietzsche says, is the ability to make promises. In accepting the feminine gesture and in the laying down of anger, the Men's Leader and his cohort become human once again. The gentleness of the gesture and the welcome it indicates is a power available to humans different both in degree and in kind from political and military power.

The Women's Leader completes the humanization of her new friend by removing a large bug from his eye. The result: tears flow from the eyes of the Men's Leader, tears of relief, tears that bear witness to human vulnerability. Though he protests at the prospect of having his tears wiped away and fairly begs not to be kissed, he relents and agrees to a complete peace. To seal the agreement between the two Leaders, their two Choruses unite into one.

In the course of this dialogue, a subtle shift in Aristophanic language occurs regarding one of the most important words: *ponēros.* In *Wasps* and in *Assemblywomen,* it signifies wretchedness or badness. In the former especially, it was employed by both father and son as an epithet of utter contempt. Suddenly, *ponēros* becomes a term of endearment, used playfully by the Women's Leader as she cares for the man opposite her. As she offers her lasting friendship, she calls him "you rascal": *ō ponēre* (1017). She will wipe the tears from his eyes "though you're quite a rascal": *kaitoi panu ponēros ei* (1035). The transformation from conflict, pain, and humiliation to *play* is signaled in the newly contextualized *ponēros,* which is itself a function of the re-humanized men. Men are "rascals," but not mere rascals. Their darker side, acknowledged by the now playful epithet, can have an endearing quality.

I divide the latter episode from the rest of the section—indeed from the rest of *Lysistrata*—because it delineates a region characterized by uniquely human grace, heightened in a context in which the possibility of grace seemed nonexistent. *Erōs* at its most chaste meets *erōs* at its most coarse. The gentle, darkness-acknowledging language of play finds its true home in this region, and in no other.

The Men's Leader calls his Choruses together in a song of peace, but the united Chorus that follows differs significantly from its predecessor. First of all, no darkness is allowed, all negative sentiments are excised. "Only good will we say / and do: since enough troubles and more / you already have": *pant' agatha kai legein kai / dran: hikana gar ta kaka / kai ta parakeimena* (1047–1049). They offer a large loan to all who need it, a loan that will be forgiven entirely if peace breaks out. They're preparing a feast for returning soldiers to which all, including children, are invited. Families are told that they are free to walk in "as if into your own home, because the door will be locked" (1070–1071) so that what goes on inside is sealed.

This Chorus returns *Lysistrata* to the purer region of comedy, where darkness is revealed by proceeding as if none existed at all. There is no badness. There's plenty of money, maybe free and clear. Finally, there is no difference between the private and the public. The playfulness signaled by the ridiculousness and impossibility of these provisions stands in stark contrast with the appropriately measured human playfulness of the individual encounter of the two Chorus Leaders that immediately precedes this song. A central Platonic theme resounds once again by means of its absence in the comedy. In the *Republic,* at the close of book 9, as has been shown, the human soul can build something honorable for itself privately although such an actual collective edifice might be excluded from possibility on earth.

Aristophanes can well be seen as enhancing the Platonic dialogues here. As I have tried to show earlier, the *Republic* shows great respect for women with regard to *tekhnē,* although Socrates seemed to regard women as weaker by nature (I also tried to show that his argument does not support this conclusion). How Aristophanes was inspired to receive it is beyond my comprehension or even speculation, but his work reflects knowledge of and sensitivity toward a peculiarly feminine wisdom and power that is not found in the Platonic dialogues. Yet another possible enhancement is the presentation of human goodness arising from horizontal interactions between people, rather than from vertical ascents and descents—although I have never thought that the latter should be regarded literally, and have always found the dialogical aspect to be primary.

The remainder of the section finds the Athenian and Spartan delegates forging an alliance based on their common interest: the relief from protracted, painful priapism. Once more, the hilarious scene of men wielding, trying vainly to hide, and complaining about their persisting erections can occur only because the men strictly honor their marital vows. The parade of erections in *Lysistrata* provides a comic image of the original phallic procession that attended the earliest Dionysian celebrations. Far from being mere surrender, the willing submission of the men to Lysistrata here—their inviting her to settle the strike—demonstrates strength of a different and nobler order.

The Men's Chorus Leader, who earlier received the darkness-acknowledging grace gifted to him by his woman counterpart, calls on Lysistrata's full humanity with its fused brightness and darkness. She must be "forceful flexible, noble (*agathēn*) vulgar, haughty sweet, much-encompassing (*polupeiron*)" (1109–1110). She will show little or none of the subtlety of the Women's Chorus Leader in the latter's private transformation of her male counterpart, for in the broader standpoint Lysistrata's is a political role. However, there is much of philosophical importance to learn from her.

LINES 1113–1189

The first noteworthy feature of Lysistrata's presentation to the men gathered to hear her, is her requirement that another person stand by her as she speaks: a very beautiful and unclad young woman named Reconciliation (*Diallagē*), a name that indicates a change from enmity to friendship. Given Lysistrata's recognized exceptional nature, why is a second woman needed? Henderson argues, "Aristophanes wants the negotiators (and the spectators) to focus on this happy end product of negotiations rather than on the issues they would face in real life negotiations. The sex-starved negotiators can only think of Reconciliation's body and agree to whatever Lysistrata says in order to make a quick end of the war."[41] Sommerstein agrees, saying "the girl is merely held before the men as 'bait' to keep their arousal and their frustration at the highest pitch so that they will remain desperately eager for peace at any price."[42]

At certain points, the text presents strong support for this view. The comments of the men never address Lysistrata's sound political arguments in which Athenians and Spartans came to one another's aid in the past. Instead, when they are not howling in pain, they comment favorably upon Reconciliation's incomparable buttocks and her lovely cunt (*kusthos*), and engage in a series of double entendres throughout the negotiation of their final settlement. However, the view that the men might settle for peace at any price in a state of the unbearably increased arousal misses the main matter, in my view.

At the beginning of her *logos,* talking with herself, she observes that arbitration of the differences between the men is not difficult when two conditions are met: if the men are "eager (*orgōntas*) for it, and not testing one another for weaknesses (*'kpeirōmenous*)" (1113). She brings Reconciliation forward in order to find out whether these two conditions are met. How—and what—does she find out? The test on the first count concerned the direction of the men's *erōs,* and their concentration upon the sexual loveliness of Reconciliation supplies Lysistrata with sufficient evidence of their eagerness to negotiate an end to the public, political dispute for the sake of the resumption of private joy—not with Reconciliation, but with their wives.[43]

The second criterion is somewhat trickier,[44] but the two sides reach a settlement without any need to consult with their similarly throbbing allies, since they will "all of them, come to the same decision we have: to fuck (*binein*)" (1178–1179). In Henderson's superb scholarship, he argues that the desire for sexual consummation guides the "negotiations" and so separates the erotic from the political.[45] However, the lens through which I read Lysistrata reaches a different result. The double entendres, through which Henderson is a good guide, contain *philosophical* significance. The Spartans covet Pylos, literally "gate," referring both to Reconciliation's anus and to the actual site.[46] By contrast, the Athenians seek Echinous, literally "sea-urchin place," referring both to Reconciliation's pubic hair and to the place so named.[47]

That is, the negotiations take place as if individual *erōs* and political *logos* were indistinguishable, or at least united so closely with one another that they can refer accurately to regionally disparate phenomena using the same word. However, the truth of the matter from which the comedy here abstracts consists precisely in the necessary asymmetry between individual *erōs* and political *logos.* Further, the thralldom of the men in the face of reconciliation's beauty recalls the first rung in Diotima's "ladder of love," bringing forth the "beautiful *logoi*" appropriate to comedy on the second. Impelled by their agreement and by their need, Lysistrata leads them rapidly up the analogous comic ladder, insisting "you remain pure (*hagneusete*), / so that we women can host you on the Acropolis / with [the food] we brought in our boxes. / There you may exchange pledges of mutual trust, that each of you may reclaim his own wife and go home" (1182–1187). The men go as quickly as they can, in service not only to their lust, but to *erōs*—in its depths, to its heights, on the earth.[48]

LINES 1188–CONCLUSION

Henderson's Oxford edition of *Lysistrata* provides an excellent survey of the prosodic and historical content of the choral songs and of the *logoi* given by the Athenian and Spartan delegates. But I will concentrate on three other matters that occur in this final section. The first echoes the conclusions of *Wasps* and of *Assemblywomen,* namely the entrance of Dionysus, in honor of whom the comedy is staged. The Second Athenian Delegate praises the *sumposion* (literally, "the drinking of wine together"), the Spartan guests, and the Athenian delegation for wisdom "in our wine drinking": *hēmeis d' en oinō sumpotai sophōtatoi* (1227). Going further, the First Athenian Delegate responds, "Right, because when we're sober we get unhinged": *orthōs g' hotiē nēphontes oukh hugiainomen* (1228). He adds that he would advise the Athenians to go to all diplomatic missions drunk.

Wine brings human beings together. Far from contravening measure, wine reintroduces it—that is the function of the Dionysian festival. The Delegate proceeds to delineate the high cost of sobriety:

> As it is, when we go to Sparta we at once start looking for ways to stir up trouble.
> And so when they say something (*ti . . . legōsin*) we don't hear it,
> And when they don't say anything (*ha d' ou legousi*) we read things into that,
> And we each come away with different reports of the same discussions. (1231–1235)

The darkly comic feature of this account of human diplomacy, in the midst of a celebration of drunkenness, is its deadly accuracy. Wine can heal this *kakia* for the city—for joyous moments on the Dionysian stage.

The respective songs and dances of the two sides also bear witness to the presence of Dionysus, once again not only at the end of the play's action but throughout. Like *Wasps* and *Assemblywomen,* and in a related way like *Clouds* as well, Dionysus is present in every line and in every pause. The entire comedy is a song and dance in his honor. *Lysistrata* honors wine, and it honors peace. I add that beyond all these, it honors *erōs,* recollecting the *erōs* that drew the mortal Semele to the embrace of the most divine Zeus, and so gave birth to Dionysus. This stretch of human *erōs* across the human-divine divide, while remaining earthbound, is *Lysistrata*'s theme, its song from beginning to end.

There remains the question of Lysistrata herself, who remains mysterious, at least for me. Her only function in this final scene is to escort the wives back to their husbands. She does not speak a word. What does she look like? At 1108, the Men's Chrous leader introduces her as *ō pasōn andreiotatē,* which both Henderson and Sommerstein translate as "bravest of all women." However, *andreiotatē* is a variant of *andreios,* from *anēr*—of or for a man. In a recent film (1987) of *Lysistrata,* the title character is portrayed by Jenny Karezi, a strikingly beautiful, forceful, and unmistakably feminine Greek actress who certainly projects every kind of womanly power, including intelligence, humor, courage, and sexual desirability to burn. The latter, at least, is nowhere indicated in the text. Could *andreiotatē* signal something about her appearance as well as about her character? I do not know and cannot even guess.

Does she have a husband to rejoin? Earlier, I raised doubts about her marital status. Though she spoke in the first person of having a husband at line 514, this may well have been merely rhetorical, and no mention of one is made either in the penultimate or the final scene, where one might expect and even hope for at least a glimpse of the man who won the heart of this mighty woman, and who was even able to inspire fear in her at one time. Again, I don't know. But here, I will guess that she is unmarried. The argument for this is certainly thin: the distance she took from the actual state of affairs in order to craft her plan and the time she takes to enact it across the country suggest that she does not find herself embroiled either in the erotic pull or the busy life of married Greek women, which the text of *Lysistrata* strongly indicates is their lot.[49] This, and the lack of a physically present husband or one named anywhere make up my reasons for this conjecture. If she is married, her marriage certainly seems not to interfere at all with her work in Athens. In this way, she resembles another well-known Athenian.

Finally, the name Lysistrata is a rich one, especially in the context of the play bearing its name, as well as in relation to the Platonic dialogues. The name suggests releasement, liberation, loosening—setting free from a habitual convention that militates against what is noblest and best in humanity, releasing into a region where what is noblest and best finds celebration. In this way, *Lysistrata* can be regarded as akin to the beginning of *Republic* book 7. The men in chains inhabiting a cave-like dwelling have the foolish warriors in *Lysistrata* as their analogue.

Socrates asks Glaucon to consider "what their release (*lusin*) and healing would be like" (515c4) if their chains were removed, then to "take a man who is released (*lutheiē*) and suddenly compelled to stand up (*anistasthai*), to turn his neck around, to walk and look up toward the light; and who, moreover is in pain" (515c6–8). The man who has been forcibly liberated has his analogue in the men who, deprived of their habitual release, are forced to stand in a different way, though the root verb is the same: *stuomai,* erection (hard-on), like *anistasthai,* is from *histēmi,* to stand. The man liberated from the cave experiences confusion and alienation, but would nevertheless rather live on the earth as a poor man than to rule among the shadows. Though he might wish to return to the cave to liberate his colleagues there, he would certainly be laughed at and killed.

At this point the difference between Aristophanic comic poetry and Platonic philosophy makes itself felt. In *Lysistrata,* the liberated men are all too happy to make a peace that they promise to uphold, and to return home and embrace their equally delighted wives. There is no unprocessed residue in the comic text, no dark remainder. The darkness is disclosed precisely through its radical absence. In Platonic philosophy, once the philosopher's comedy in *Republic* book 5 is disrupted by . . . the philosopher (!), whose nature comes into question in books 6 and 7, there can be no more pretense of a happy merger of the personal and the political, and life in the city proves to be riddled with obstruction, injustice, and pain. Lysistrata receives encomiums from her fellow citizens. Socrates receives a death sentence. Lysistrata walks silently at the play's close. Socrates drinks the hemlock.

The man who liberated the first cave-dweller is even more mysterious to me than Lysistrata. The first liberated man is apparently left to his own devices by his liberator, devices that prove sufficient after a time to orient himself happily in his new environs. I am tempted to say that the liberator is Socrates who, through his challenge to the people of Athens, forced them to face their bond to shadowy opinion: this challenge angered many, but allowed several to achieve a much better humanity. I am also tempted to say the same of Lysistrata: by means of her inspired plan, she effected analogous progress in the men and women of Greece on the Dionysian stage. Both

Socrates and Lysistrata somehow stood apart from and within their social order, and so were positioned to serve as liberators who stood aside as their charges found their strength and their true humanity.

But something stronger urges me to allow the liberator to remain nameless. Further, I do not even want to assume that the liberator is a human being. Rather, *Erōs*—neither mortal nor immortal—finds itself located in certain works and in certain individuals at propitious times, drawing us out of ourselves toward . . .

Conclusion

Ridicule and Measure

Throughout this book, the issue of *measure* arose again and again. Perhaps strangely, if a single theme could be said to characterize the *huponoia* or "underlying sense" of Aristophanic comedy, it is this one. Viewed through a philosophical lens, all four plays bear directly upon the proper measure for a human life. Aristophanes' inspired comic gift creates both scenarios that raise the question of proper measure, and characters whose words and actions illustrate proper measure, most often by dwelling—or appearing to dwell—very far from its vicinity. In this conclusion I will address this theme, toward which all of the previous analyses have pointed.

The key scenarios in the four comedies are one and all ridiculous. In terms of the comedy, however, they provide a standard of sobriety that is itself intoxicated with folly, a standard for sanity that is itself insane. In their fruitless and uproarious efforts to gain their bearings within these scenarios, comic figures disclose something of that measure that we humans seek within our own perplexing scenario. Thus Strepsiades sets fire to the Socratic *phrontistērion* in *Clouds,* destroying sophistical use of language and disrespect for the gods. Philocleon "introduces measure" into the aristocratic symposium by drunkenly demolishing its order and decorum, thereby destroying the pretense that goodness consists of luxury, fashionable manners, and snobbishness. Praxagora's cohort of bearded women in the Assembly succeeds in taking over the government of Athens, but her strict regulation of *erōs* destroys its essential affiliation with beauty. The sex strike in Lysistrata, leading to the gathering of faithfully erect Athenians and Spartan husbands who enter into a political pact for peace, collapses the distinction between private and public that is fundamental to a well-measured human life.

It would be mistaken, and this interpretation would be badly misunderstood, if the comedies are taken in any way as cautionary tales. The Dionysian festival celebrates our humanity. The laughter provoked by the comedies belongs essentially to its celebratory nature. *Wasps, Assemblywomen,* and *Lysistrata* all conclude with the players dancing and singing joyfully as they exit the stage; at the end of *Clouds,* Strepsiades undertakes his measure-restoring arson with great glee, as the Chorus signs off cheerfully. Human vulnerability and human folly belong to who we are. They deserve acknowledgement. The ridicule they receive in Aristophanic comedy is the direct analogue of the careful attention they deserve. The laughter they provoke is the complement of the thoughtful treatment they require.

Thus, the so-called "ancient quarrel" between poetry and philosophy, if indeed it is rightfully regarded as a quarrel, issues from a close kinship that derives from a common source: care for the human soul. Through the lens of inspired comic poetry, this care shows itself in the nobility discernible in human beings even at their basest and most laughable. And what is foolish, vulgar, or both dwells not far from the surface of even the most cultivated among us. This is the power of Aristophanes' work. It is therefore at least a very incomplete picture of his achievement, if not a badly misleading one, to regard him merely or even primarily as a highly skilled satirist commenting upon Athenian politics and society.

Toward the establishment of the philosophical import of Aristophanic comedy, I have endeavored throughout to connect his comic image-making with the kind of philosophical questioning and image-making in its service that takes place in the dialogues of Plato. This connection is most direct in cases that seem to mimic Platonic dialogue, such as the many Socrates-Strepsiades exchanges and the refutation of Stronger *Logos* by Weaker *Logos* in *Clouds,* the trial involving the two dogs in *Wasps*, the disagreement between Man and Neighbor in *Assemblywomen,* and the dispute between the Men's and Women's Chorus Leaders in *Lysistrata.* But it is also present in those many instances where the comic action is so very excessive that the provoked laughter discloses wonder concerning proper measure. Strepsiades' difficulty with bowel control, Philocleon's version of the Trojan horse, Blepyrus' first appearance wearing his wife's slip and slippers and seeking a suitable place to relieve himself, and Kinesias' mad cries uniting love and outrage indicate both the dignity and goodness of human beings and bring forth considerations of the proper measure for a human life in proportion—sometimes inverse proportion—to their coarse hilarity.

Through this philosophical lens, Aristophanic comedy also displays several crucial areas in common with the Platonic dialogues that are related to proper measure as narrower instances of philosophical import. I list three of the most general ones: (1) the indication for both proper criteria for truth-seeking argumentation, shown by the way the characters outrage and ignore them; (2) the outlines of human wisdom, seen in the wantonly displayed folly in which so many of the characters revel; (3) the ignorance to which we are all given over, in the words and actions of serenely confident but foolishly misguided figures.

In another likeness to the Platonic dialogues, we find nothing remotely resembling a formula for a good life. Instead, we find human beings with strengths and weaknesses trying to make their way. Recall that Socrates has no exemption from this condition: in *Republic* book 7, after Glaucon remarks that the image of the cave is strange, as are the prisoners, Socrates responds, "They're like us." We are, one and all, bound in some way to the shadowy opinions amidst which we live. Our task is to test them, to select the ones that prove best as our guides, and to continue to question and to examine.

Again, the ignorance to which we are all given over deserves no rebuke. Together with this ignorance, we have been granted the means to become aware of it and, through philosophy, to seek what is best within its limits. A crucial aspect of that ignorance concerns our fate after death, another matter treated in differing but kindred ways in the dialogues and in the comedies. In Plato's *Phaedo,* Socrates argues that since philosophy is the activity that seeks most of all to separate concerns of the soul from those of the body, and that death is precisely this separation for which the philosopher strives in life, "those who philosophize rightly make dying their care, and of human beings to them least of all is death terrifying" (67e).[1] In this light, his frequent discussions of death are occasioned by the fear of his interlocutors, both friends and enemies, who regard death as a great evil. His remark toward the end of the *Apology,* that "to a good man no evil (*kakon*—perhaps 'nothing bad') can come, whether in life or in death" (41d1–2) can certainly be regarded as an attempt to comfort his supporters. But since Socrates calls philosophical yield a *truth* to which one must hold, I regard it as something worthy of pondering. My view: for Socrates, and for those who philosophize rightly, badness or evil means only *becoming worse, becoming more unjust.* Whatever fortune should deliver, the good human being remains steadily concerned with the goodness of her/his own soul.

In the *Apology,* Socrates is sentenced to death. In the *Crito,* he argues for accepting the judgment of the Athenians, however unjust the verdict. In the *Phaedo,* he drinks the hemlock and dies. Many other dialogues include what we would today call arguments for the immortality of the soul. These would not attract the attention that they do, if they would arise at all, if it were not for the inevitable, visible death that all human beings undergo, and that so many fear.

Holy madness, which Socrates ascribes to the poet, makes possible the transmission of important truths to human beings in a non-rational manner. In the comedies, by contrast to the dialogues, no comic character ever dies, or even fears death with any seriousness. Strepsiades worries about financial ruin. Bdelocleon is troubled by his father's folly and by his uncouth behavior. Among Blepyrus' concerns are age, sexual potency, and the fidelity of his wife. The men at war do not show the slightest fear of death, but are brought low by ever more throbbing erections that they refuse to . . . defuse. The oblivion of death in the souls of the comic figures is balanced by the pettiness of their concerns, which stand in both aptly and ridiculously for the knowledge of human finitude that death-awareness provides. The philosopher and the comic poet share the same appropriate care for death, the former by attempting to relocate fear away from death, the latter by proceeding as if death did not enter human consideration at all.

But unlike the dialogues, the last two comedies treated here seem to provide a source of wisdom that is missing there, the insight and strength of *women.* In their different ways, both Praxagora and Lysistrata demonstrate intelligence, forcefulness, and persuasiveness. They are able to convince their charges to follow them courageously, and in both cases their confidence is rewarded with success. In the first case, Athens becomes happy and prosperous. In the second, peace is made and erotic bliss recommences. But the prosperity and the recommencing of erotic bliss are *poetic* creations just as Praxagora and Lysistrata are, to be vicariously enjoyed and considered rather than regarded as actual.

What, then, can be concluded about Aristophanes' remarkable women? They *might* be seen as standing in for the missing insight that would make a human being able to know something worth knowing. Their mere *not-being-men* strengthens this suggestion. However, even in their poetic reality, the political exploits of the women fall short of Socrates' so-called philosopher-king in important ways, however much their traits resemble the latter's. In Praxagora's Athens, the sexual infighting that results from her "equal erotic access for all" law disrupts the harmony she promised; and Lysistrata abdicates her leadership role immediately after the peace is made.

That said, I must digress in order to comment upon Hegel's observation that the historical authentication of the comedies of Aristophanes certified that ancient Greece possessed a freedom that we could not have otherwise imagined. To this, I add the following: were it not for these plays we could have no knowledge of the pure intelligence[2] accorded to women by at least some of its most enlightened citizens. Further, Aristophanes displays remarkable sensitivity to their pain and frustration, and for the injustice and abuse to which they were often and habitually subjected. While Aristophanes may not have been "the first feminist," it is certain that he wrote with an artistic sensitivity that is able to ascribe full humanity to women in a historical era that denied it.

In conclusion, awareness of measure is everywhere, not only in the comedies of Aristophanes, the tragedies with which they shared the festival stage, and the Platonic dialogues, but also in every human being and every human undertaking. In their own ways, the comedies, tragedies, and dialogues serve to draw human beings vicariously into that most human of endeavors, namely *raising the question* of measure, making the attempt to determine proper measure. It is a wise truism that the Platonic dialogues should each be read separately, and that commingling them must be done with the greatest of care. Nevertheless, I risk the opinion that the one dialogue in terms of which all the others can best be read is the *Philebus,* in which measure and moderation are regarded as the most valuable possessions for a human being. Though the axiological order of possessions given there may complicate existing interpretations of other dialogues and may possess aporetic elements of its own,[3] there is little doubt in my view that each of the other dialogues is importantly concerned with measure, and that no dialogue other than the *Philebus* so clearly asserts and enacts its primacy. The four comedies treated here provide much assistance in determining this primacy.

So let us honor the flatulent Strepsiades, the loutish Philocleon, the hapless Blepyrus, the hoodwinked Kinesias, and all the others for directing us so splendidly toward our goal: an appropriately measured humanity. Let us thank them for the entire panoply of Socratic goods listed in the *Philebus:* measure, beauty, intelligence, art, and harmless pleasure. And when the occasion beckons, let us celebrate our humanity with wine, song, dance, and laughter.

Notes

INTRODUCTION

1. Schmidt, *On Germans and Other Greeks* (Bloomington, 2001), p. 19.

2. His last play, *Ploutos* (*Wealth*), is an exception. It has more characteristics of the newer comedy.

3. Solomos, *The Living Aristophanes* (Ann Arbor, 1974), p. 27.

4. Hegel, *Sämtliche Werke* (Stuttgart, 1964), vol. 14, p. 560. (The page number refers to the publisher's pagination.) Translations mine.

5. Hegel, *Lectures on the History of Philosophy* (New York, 1963), vol. 1, pp. 426–427.

6. Ibid., p. 427.

7. "It is *Schiller* [1759–1805] who must be given great credit for breaking through the Kantian subjectivity and abstraction of thinking and for venturing on an attempt to get beyond this by intellectually grasping the unity and reconciliation as the truth and by actualizing them in artistic production."

"Schiller . . . had succeeded in asserting, against the Understanding's treatment of willing and thinking, the idea of the free totality of beauty. A number of Schiller's writings are devoted to this insight into the nature of art, especially his *Letters on Aesthetic Education.*" Hegel, *Sämtliche Werke* (Stuttgart, 1964), vol. 12, pp. 96, 97.

8. Schiller, *Naive and Sentimental Poetry and On the Sublime* (New York, 1966), p. 122.

9. Ibid., p.122.

10. Ibid., p. 122.

11. Hegel, *Sämtliche Werke* (Stuttgart, 1964), vol. 14, p. 576.

12. Schiller, *Sämtliche Werke* (Munich, 1960), vol. 5, p. 539.

13. In Freydberg, *The Play of the Platonic Dialogues* (New York, 1997), I attempted to develop a notion of philosophical playfulness that included the highest seriousness.

14. While an occasional reference to "lovers" is made by one of the characters, it is clear that husbands are the target.

15. "The Old Comic poet did not have to dare to smash taboos; he was supposed to smash them, and his challenge lay in trying to discover how ingeniously he could smash them. There were taboos, of course, and the place to smash them was the comic stage . . . The proper words [for the reproductive organs] occur with reasonable frequency from Homer to Aristotle . . . but they never occur in comedy; they would have been as out of place there as the improper words would have been in Homer." Whitman, *Aristophanes and the Comic Hero* (Cambridge, Mass., 1984), pp. 209–210.

16. Hegel, *Sämtliche Werke* (Stuttgart, 1964), vol. 14, p. 561.

17. Aristophanes, *Clouds, Wasps, Peace* (1998); *Birds, Lysistrata, Women at the Thesmophoria* (2000); and *Frogs, Assemblywomen, Wealth* (2002), ed. and trans. Jeffrey Hen-

derson (Cambridge, Mass.). I am grateful for Henderson's translations and for the many fine translations by other classicists.

1. *CLOUDS* AND THE MEASURING OF *LOGOS*

1. Hornblower and Spawforth, eds., *The Oxford Classical Dictionary* (Oxford, 1996), s.v. "Old Comedy," p. 369: "the vocabulary used in these kinds of humor [i.e., sexual and excretory] eschews the euphemism characteristic of prose literature."

2. *Clouds* was originally performed in 423 BCE. The first version is lost. (Although one scholar, Hartmut Erbse, has maintained that there never was a "first" version; see his "Über die ersten 'Wolken' des Aristophanes," in Newiger, *Aristophanes und die alte Komödie* [Darmstadt, 1975], pp. 198–211.) We work with what seems to have been a revision, which was never performed at the Dionysiad. For a standard account, see Dover, *Aristophanic Comedy* (Berkeley, 1972), pp. 103–135. The "revision" issue has no effect upon the nature of this study, although it has played a large role in many others. I would rather avoid speculation in the absence of textual evidence.

3. In his *Second Letter,* the authenticity of which is disputed, Plato says that he will not write in his own name but in that of a "Socrates become beautiful and new" (314c2–4). It is the creation of the philosopher in the dialogues that I call "genuine," apart from historical considerations.

4. My view is in strong disagreement with the view expressed in Kenneth J. Dover's classic study, *Aristophanic Comedy* (Berkeley: 1972). Dover argues "that Aristophanes decided to treat Socrates as the paradigm of the sophist and attached to him any attribute of the whole genus which lent itself to ridicule" (ibid., p. 118). In support of his view, he notes that several other comedians were supposed to have written comedies ridiculing Socrates in this manner, and that ordinary citizens uninterested in fine distinctions between philosophy and sophistry would likely confound the two, an impression that, Dover suggests, Aristophanes would not mind making at all, given his loathing of Socrates (ibid., pp. 188–189). The friendly exchanges between Socrates and Aristophanes in Plato's *Symposium,* the Platonic fragment that heads this section, and other details serve at least to call such views as Dover's into question.

5. As Whitman has argued, "There could never have been any question of representing [Socrates] seriously and accurately. Had there been, Aristophanes would scarcely have accredited him with practically all the intellectual accomplishments of the whole Sophistic movement"; and, "Had Plato really felt an enemy in Aristophanes, he surely possessed the articulateness to say so clearly." Whitman, *Aristophanes and the Comic Hero* (Cambridge, Mass., 1984), pp. 142, 143. But the main issue here is not a contest of historical speculation, but concerns the text and what it shows upon treating it as a work of art.

6. Aristotle, *The Basic Works of Aristotle* (New York, 1968), p. 1455. (Greek 1449a 31–35.)

7. This is Whitman's interpretation of *ponēros.*

8. Henderson, for example, writes: "[Strepsiades] is an ignoramus, puzzled and confused by the city and its ways but unable either to transcend or transform them. The reason is simple, he is selfish and without the strongly developed sense of morality that characterized [Dicaeopolis and Trygaeus]; he wants his share of the corruption." Henderson, *The Maculate Muse* (New Haven, 1975), p. 72.

9. I employ the Henderson translation in all quotations, but often change a word or a line. In every case, I indicate the change(s); also, I insert the Greek where it seems appropriate.

10. Literally, to a "good wife," but this is said with obvious irony.

11. The name means "great renown."

12. Hume, *An Inquiry Concerning the Principles of Morality* (Indianapolis, 1957), p. 20.

13. Plato, *Protagoras,* trans. Jowett (New York: 1956), p. 36.

14. The paradigm that Socrates presents is the question, "what is . . . figure (*skhēma*)" (75b8)? A stumped Meno dodges it, and entices Socrates to respond. When Socrates offers his answer, "figure is the only thing that always follows color," Meno feigns ignorance, asking Socrates how he would respond if someone were to ask what color is. An irritated Socrates then lays out the two conditions for genuine argumentation listed above (75c8–e5).

15. As neither father nor son ever poses a direct thesis that the other attempts to refute rationally, *elenkhos* plays a minor and mostly subterranean comic role in *Clouds.* There are some comic "refutations" later, especially by Weaker *Logos* (see ll. 1046–1050, 1059–1070).

16. For an opposite view, see O'Regan, *Rhetoric, Comedy and the Violence of Language* (Oxford, 1992). This excellent book-length study also focuses on the role of *logos* in *Clouds,* and offers a close reading that neither sugarcoats Aristophanes' treatment of *logos* and its limits nor makes comedy subordinate to other interests. It views *Clouds* in the context of the role of rhetoric in general and sophistry in particular at the time of Aristophanes. Also (and more problematically in my view), it treats extensively the supposed difference between the two versions, accepting Dover's view that the version we have represents a radical revision of the earlier one. We do, however, disagree clearly on the Aristophanic Socrates. O'Regan writes: "Strepsiades neither understands what the elevated Socrates is doing, nor does he care" (ibid., p. 43). For progenitors of this view, see two standard works: Aristophanes, *Clouds,* trans. Dover (Oxford, 1968), p. xxvii: "He is ignorant, stupid and boorish, a son of the soil and smelling of the soil . . . but one of its richer sons"; and Wilamowitz-Moellendorff, *Platon* (Berlin, 1948), p. 72: "so fasste er nun Socrates als [sophistitische] Vertreter, unbekümmert, wessen Inhalt dessen Gespräche mit der Jugend hatten, und auch darum unbekümmert, dass er keine Schulstube hätte und überhaupt keinen förmliche Unterricht erteilte. Er war eben Sophist; das hielt man für feststehend und beurteilt ihn danach."

17. For the fullest of my accounts, see Freydberg, *The Play of the Platonic Dialogues* (New York, 1997), chap. 7.

18. An intriguing article that would almost surely escape the attention of American readers is Andreas Patzer, "Die Wolken des Aristophanes also philosophiegeschichtliche Dokument," in Neukam, *Klassische Sprachen und Literaturen* (Munich, 1993), vol. 27, pp. 72–93. Patzer shows how the Socrates of *Clouds* comically (artistically) conflates three philosophical types: the Pythagorean, the Sophist, and the naturalist.

19. The history of philosophy consists of such *logoi* at every turn, from Plato's *Parmenides* through virtually all of medieval, modern, and contemporary philosophy.

20. See Spatz, *Aristophanes* (Boston, 1978). "This comic transformation of the real Socrates is typical of the art form and can be paralleled in Aristophanes' distortion of other contemporaries. Socrates himself seems to have appreciated the joke" (ibid., p. 51). In her notes, she cites Plutarch, *Moralia,* bk. 1, 10 C–D, as her source (ibid., p. 154).

21. *Themis* in this context means, as Henderson indicates, "what is laid down by the gods." So "sacrilege" is a good translation of *ou themis.*

22. This also has the sense of "re-measuring the earth."

23. In his conclusion to *Socrates and Aristophanes* (New York, 1966), Leo Strauss indicates that something along the lines of the ancient quarrel obtains between the depic-

tion of Socrates by Aristophanes on the one hand, and by Xenophon and Plato on the other. "Accordingly the wisdom of the Platonic Socrates is superior to the wisdom of the poets: The truth discerned by the poets must be integrated into the all-comprehensive truth with which the philosopher is concerned." He even supposes, "One can easily receive the impression that Plato and Xenophon presented their Socrates in conscious contradiction to Aristophanes' presentation" (ibid., p. 314). In my interpretation, the poetic and the philosophical are inextricably intertwined.

24. Gregory Vlastos claims, "The anti-hero of the *Clouds* is many things to many men, but an ironist to none," in Vlastos, *Socrates* (Ithaca, 1991), p. 29. However, it seems clear to me from the two-edged nature of so many of Strepsiades' remarks, as well as from his prior distance from any kind of sophistry, that he is indeed a wonderfully coarse ironist.

25. Henderson has "the flower of orators," which includes the metaphorical overtone of roguery. I simply wanted to make this more explicit.

26. The search for justice in bk. 1 "fails" anyway, and Socrates blames himself for proceeding in an improper way. However, this failure leads to Socrates' necessary conclusion of his own ignorance, and that he must first inquire as to what the just is before seeking to praise its benefits.

27. In the *Apology,* these charges were made by Meletus, one of Socrates' "new accusers." The "old accusers" to which Socrates referred are those who maintained that he "investigated matters below the earth and beyond the heavens" and that he "made the weaker argument appear stronger." We have already seen Aristophanes' mockery of the first stock charge, and must await that of the second one. Socrates does refer to Aristophanes in the *Apology* as the possible source of the old accusations and prejudice, and this single text inspired Voltaire's "fiery attack" on Aristophanes, in which he called the comic poet "much lower and more despicable than Plutarch depicts him." Plutarch claimed that "all good men detest his malignity." Both cited in Van Steen, *Venom in Verse* (Princeton, 2000), p. 16. However, there is much evidence of friendship, cordiality, and respect between Socrates and Aristophanes.

28. Of the three speeches, only Agathon's capitalizes the opening epsilon.

29. The dialogue between Socrates and Agathon that occurs immediately after Agathon's speech is often obscured by the recitation of Socrates' beautiful *logos* on *erōs* that was inspired by Diotima. However, this "intervening" dialogue deals with matters of major philosophical import. For a splendid reading of this exchange, see Geier, *Plato's Erotic Thought* (Rochester, 2002), pp. 3–17.

30. One can certainly see a certain comedy in the entrance of Alcibiades. After Socrates culminates his *logos* with Diotima's praise of disembodied beauty, beautiful-bodied Alcibiades arrives, and is—perhaps oddly—entirely welcome. Alcibiades' subsequent "praise" of Socrates might well indicate a re-ascent of the ladder of love.

31. Geier, *Plato's Erotic Thought* (Rochester, 2002), p. 49.

32. Chaos and the Tongue are mentioned here for the first time. Taken together with the Clouds, they name the atmosphere in which an unjust *logos* can triumph over a just one.

33. Liddell and Scott, *A Greek-English Lexicon* (Oxford, 1989), p. 1654.

34. Cratinus' *Wine Flask* (*Putinē*) took first prize. (Amepsias' *Konnas,* another comedy featuring Socrates, taking second prize.) Though no entire works of Cratinus survive, he is credited with merging iambics with the *kōmos,* with the standard form of *prologos* (prologue spoken to the audience or to another character), *parodos* (entrance of the Chorus of twenty-four members), *agon* (argument between two characters), *parabasis* (Chorus ad-

dressing the audience), *kōmos,* and *exodus,* and is also credited with initiating the practice of public ridicule.

35. See Rosen, "Cratinus' *Pytine* and the Construction of the Comic Self," in Harvey and Wilkins, eds., *The Rivals of Aristophanes* (London, 2000), pp. 23–29. Rosen provides a splendid argument on the creative, poetic construction of the parabasis in Old Comedy, noting that the move from the poetic parabasis to genuine autobiography is a non sequitur and should be resisted at every turn. "As responsible scholars we must remind ourselves that however autobiographical the parabases might appear, they still remain poetic creations composed for a dramatic competition, and delivered by fictional characters decked out in masks and costumes" (ibid., pp. 23–24). A bit later, he writes: "even those who want to see the real Aristophanes behind a parabitic 'I' must confront the fact that not once in all the surviving plays does a character by that name actually ever appear" (ibid., pp. 23–24). Rosen uses the plot, as related by the scholiast, of Cratinus' *Pytine* as an example of an Old Comic poet constructing a fictional parabitic self. In this comedy, which famously defeated *Clouds,* the Chorus Leader claimed to be married to Comedy, which he had given up for drink.

36. See ll. 177–179, where Aristophanes puns on a Socratic experiment and his stealing food from a passive homosexual. See Henderson, *The Maculate Muse* (New Haven, 1975), pp. 30–31.

37. An extensive study of Aristophanic choral interludes of this kind is Hubbard, *The Mask of Comedy* (Ithaca, 1991). Hubbard argues, as do others that he cites, from the traditional position in the parabasis, that the poet directly proclaims his own view to the audience. His theory here is that Aristophanes is playing on editions of *Clouds,* attempting to win over those who voted against it the first time while winking knowingly at the "more sophisticated" who appreciated the first version. In particular, Aristophanes did not appeal to "cheap tricks" the first time around such as the concluding conflagration, but in the second edition he uses them all. "The text thus manipulates its audience by appealing to more than one level of understanding and more than one level of irony" (ibid., p. 112). However, this seems both more labored interpretively, and also to miss the inherent self-alienating ridiculousness of any such parabasis.

38. Nietzsche, *Jenseits von Gut und Böse und Zur Genealogie der Moral* (Munich, 1999), p. 47.

39. Murray, *Aristophanes* (New York, 1964), p. 99. In Murray's interpretation of *Clouds,* even the comic Socrates is treated favorably. "There is no attack on his honor. He is not represented as charging high fees . . . His morals, in the narrower sense, are left unassailed." The "joke" of *Clouds* consists of "a stupid and dishonest low-brow, like Strepsiades" being "brought into the school of ascetic contemplative students" (ibid., p. 94).

40. It has been well noted that the historical Aristophanes despised the historical Cleon. A supposedly thinly veiled "fictionalized" Cleon made important and villainous appearances in several of Aristophanes' comedies, two of which I will treat in later chapters. However, once again I am not interested in Cleon except as he occurs in the Aristophanic text. Any import of often speculative historical details will be held to an absolute minimum, and will always be employed in service to the interpretation of the comedy.

41. In Niall W. Slater's recent and often intriguing *Spectator Politics* (Philadelphia, 2002), in which he attempts to fuse political and aesthetic interpretations by means of meta-theatrical elements (i.e., elements *in* the comedy which demonstrate self-consciousness *of* the comedy), he writes "Aristophanes is not just worried about tragedy's state of artistic health; he offers his own comedy as an alternative way of thinking and talking directly, not mythically, about Athens and its problems" (ibid., p. 6). I would argue that

there is *much* indirection and also much attention to *muthos* along with the more obvious connection to contemporary Athens.

42. This *logos* consists of the *eidē* of which he has always spoken: "the beautiful itself according to itself, and the good and the great and all the rest." See *Phaedo* 100b1–8. The entire passage will be treated in chap. 3 of the present volume.

43. After having several of his *logoi* on the forms (*eidē*) refuted, and upon being challenged by Parmenides to say which philosophical resources he has available to meet these objections, Socrates replies: "I seem to have no clear one at present": *Ou panu moi dokō kathoran en ge tō paronti* (135c7).

44. Sallis, *Being and Logos* (Bloomington, 1996), p. 30.

45. After Chronos lopped the genitals off his father Ouranos, he began devouring his own children so that his rule could not be usurped. With the help of his mother Rhea, Zeus tricked his father Chronos into swallowing a stone, then bound his father and caused him to vomit up all of his (grateful) children, and established order among the gods. See *Theogony* (ll. 453–506) in Hesiod, *The Homeric Hymns and Homerica,* trans. Evelyn-Whyte (Cambridge, Mass., 1974), pp. 112–117.

46. Solomos has argued that Aristophanes chose to ridicule Socrates for many reasons. The main one was the poet's desire to criticize the newer education, which he had Socrates represent because the latter was not associated with any particular school and so the poet would not face any specific rebuke, and because it was well known that Socrates "was himself a man with a an acute sense of humor, always ready to laugh when people teased him." Solomos, *The Living Aristophanes* (Ann Arbor, 1974), p. 111.

47. Henderson has "decency."

48. In *Formen und Darstellungsweisen in der aristophanisischen Kömodie,* Paul Händel argues: "Die beiden mitwerkenden Personen sind Allegorien, weiter nich individualisierte Verkörperungen der beiden Thesen, die zur Diskussion stehen und die sich hier selbst verteidigen . . . Der dramatische Einfall besteht also hier in der Abstraktion, im Auftretenlassen von Allegorien zu einem theoretischen Kampf." Cited in Gelzer, "Der epirrhematische Agon bei Aristophanes," *Zetemata* (Munich, 1960), p. 15. However, the clear gestural components of both *Logoi* indicate that they are *not* mere abstractions, but rather are indeed personifications who in individualized ways embody the *erga* as well as the positions articulated.

49. Victor Ehrenberg observes: "There are undoubtedly many features of the comic Sokrates which, however exaggerated, fit Sokrates better than the sophists . . . It is he to whose teaching the 'know thyself' refers which Strepsiades has learnt to use as a maxim . . . [however] what the Sokrates of the *Clouds* is chiefly concerned with has very little to do with the historical person." Ehrenberg, *The People of Aristophanes* (New York, 1962), p. 275.

50. This might refer to "the sapient ones" generally, or could refer only to the inhabitants of the *phrontistērion,* given the linguistic kinship.

51. Aristophanes, *Clouds,* ed. Dover (Oxford, 1968), p. 226.

52. Ibid., p. 226.

53. Henderson, *The Maculate Muse* (New Haven, 1975), p. 59n.

54. Henderson has "rhetoric." The Greek is *legein.*

55. See *Meno* 95c4–5: "I admire this most in Gorgias, Socrates, that you would never hear him promising this. Indeed, he ridicules the others when he hears them making this claim. He thinks one should make people clever speakers [*alla legein oietai dein poiein deinous*]." Grote trans., in *Plato: Complete Works,* ed. Cooper (Indianapolis, 1997), p. 893.

56. See Landfester, *Handlungsverlauf und Komik in den frühen Komödien des Aristophanes* (Berlin, 1977), p. 104: "Die freudige Stimmung der 12. Szene setzt sich auch in

der 13. Szene (v. 1171–1213) fort, in der Strepsiades seinen Sohn überschwenglich begrüsst. Von diesem ist alle Verdriesslichkeit und aller Widerstand gegen die neue Lehre gewichen; er ist das geworden, was sich sein Vater immer gewünscht hat: ein rechter Sophist, der die Sorgen des Vaters als gegenstandlos und die wirtschaftliche Zukunft als gesichert ansieht." (Of course, he divides the scenes differently than they are divided here.) Landfester's analysis of *Clouds* also pays close attention to Aeschylean motifs.

57. See *Frogs,* where for Dionysus it's a close call. (And it is hasty even to assume that the comic Dionysus speaks for Aristophanes!): "These men are my friends, and I'll not judge between them; I don't want to get on the bad side of either of them. One I consider wise, and the other delights me" (ll. 1411–1413). He chooses Aeschylus to ascend from Hades . . . but not right away.

58. Hegel, *Phänomenologie des Geistes* (Hamburg, 1952), pp. 519–520.

59. Lois Spatz makes the intriguing suggestion that in *Clouds* "the truth about man is that he must assert himself, must not deny his body, his passions or his will." Finally, "The shambles he made of the Thoughtery is the dramatic depiction of the shambles the comedy has made of the metaphysical structures man creates to oppress and control his true nature." Spatz, *Aristophanes* (Boston, 1978), p. 59. This author notices, more than most others, that the *logoi* in *Clouds* cancel one another out. In this light her conclusion is genuinely thought-provoking. However, these lines of Strepsiades seem clearly to work against her thesis.

60. Dover, *Aristophanic Comedy* (Berkeley, 1972), p. 268.

61. Ibid., p. 266.

62. Liddell and Scott, *A Greek-English Lexicon* (Oxford, 1989), p. 401.

63. The standard source for viewing Aristophanes historically as a conservative is de Ste. Croix, *The Origins of the Peloponnesian War* (Ithaca, 1972). However, even this spectacularly learned Marxist historian does not call Aristophanes a straightforward conservative, as some seem to think: "There is no indication at all that he was an oligarch, in the literal sense of wanting to limit the franchise and . . . reduce the lower classes to complete political subjection, *donleia.* Indeed, he can sometimes show some real sympathy for the lower orders. . . . But he had an essentially *paternalist* attitude toward them" (ibid., p. 357, emphasis in original).

In a somewhat confusing manner, Moses Hadas writes (correctly, in my view): "many have thought that advocacy of a particular set of doctrines was his prime object . . . and some have thought he was actually in the pay of the conservative oligarchy. Nothing could be more mistaken. The proper description of Aristophanes is poet and comic genius." However, the very next paragraph begins with the words, "The direction is at all points conservative." Aristophanes, *The Complete Plays of Aristophanes,* ed. Hadas (New York, 1988), pp. 7–8.

2. *WASPS* AND THE LIMITS OF *LOGOS*

1. Aristophanes, *Clouds, Wasps, Peace,* ed. and trans. Henderson (Cambridge, Mass., 1998), p. 214.

2. Ibid., p. 216.

3. Ibid., p. 225n.

4. Henderson translates *phallaina* as "dragon." Hadas has "shark." It could stand for a monster of many kinds. In l. 4, Sosias speaks of the *knōdalon,* another word that points to general monstrousness.

5. See *Theaetetus* 191c9ff. and especially 194c4–195a10 for a discussion of the soul in the image of waxedness.

6. Aristophanes, *Clouds, Wasps, Peace,* ed. and trans. Henderson (Cambridge, Mass., 1998), p. 232.

7. *Onoma* means both "name" and, in an attenuated sense, "word" as well, but "word" only in the sense of a language unit that points to a thing, while clearly many, many "words" in the usual sense do not. *Onoma* can thus be translated sometimes as "noun."

8. As a "preamble" to the way of presenting the divine names, the names Zeus and Cronos were derived at 396d1–c3; the sustained derivation takes place from 401b1–407d5.

9. Sallis, *Being and Logos* (Bloomington, 1996), p. 185.

10. Ibid., p. 186.

11. Hornblower and Spawforth, eds., *The Oxford Classical Dictionary* (Oxford, 1996), p. 445.

12. The context is unclear as to whom the threat is directed.

13. The "Trojan horse" is not treated in the *Iliad* or the *Odyssey,* but in Virgil's *Aenead.* Conceived by Odysseus and brought into Troy by night under pretense of guaranteeing a Trojan victory, it contained scores of Hellenic soldiers within, who were released and subsequently brought Troy to ruin.

14. Aristophanes, *Wasps,* ed. MacDowell (Oxford, 1971), p. 156.

15. Literally "feast" me, regale me with feasting.

16. Dover admits sympathy for Philocleon, but then proceeds to document his extreme reprehensibility, his desire only to do harm (*kakia*). But this is all that is left to him! Dover, *Aristophanic Comedy* (Berkeley, 1972), pp. 125–126.

17. Aristophanes, *Clouds, Wasps, Peace,* ed. and trans. Henderson (Cambridge, Mass., 1998), p. 271n.

18. Aristophanes, *Wasps,* ed. MacDowell (Oxford, 1971), p. 185.

19. In Murray, Philocleon and the wasps are regarded in such a manner. Despite their unjust propensities, "the curious thing is that Philocleon and his waspish colleagues are treated with a kind of personal sympathy . . . The truth is that the juries were composed of just the class of men that Aristophanes liked and championed . . . the old men from the country . . . respectable, very poor, embittered and angry, able to serve on juries or sit in the ecclesia, and—according to Aristophanes—easy prey to any smart and unscrupulous speaker who chose to gull them." Murray, *Aristophanes* (New York, 1964), p. 82.

20. Aristophanes, *Wasps,* ed. MacDowell (Oxford, 1971), p. 191.

21. Ibid., p. 203.

22. Henderson has "commanding." Again, this is fine, but does not quite capture the sense of power Philocleon is expressing here.

23. Henderson has "formidable intellect." I want to keep the connection between this use of *deinēs* and its earlier uses.

24. Aristophanes, *Wasps,* ed. MacDowell (Oxford, 1971), p. 223.

25. The Greek has the sense of "animal tamer" as well.

26. Henderson maintains that *Wasps* is free of the "moralizing and dispassionate analysis" that he finds in *Clouds,* which he judges to be "unsatisfying and ambivalent" for that reason. But there is *nothing but* "moralizing and dispassionate analysis" in the contest of *logoi* between father and son here. Thus, I cannot concur in any respect with his effort to set *Wasps* apart, both ethically and aesthetically, from what he called the "unsatisfying and ambivalent" *Clouds.* See Henderson, *The Maculate Muse* (New Haven, 1975), p. 78.

27. Plato, *Plato's Sophist,* trans. Brann, Kalkavage, and Salem (Newburyport, Mass., 1996). "Speech" is *logos.* "Conversation" is *dialogos.*

28. Glaucon alone remains in conversation with Socrates until the end of the *Republic,* and shows astuteness and passion that are superior to these qualities in the other interlocutors. It is easy to forget that Socrates regarded the question as settled as early as bk. 2, 368b5–6, where Socrates says, "I thought in what I showed to Thrasymachus that justice was better than injustice . . ." Then he notes that the brothers didn't accept it, but never says that this proof was insufficient.

29. Aristophanes, *Clouds, Wasps, Peace,* ed. and trans. Henderson (Cambridge, Mass., 1998), pp. 324–325n.

30. Here, *halōsetai* has both the legal meaning of "he'll be convicted" and the commonplace meaning of "he'll be thrashed" or "he'll be destroyed." Henderson's translation is therefore excellent, in that it effortlessly captures both meanings.

31. Although "form" or "Form" (without scare quotes) is the traditional translation of *eidos,* it conceals much of its Greek sense. *Eidos* comes from *eidenai* (to know), which itself is the perfect tense of *horaō,* to see. "Form" obscures both this visual and temporal connection.

32. Henderson translates *Kuōn* as "Demadogue" in order to capture the pun on Cleon's name and the latter's reputation as a demagogue. He translates *Labēt'* as "Grabes" in order (I suppose) to capture this dog's having "grabbed" all of the Sicilian cheese. I have left it "Grabes," to keep the pun on Laches' name, which is surely intended by Aristophanes.

33. There is also something of a pun involving *sukinos,* "fig-wood" or, as Henderson has it, "impeach wood." See Aristophanes, *Clouds, Wasps, Peace,* ed. and trans. Henderson (Cambridge, Mass., 1998), pp. 239, 239n., and 337.

34. See Aristophanes, *Wasps,* ed. MacDowell (Oxford, 1971), commenting on l. 895, p. 250.

35. See Aristophanes, *Clouds, Wasps, Peace,* ed. and trans. Henderson (Cambridge, Mass., 1998), p. 339n.

36. Aristophanes, *Wasps,* ed. MacDowell (Oxford, 1971), p. 253.

37. Aristophanes, *Clouds, Wasps, Peace,* ed. and trans. Henderson (Cambridge, Mass., 1998), p. 341.

38. See Cunliffe, *A Lexicon of the Homeric Dialect* (Norman, 1963), p. 310.

39. Aristophanes, *Clouds, Wasps, Peace,* ed. and trans. Henderson (Cambridge, Mass., 1998), p. 345; also Aristophanes, *Wasps,* ed. MacDowell (Oxford, 1971), p. 255.

40. See Liddell and Scott, *A Greek-English Lexicon* (Oxford, 1989), pp. 1057–1059.

41. See Aristophanes, *Wasps,* ed. MacDowell (Oxford, 1971), p. 256, note to l. 958, where MacDowell argues persuasively that the conditional *ei d' hupheito* amounts to a concession to the charge of theft.

42. Ll. 1014–1015: "[Letting good words fall to the ground] is what happens to crude spectators, but not from you."

43. See Aristophanes, *Wasps,* ed. MacDowell (Oxford, 1971), pp. 268–269; and Aristophanes, *Clouds, Wasps, Peace,* ed. and trans. Henderson (Cambridge, Mass., 1998), p. 357.

44. For extensive discussion of this topic, see Freydberg, *The Play of the Platonic Dialogues* (New York, 1997), chap. 6.

45. Plato, *Republic,* trans. Bloom (New York, 1968), p. 189.

46. I'm supposing that the prefix *ka-* is *kakia* abbreviated. Hence the clunky "badly educated" for *kapaideute.* A *skia* is a shadow. Henderson has "oaf," but I think that the literal rendering is crucial here, as is the literal translation of "men" rather than "gentleman" for *andrasin.*

47. The remaining vocal exchanges are obscure. See Aristophanes, *Wasps,* ed. MacDowell (Oxford, 1971), p. 294.

48. *Sumposion* (symposium) literally means "the drinking of wine together."

49. While the comic chorus will praise Bdelocleon "comically," Solomos does so seriously: "In the case of [Bdelocleon] . . . we have a character most rare in Attic comedy: a serious, tender, practical, ingenious, dashing and enduring young man." See Solomos, *The Living Aristophanes* (Ann Arbor, 1974), p. 135. There are many reasons to disagree with this that are built into the play, as I have taken pains to show. In *The Mask of Comedy,* Hubbard correctly observes that "in different forms, both father and son pursue ultimately selfish ends under the guise of upholding law and social order." See Hubbard, *The Mask of Comedy* (Ithaca, 1991), p. 124.

50. Much of the material in the choral songs would be familiar to Aristophanes' spectators. Information on the figures and events mentioned can be found in Aristophanes, *Wasps,* ed. MacDowell (Oxford, 1971), pp. 295–308. Except for the Chorus Leader's speech on Cleon, this material will play a very little role in the interpretation of this section. Its philosophical material trumps all else.

51. Aristophanes, *Wasps,* ed. MacDowell (Oxford, 1971), p. 295.

52. Aristophanes, *Clouds, Wasps, Peace,* ed. and trans. Henderson (Cambridge, Mass., 1998), p. 386; Liddell and Scott, *A Greek-English Lexicon* (Oxford, 1989), p. 270; also Aristophanes, *Wasps,* ed. MacDowell (Oxford, 1971), p. 301.

53. This is MacDowell's translation; Henderson has "sweet-talked."

54. Douglass Parker recognizes the complexity of Aristophanes' characterizations, and formulates it in this interesting fashion: "In one sense, then, our choice lies between doing the right things for the wrong reasons [Bdelocleon] and doing the wrong things for the right reason [Philocleon]. Not an easy choice, and the despair of the seeker after black and white—but an intensely comic polarity. Thus is irony ironized beyond pamphleteering, incident endowed with the cross-welter of meanings, the coexistence of mutual exclusives, which marks great drama of any sort." See Aristophanes, *Four Comedies,* trans. Parker, ed. Arrowsmith (Ann Arbor, 1975), p. 3.

55. Solomos, echoing many others, writes, "The *Wasps* is a social satire, aiming at the abuses of the judicial system. In spite of its courtroom subject, however, the play's overall theme is political." Solomos, *The Living Aristophanes* (Ann Arbor, 1974), p. 127.

56. Nietzsche, *The Birth of Tragedy and The Case of Wagner* (New York, 1967), pp. 36–38.

57. Following Henderson, *The Maculate Muse* (New Haven, 1975), p. 132.

58. Aristophanes, *Wasps,* ed. MacDowell (Oxford, 1971), pp. 307–308.

59. Ibid., pp. 307–308.

60. In his thought-provoking *Formen und Darstellungsweisen in der aristophanischen Komödie* (Heidelberg, 1963), Paul Händel argues forcefully for the view that Philocleon's character undergoes radical change, and that Bdelocleon has been successful at curing his father of his obsession with jury service. The transition, however, is not to some respectable state, but to the pursuit of erotic pleasure. At the conclusion of his *Wasps* chapter, he writes: "Am Ende des *Wespen* steht also der völlig verwandelte Philokleon. Von v. 1003 bzw 1122 an ist er plötzlich von seiner Richterwut geheilt. Das ist ein Faktum, an dem keine Interpretation vorbeigeben kann. Soweit hat Bdelykleon also durchaus Erfolg gehabt" (ibid., p. 149).

However, the evidence upon which he bases this "fact" is entirely decontextualized. At l. 1337, when Philocleon urges that the voting urns be thrown out, this clearly obtains when he is drunk and *only when **he** will be the defendant in a lawsuit.* Also, Philocleon's erotic pursuits will be limited by his one "non-rejuvenated" element. Philocleon retains a heroic unity of *thumos* (spirit) and *timē* (honor) throughout, as wasp-juror, as juror in his own home, as "guest" at an aristocratic symposium, as danger to the public thereafter . . . and as the embodiment of Dionysus that he remained throughout.

61. "And what does it take to make the slave weep? The misfortune of his master, oppressor, despoiler, pillager, of the man who laid waste his town and killed his dear ones under his very eyes. This man suffers or dies; *then* the slave's tears come. And really why not? This is for him the only occasion on which tears are permitted, are, indeed, required. A slave will cry whenever he can do so with impunity—his situation keeps tears on tap for him.

> *She spoke, weeping, and the women groaned,*
> *Using the pretext of Patroclus to bewail their own torments.*"

Simone Weil, *The Iliad or The Poem of Force* (Wallingford, Penn., 1976), p. 9.

62. As MacDowell notes, this word was used at l. 744, when the Chorus noted that Philocleon criticized himself for the deeds he "was crazy about (*epemainet'*) before." (Henderson has "ecstatic.")

63. See Aristophanes, *Wasps*, ed. MacDowell (Oxford, 1971), p. 319.

64. Leo Strauss argues that Philocleon "can be cured of his eagerness to judge or to condemn strictly speaking, or for his longing for the greatest stateliness, or Zeuslike grandeur. He retains to the end his natural inclination to malice and mischief, his natural nastiness and bitterness. It is obvious that malice is a necessary ingredient of the Aristophanic comedy." Strauss, *Socrates and Aristophanes* (New York, 1966), p. 134. While one might quarrel with some of these claims (especially concerning the "natural" status of Philocleon's qualities, as well as the cure for his love of jury service and of condemnation), Strauss' observation on the necessary role of *malice* in the poetry of Aristophanes is well made. He may see such malice as belonging specifically to comedy. It seems to me that it belongs essentially to the human condition. Therefore, it would not be appropriate to call it *kakia*, any more than it would in the case of the digestive process. Rather, *kakia* can be said rightly of it only when it is out of control and improperly directed.

65. For a sustained treatment of the dancing (and the dancers) with which Wasps concludes, see Aristophanes, *Wasps*, ed. MacDowell (Oxford, 1971), pp. 322–332.

66. In her excellent little book, Lois Spatz takes issue with the opinions of many scholars who maintain that the final scenes of Wasps mistakenly dropped the satire against the jury system, in order to satisfy the public with slapstick and obscenity: "But its very vulgar form is absolutely necessary to dramatize the triumph of the life-force in nature which Old Comedy celebrates." However, she interprets Philocleon's dance as an expression of "man's freedom to assert his individuality and to seek satisfaction without restraint," and accordingly concludes that "he embraces hedonism." I do not identify "the triumph of the life-force in nature" with hedonism and the pursuit of individual pleasure. Hedonism is a function of human choice. Bdelocleon exemplifies it. The life-force to which Spatz so aptly refers lies beyond and beneath, in any case outside of, human control. Its assertion in the dance of Philocleon reminds that the god in whose name the festival takes place is ever-present. See Spatz, *Aristophanes* (Boston, 1978), pp. 68–69.

67. This is why I cannot agree with Hubbard, who says that *Wasps* (like *Clouds*) ends with the hero's failure "and it is no surprise that the plays themselves were relative failures with the public. Neither play is able to articulate a positive vision of the world as it ought to be . . ." Hubbard, *The Mask of Comedy* (Ithaca, 1991), p. 136.

Comedies do not resemble sermons at all in my view, but rather serve to remind us of and to take joy in our common humanity, with both its virtues and its flaws. In one of Hubbard's most provocative remarks, he writes: "The power of comedy is the power to manipulate public imagination into new modes of perception" (ibid., pp. 132–133). *Clouds* and *Wasps* both do so, by displaying complex human characters and situations in ways that provoke thoughtful laughter, not by offering alternative positive visions, which is the (very difficult!) work of political scientists and political philosophers.

3. *ASSEMBLYWOMEN: ERŌS* AND HUMAN LAW

1. This will conflict with the "throng of lies" that the founders must tell not long after these "principles" are declared. This "principle" is also comic.

2. See Freydberg, *The Play of the Platonic Dialogues* (New York, 1997), esp. chap. 3: "Play and Brightness: Intellect and Knowledge of Being."

3. Aristophanes, *Frogs, Assemblywomen, Wealth,* ed. and trans. Henderson (Cambridge, Mass., 2002), p. 247.

4. Henderson renders *GUNĒ Á, GUNĒ B,* etc., "First Woman," "Second Woman," etc.

5. Aristophanes, *Frogs, Assemblywomen, Wealth,* ed. and trans. Henderson (Cambridge, Mass., 2002), pp. 157, 257.

6. Henderson, *The Maculate Muse* (New Haven, 1975), p. 172.

7. Could be translated "way of life," "habit," "custom," or "temper."

8. "A women's festival in honor of Demeter, common to all Greeks, celebrated in autumn . . . before the time of sowing. Men were excluded . . . The festival included obscenity and a sacrifice." See Hornblower and Spawforth, eds., *The Oxford Classical Dictionary* (Oxford, 1996), p. 1509.

9. Grene and Lattimore, eds., *Greek Tragedies* (Chicago, 1960), vol. 1, p. 194.

10. Sophocles, *Antigone, The Women of Trachis, Philoctetes, Oedipus at Colonus,* trans. Lloyd-Jones (Cambridge, Mass., 1994), p. 34.

11. Liddell and Scott, *A Greek-English Lexicon* (Oxford, 1989), p. 374.

12. This is how Schmidt translates *unheimlich.*

13. Heidegger, *An Introduction to Metaphysics* (Garden City, 1961), pp. 123–127.

14. In Ast's Plato concordance, the following synonyms, all denoting the fearful, evil side, are listed: *timendus, horribilis, atrox, dirus, malus, perniciosus.* See Ast, *Lexicon Platonicum* (New York, 1969), p. 431.

15. See Kant, *Critique of Judgment* (New York, 1951), p. 86.

16. Ibid., pp. 96–99.

17. In so rendering *kalos,* I am attempting to capture something like "manifest magnificence," whether in terms of what we today might distinguish as outward and inward splendor.

18. For a splendid essay on the *Philebus,* see Figal, "The Idea and Mixture of the Good," in Sallis and Russon, eds., *Retracing the Platonic Text* (Evanston, Ill., 2000), pp. 85–95.

19. Liddell and Scott, *A Greek-English Lexicon* (Oxford, 1989), p. 1094. Henderson has "a dangerous psychopath."

20. Aristophanes, *Ecclesiazusae,* ed. and trans. Sommerstein (Warminster, 1998), p. 165.

21. The pay had recently been raised from a paltry one obol. This increase was sufficient to draw a large crowd, where the previous amount attracted few—another commentary on the civic-mindedness of the Athenian men.

22. Henderson has “in the role you’ve got to play.”

23. This reference was found in Aristophanes, *Frogs, Assemblywomen, Wealth,* ed. and trans. Henderson (Cambridge, Mass., 2002), p. 293.

24. This is also true of the guardians in *logos.*

25. The midwife characteristically received extra payment if she delivered a boy.

26. A literal rendering of *ton bion* can certainly be “life.”

27. Aristophanes, *Ecclesiazusae,* ed. and trans. Sommerstein (Warminster, 1998), pp. 184–185.

28. “Unless” is logically equivalent to “if not.”

29. Solomos believes that “the *Assembly of Women* aims anonymously at Plato’s extremist views. The heroine of the play . . . proposes a political system which is a distillation, one might say, of the fifth book of Plato’s *Republic:* a socialistic system abolishing family and private property.” Solomos, *The Living Aristophanes* (Ann Arbor, 1974), p. 232. In this chapter, I hope it becomes clear both that Plato “proposed” no such thing, and that the comedy of Aristophanes here is in no sense a commentary on this non-proposal. Still, like Murray’s, Solomos’ appreciation of Aristophanes remains a delight to read.

30. Aristophanes, *Frogs, Assemblywomen, Wealth,* ed. and trans. Henderson (Cambridge, Mass., 2002), p. 171. Henderson restricts this interpretation to later in the play, but it seems to fit here as well.

31. Ibid., p. 168. Henderson points out that this is an Aristophanic neologism uniting *skallein* (poke) and *thura.*

32. *Hōraiotatēn* has many shades of meaning. Henderson has “prettiest.” Sommerstein has “most attractive.” The principal meaning given for persons in Liddell and Scott is “seasonal, ripe.” It seems to me that the leering salaciousness of Blepyrus should be reflected in the translation.

33. In the introduction to his edition of *Ecclesiazusae,* Ussher seems to believe that Praxagora’s proposal was intended seriously, since the idea of such a society was in the air at the time. What he finds new is her suggestion that wives and children be held in common. “Praxagora knows too that desperate situations require desperate means to correct them. And in fact the last hope of salvation (*sōtēria*) for Athens is the reversal of the whole existing order, the turning upside-down of *all* accepted attitudes, towards sex or economics or the State.” See Aristophanes, *Ecclesiazusae,* ed. Ussher (Oxford, 1973), p. xv.

34. As Heidegger has said, poetry and philosophy are as close as can be, but they dwell on different mountain peaks.

35. Note a possible anomaly. Perhaps this is what Whitman means when he singles out *Assemblywomen* as the only one of Aristophanes’ plays in which the plot might not hold together: “it is still hard to read any play, except possibly the *Ecclesiazousae,* and feel that it is falling apart, at least, if one reads with an eye open to poetic coherence.” Whitman, *Aristophanes and the Comic Hero* (Cambridge, Mass., 1984), p. 9. But perhaps he is thinking of the dissolution of Praxagora’s city due to erotic conundrums following from her edict of equality. I would argue that the latter is precisely its point, and that accordingly the plot is exceptionally coherent.

36. Aristophanes, *Ecclesiazusae,* ed. and trans. Sommerstein (Warminster, 1998), p. 196.

37. Ibid., pp. 196–197.

38. In “Utopianism and the Sophistic City,” Thomas K. Hubbard astutely notes: “The plot of *Ecclesiazousae* unfolds itself as a progressive demonstration of the unworkability of Praxagora’s communistic program.” It shares this quality with *Republic* bk. 5, as

I have endeavored to show. Hubbard is the interpreter who best grasps *Assemblywomen*'s wonderful unity. See Hubbard, "Utopianism and the Sophistic City," in Dobrov, ed., *The City as Comedy* (Chapel Hill, 1997).

By contrast, Gilbert Norwood holds the opposite view. In his much earlier *Greek Comedy,* Norwood finds *Ecclesiazusae* to be among Aristophanes' weakest works, arguing that it is "more rational than its predecessors: it insists, for better or for worse, on consistency, common sense." Norwood, *Greek Comedy* (London, 1931), p. 267. While I cannot agree with his overall assessment, his evidence in its support are worthy. He finds the plot less ingeniously far-fetched than those of *Frogs* and *Peace,* and adduces situations where characters give plausible accounts—such as Praxagora's explanation of her oratorical skill—"worthy of Xenophon," rather than inspired nonsense (ibid., p. 268).

Norwood, however, calls *Ecclesiazusae* "the work of a broken-hearted man" (ibid., p. 265), itself a "more rational" but less well-founded account of its poet, whom he so much admires. According to my interpretation, which starts from a far different point of view, its coherence is precisely what allows for its fundamental ridiculousness to shine forth.

39. There is one moment, which seems out of place, in which Praxagora speaks of children singing songs that praise the brave in war but shame the cowardly so that the latter would not join the rest at dinner (ll. 678–679). Sommerstein finds it "surprising that the blessings of Praxagora's new order apparently do not include peace." Aristophanes, *Ecclesiazusae,* ed. and trans. Sommerstein (Warminster, 1998), p. 199. This line presents a problem. However, since there is no other mention of warfare nor an expression of the slightest concern with it, I venture a guess that this is an ad hoc answer she gives to quiet the men. After all, who will fight if they are all sleeping in!?

40. See Hegel, *Reason in History* (New York, 1953), pp. 23–24. I have replaced "man" with "humanity."

41. Aristophanes, *Ecclesiazusae,* ed. and trans. Sommerstein (Warminster, 1998), p. 214.

42. Regarding the staging, Sommerstein theorizes that three two-floor flats are on stage, with the old women occupying the bottom ones and the girls occupying the top ones. The directions (i.e., up and down) support this claim, and I can find no reason to call it into question.

43. See Aristophanes, *Ecclesiazusae,* ed. and trans. Sommerstein (Warminster, 1998), p. 215.

44. Davidson observes that this section of *Assemblywomen* "has always seemed a bit odd," and displays "a humour that seems rather savage and bad-tempered." He attempts to solve this "problem" by suggesting that the scene resembles a kind of play within the play designed to be the entertainment for the dinner-party, rather than a discrete part of the action of he play. See Davidson, "Gnesippus paigniagraphos: the Comic poets and the Erotic Mime," in Harvey and Wilkins, eds., *The Rivals of Aristophanes* (London, 2000), pp. 41–64.

While Davidson's suggestion is intriguing, it hangs upon two very weak premises. The first premise consists of the "oddness" of the scene, and the putative anomaly of its savage humor. Firstly, this scene follows directly from Praxagora's sexual law; secondly, as we have seen throughout (and as Strauss has aptly said), malice belongs essentially to Aristophanic comedy (and, I add, to the constitution of our humanity). The second premise, that the scene is entertainment for the dinner-guests, is nowhere indicated in the Aristophanic text.

45. Aristophanes, *Ecclesiazusae,* ed. and trans. Sommerstein (Warminster, 1998), p. 214.

46. Though I changed some key words, I made use of the Nehemas and Woodruff trans. in *Plato: Complete Works,* ed. Cooper (Indianapolis, 1997), p. 489.

47. L. P. E. Parker observes that the speeches of the First Old Woman and of Epigenes both "trumpet out their conflicting assertions of civil rights to the tune of the anthem of Athenian democracy, each concluding with a key word: *eleutherō* (liberty) . . . *dēmokratoumetha.*" See Parker, *The Songs of Aristophanes* (Oxford, 1997), pp. 544–545.

48. As Hubbard observes, "The most ridiculous extension of Praxagora's program of sexual equality is in the sphere of attempting to equalize sexual attractions, so as to guarantee that all citizens have equal opportunity for sexual activity, whether young or old, beautiful or ugly. It is an inevitable fact of nature that not all of us are equally endowed; the aging process is also an irreversible fact of life." Hubbard, "Utopianism and the Sophistic City," in Dobrov, ed., *The City as Comedy* (Chapel Hill, 1997), p. 29. Aristophanes both "knows" this and *celebrates* it by means of thoughtful, laughter-provoking ridicule that is always *self*-ridicule.

49. Watkins, *African-American Humor* (Chicago, 2002), p. 184.

50. Xenophon, *Anabasis IV–VII, Symposium, and Apology,* trans. Todd (Cambridge, Mass., 1961), p. 446.

51. Hölderlin, *Werke und Briefe* (Frankfurt am Main, 1969), vol. 1, p. 39.

52. Hornblower and Spawforth, eds., *The Oxford Classical Dictionary* (Oxford, 1989), p. 484.

53. The word has "vagina" at its root.

54. Strauss, *Socrates and Aristophanes* (New York, 1966), p. 134.

55. Heidegger, *Sein und Zeit* (Tübingen, 1927), p. 250. Translation mine.

56. Could the usually astute, sympathetic, and delightful companion Gilbert Murray have been overwhelmed by the vulgarity in *Assemblywomen*? Could his classical erudition, which led him to note prosodic affinities with the New Comedy, have misled him into missing its kinship with its predecessors? Finally, and more significantly, could he really have supposed that this ridiculous appeal, together with its ringing insults, was designed to win the favor of the multitude? Perhaps he could. Murray writes, "One can imagine him working up the joke about Blepyrus' nocturnal troubles, of the long one with the Three Hags, and saying to himself 'Surely they cannot say it is too high-brow now!'" See Murray, *Aristophanes* (New York, 1964), p. 186.

57. Aristophanes, *Frogs, Assemblywomen, Wealth,* ed. and trans. Henderson (Cambridge, Mass., 2002), p. 411.

58. Though he admires other Aristophanic neologisms, Norwood expresses contempt for this "famous longest word," which he calls "a mechanical monstrosity." He claims that "Any Greek on any street corner could have manufactured this: it is entirely different from his earlier witty fabrications such as the delightful *arkhaiomelisidōnophrunixērata.*" But no other Greek, irrespective of location and status, created anything like it! Norwood, however, is a most worthy reader. His comment is not so much a disinterested appraisal as a personal lament: "The mighty irresponsible genius has dwindled into a mere accomplished writer." See Norwood, *Greek Comedy* (London, 1931), p. 266.

59. Hubbard's view on this point is curious, to say the least: "Just as in the *Birds,* we perceive [*Assemblywomen*'s] utopian vision of a return to Nature turning into a dystopian totalitarianism of the worst sort, in which words come to mean their opposite, as manipulated by the sophistic will to power." This conclusion springs, I suppose, from Praxagora's appeal to the family as the traditional and natural basis of society. But it is a gross non sequitur to infer from this that Praxagora's quite obviously non-natural pro-

posal is a "utopian vision of a return to Nature." Further, I can find no evidence of totalitarianism, nor of words meaning their opposites, and Hubbard does not offer any examples. See Hubbard, "Utopianism and the Sophistic City," in Dobrov, ed., *The City as Comedy* (Chapel Hill, 1997), p. 251.

60. Schiller, *Naive and Sentimental Poetry and On the Sublime* (New York, 1966), p. 122.

61. Strauss, *Socrates and Aristophanes* (New York, 1966), p. 279.

62. Hegel, *Sämtliche Werke* (Stuttgart, 1964), vol. 14, p. 561. Translation mine.

4. *LYSISTRATA: ERŌS* AND TRANSCENDENCE

1. Solomos gives a good contemporary slant: "Perhaps the most significant thing about her, all contrasts included, is that she is the first feminist in history. She strives not only to bestow upon women the happiness of peace but to awaken them from their apathy toward the problems of life by giving them the right to have an opinion." Solomos, *The Living Aristophanes* (Ann Arbor, 1974), p. 189. Some scholars (see n. 6, below, on Xavier Riu) seek to dispute this, arguing that Lysistrata reinstates male dominance. While I seek an avenue apart from both of these, the latter interpretation seems both labored and contradicted by textual evidence.

2. Two standard editions supply the basic historical and linguistic material, and other references: *Lysistrata,* trans. Henderson (Oxford, 2002); and *Lysistrata,* trans. Sommerstein (Warminster, 1990).

3. Francis Cornford, among others, assumes that Lysistrata, like Praxagora, has a husband: "In the two Women plays, the heroines, Praxagora and Lysistrata, are married women supposedly in the prime of life." Cornford, *The Origin of Attic Comedy* (Gloucester, 1968), p. 150. But "he" is surely not named.

4. See chap. 3, above.

5. See Freydberg, *The Play of the Platonic Dialogues* (New York, 1997), esp. chap. 12: "Play and Immortality."

6. The following unfounded position, contradicted directly by the material in Aristophanes' text referred to above, appears in a distinguished classics volume and was written by a respected classicist: "Women embody that foreign, alien, external element . . . that comedy, under the patronage of Dionysus, has to introduce at the very heart of the city. The disfoundations of Dionysus, structurally opposed to the foundations of Apollo, are carried out by women. This is their role, and we have no reason to believe that in comedy it should be different, mainly because it is not different in daily life either: the exclusion from public affairs to which they are subjected is clear on that point." Riu, *Dionysism and Comedy* (London, 1999), p. 171.

I must admit that I have no sympathy for this entire line of argumentation, though the author pursues it consistently. From its *ad ignorantiam* fallacy to its crude treatment of the Apollo/Dionysus distinction to its presupposition that the sketchy knowledge we have of actual women's lives in ancient Greece leads to the real nature of Aristophanes' plays—Riu believes that the plays are aimed exclusively at men and at restoring the established order (ibid., p. 183)—there is little that I find persuasive. Like his mentor Gregory Nagy (brilliant classicists both), I find an absence of any appreciation of the genuine creativity belonging to the materials they study, but a great deal of another kind of "creativity" in their speculations.

7. Murray supposes, "Aristophanes has the thought that these very [women's] lusts might be made an instrument to save Athens." Murray, *Aristophanes* (New York, 1964),

p. 165. I would rather ascribe this "thought" to the realm of art, and to Aristophanes' Muse.

8. Aristophanes, *Lysistrata,* trans. Henderson (Oxford, 2002), pp. 75–76.

9. Spatz, *Aristophanes* (Boston, 1978), pp. 91–92.

10. See Hegel, *Reason in History* (New York, 1953), pp. 23–24.

11. All page numberings in my text are from the Knox translation of Hegel's *Aesthetics,* vols. 1–2 (Oxford, 1973, 1975). I have emended the translations where appropriate, always substituting more literal terms.

12. See Aristophanes, *Lysistrata,* trans. Henderson (Oxford, 2002), pp. 117–118.

13. Henderson has "riotous extravagance." Mine is the more literal.

14. Aristophanes, *Lysistrata,* trans. Sommerstein (Warminster, 1990), p. 176.

15. See chap. 3.

16. Only by taking it out of context can this be maintained.

17. See chap. 3.

18. So much Aristophanes scholarship, and other scholarship on ancient literature, takes place in terms of these two "categories." I do not find them useful in any general or structural way, as they impose something onto the texts from outside them. Too often, they are obstacles to discovering both their wondrousness and their insight.

19. Aristophanes, *Lysistrata,* trans. Henderson (Oxford, 2002), p. 133.

20. See chap. 3.

21. In a convincing discussion of the wool image from another direction, Carroll Moulton approaches the "tangled" wool as emblematic of the disorder and confusion in cities, and analyzes Aristophanes' ingenious interweaving of domestic and political motifs in Lysistrata's speeches. See Moulton, *Aristophanic Poetry* (Göttingen, 1981), pp. 48–53.

22. At such moments as these, Lord finds "in Aristophanes too an unexpected gentleness and a quality akin to tears . . . The *lacrimae rerum* are never far from his thoughts, and the laugh of the jester often ends in a choking sob . . . In the *Lysistrata* an Athenian Magistrate is arguing that women should have nothing to say in the decisions of the state for war or peace: LYS: *nothing to do with it, wretch that you are!*" Lord, *Aristophanes* (New York, 1963), p. 72.

23. Aristophanes, *Lysistrata,* trans. Henderson (Oxford, 2002), pp. 150–160.

24. Aristophanes, *Lysistrata,* trans. Sommerstein (Warminster, 1990), pp. 187–193.

25. Ibid., pp. 190–191.

26. I do not see how Strauss can write, "The laughable character of the action of the play is limited to the sex strike. One wonders whether the change of regime [that would consist of a secret plot by Athenian men to work with Sparta] . . . is not the poet's serious proposal." Strauss, *Socrates and Aristophanes* (New York, 1966), pp. 212–213. This *agōn* on the Acropolis is at least equally laughable as the sex strike; and Strauss' "wondering" concerning Aristophanes' "serious" proposal seems to be nothing more than the merest speculation.

27. See Sallis, *Being and Logos* (Bloomington, 1996), p. 185.

28. Sallis, "Hades: Heraclitus, Fragment B 98," in Sallis and Maly, eds., *Heraclitean Fragments* (University, 1980), pp. 61–68.

29. Ibid., pp. 61–68.

30. Ibid., p. 66.

31. See *Republic* 357b4–8; *Philebus* 66c4–6.

32. Hornblower and Spawforth, eds., *The Oxford Classical Dictionary* (Oxford, 1996), p. 444.

33. Ibid., p. 1071.

34. This is Sommerstein's translation.

35. Here is one of many instances where Whitman's observation rings true: "the *Lysistrata,* despite its evident bawdry and the coarseness of numerous episodes, possesses a delicacy of charm very difficult to convey in translation, but pervasively felt in the Greek. Far from being a pornographic orgy, as it often supposed, the play is a celebration of the life-giving properties of love." Whitman, *Aristophanes and the Comic Hero* (Cambridge, Mass., 1984), p. 205.

36. The men are "apparently unable even to masturbate, fornicate with slave-girls or prostitutes, or find a man or boy on whom to exercise their lusts. If Cinesias is to have any sexual release, he must come to the acropolis and petition for his wife. The assumption of the plot is that no sexual fulfillment is possible outside the context of traditional family life." Henderson, *The Maculate Muse* (New Haven, 1975), pp. 94–95. This structures the play, and makes it *this* celebration of *erōs,* or a celebration of *erōs* understood properly within the Dionysian festival.

37. I saw it performed as an excerpt in Ancient Olympia, Greece, in August 2001, where I learned that many young actors use it as an audition piece.

38. The references to other avenues of sexual release are not meant seriously.

39. Aristophanes, *Birds, Lysistrata, Women at the Thesmophoria,* ed. and trans. Henderson (Cambridge, Mass., 2000), p. 403.

40. Murray, who reads the play in a historical manner similar to Norwood's, nevertheless grasps its internal artistic logic: "The play is, of necessity, indecent and more than indecent. The *phallus erectus* is treated as a kind of symbol, standing for all of the thwarted desires and expectations that would arise in men alienated from their womankind." Murray, *Aristophanes* (New York, 1964), p. 167. Of course the *phallus erectus* also guides the ancient Dionysian procession.

41. Aristophanes, *Lysistrata,* trans. Henderson (Oxford, 2002), p. 196.

42. Aristophanes, *Lysistrata,* trans. Sommerstein (Warminster, 1990), p. 212.

43. "Die Scherze, zu denen sie benutzt werden, hängen über meist recht heftige Obszönitäten mit den Begriff, den sie verkörpern, zusammen. Im Grunde genommen gilt für sie alle, was Wilamowitz von Diallage sagt: die Sehnsucht nach Freiden wird in Begierde nach den Reizen der Frauenzimmer verkehrt. Darin allein liegt schon eine Übertragung." Newiger, *Metapher und Allegorie* (Munich, 1957), p. 120.

44. Henderson opines that the Athenians got the better of the negotiations. Aristophanes, *Lysistrata,* trans. Henderson (Oxford, 2002), p. 204.

45. Ibid., p. 204.

46. Aristophanes, *Birds, Lysistrata, Women at the Thesmophoria,* ed. and trans. Henderson (Cambridge, Mass., 2000), p. 425: "exploiting the stereotype of Spartan predilection for anal intercourse with either sex."

47. Ibid., p. 425: "the Athenians will opt for the vagina, and so the settlement will be mutually satisfactory."

48. "The exodus of this feminist comedy, named after Lysistrata, in giving—positive—importance only to its male characters, is intended to show that the women's scheme has indeed restored the men, provided Athens and Sparta once more with men (cf. 528, 524). In such an atmosphere of male restoration it would hardly seem appropriate were a woman, Lysistrata, to concede permission to the Spartans and Athenians to lead off their womenfolk, particularly when for these precise ends she has provoked an autonomy on the par of the men . . . She does not say, I will reconsign you to the women, but rather: you, having sealed the pact of friendship, retake them and go." Russo, *Aristophanes* (London, 1994), p. 172. Russo's interpretation, which is driven by the re-prioriti-

zation of gender, misses the inspired and divine dimension of both the poem and of the Dionysian festival, in my opinion. Although he may be correct about the re-instantiation of traditional ritual, it is *Erōs* who prevails, and not the men.

49. David Konstan is one of the very few scholars who agrees. "Unlike the rest of the women, Lysistrata seems free from domestic constraints and has no difficulty organizing and participating in the plans for the sex strike . . . She also stands above the sexual obsessions of the others. Her age and marital status are indeterminate." Konstan, *Greek Comedy and Ideology* (New York, 1995), p. 59.

CONCLUSION

1. Plato, *Phaedo,* trans. Brann, Kalkavage, and Salem (Newburyport, Mass., 1998), p. 39.

2. In the epics and tragedies, mortal women show traits of courage, cunning, adherence to principle, viciousness, and so on. Goddesses such as Athena have wisdom, but no mortal woman that I know of has intellect as her most prominent trait.

3. Recalling the order in the *Philebus,* the second is beauty and proportion; the third is intellect (*nous*) and good sense (*phronesis*); and the fourth is comprised of the arts and sciences. The last consists of the harmless and pain-free pleasures associated with knowledge and, in certain cases, perception. As to the "complication," in my opinion the role of beauty in the Platonic dialogues has always been underplayed—but that is a matter for another occasion.

Bibliography

Aristophanes. *Clouds.* Ed. Kenneth Dover. Oxford: Clarendon Press, 1968.

———. *Wasps.* Ed. with intro. and comm. Douglas M. MacDowell. Oxford: Clarendon Press, 1971.

———. *Ecclesiazusae.* Ed. Robert G. Ussher. Oxford: Clarendon Press, 1973.

———. *Four Comedies by Aristophanes.* Trans. Douglass Parker. Ed. William Arrowsmith. Ann Arbor: University of Michigan Press, 1975.

———. *The Complete Plays of Aristophanes.* Ed. Moses Hadas. New York: Bantam, 1988.

———. *Lysistrata.* Trans. Alan H. Sommerstein. Warminster: Aris & Phillips, 1990.

———. *Ecclesiazusae.* Ed. and trans. Alan H. Sommerstein. Warminster: Aris & Phillips, 1998.

———. *Clouds, Wasps, Peace.* Ed. and trans. Jeffrey Henderson. Cambridge, Mass. and London: Harvard University Press, 1998.

——— *Birds, Lysistrata, Women at the Thesmophoria.* Ed. and trans. Jeffrey Henderson. Cambridge, Mass. and London: Harvard University Press, 2000.

——— *Frogs, Assemblywomen, Wealth.* Ed. and trans. Jeffrey Henderson. Cambridge, Mass. and London: Harvard University Press, 2002.

———. *Lysistrata.* Trans. Jeffrey Henderson. Oxford: Clarendon Press, 2002.

Aristotle. *Poetics.* In Richard McKeon, ed. *The Basic Works of Aristotle.* New York: Random House, 1968.

Ast, Friedrich. *Lexicon Platonicum; sive, Vocum Platonicarum index.* New York: B. Franklin, 1969.

Cornford, Francis Macdonald. *The Origin of Attic Comedy.* Gloucester: Peter Smith, 1968.

Cunliffe, Richard John. *A Lexicon of the Homeric Dialect.* Norman: University of Oklahoma Press, 1963.

Davidson, James. "Gnesippus paigniagraphos: the Comic poets and the Erotic Mime." In David Harvey and John Wilkins, eds. *The Rivals of Aristophanes.* London: Duckworth and the Classical Press of Wales, 2000.

de Ste. Croix, G. E. M. *The Origins of the Peloponnesian War.* Ithaca: Cornell University Press, 1972.

———. *The Class Struggle in the Ancient Greek World.* Ithaca: Cornell University Press, 1998.

Dobrov, Gregory. *The City as Comedy: Society and Representation in Athenian Drama.* Chapel Hill: University of North Carolina Press, 1997.

Dover, Kenneth J. *Aristophanic Comedy.* Berkeley: University of California Press, 1972.

Ehrenberg, Victor. *The People of Aristophanes: A Sociology of Old Attic Comedy.* New York: Schocken, 1962.

Erbse, Hartmut. "Über die ersten 'Wolken' des Aristophanes." In Paul Händel, ed. *Formen und Darstellungsweisen in der aristophanischen Komödie.* Heidelberg: C. Winter, 1963.

Figal, Günter. "The Idea and Mixture of the Good." Trans. Michael McGettigan and Cara Gendel Ryan. In John Sallis and John E. Russon, eds. *Retracing the Platonic Texts.* Evanston, Ill.: Northwestern University Press, 2000.

Freydberg, Bernard. *The Play of the Platonic Dialogues.* New York: Peter Lang, 1997.

Geier, Alfred. *Plato's Erotic Thought: The Tree of the Unknown.* Rochester: University of Rochester Press, 2002.

Gelzer, Thomas. "Der epirrhematische Agon bei Aristophanes: Untersuchungen zur Struktur der attischen Alten Komödie." *Zetemata; Monographien zur klassischen Altertumswissenschaft,* no. 23. Munich: Beck, 1960.

Grene, David, and Richmond Lattimore, eds. *Greek Tragedies,* vol. 1. Chicago: University of Chicago Press, 1960.

Händel, Paul, ed. *Formen und Darstellungsweisen in der aristophanischen Komödie.* Heidelberg: C. Winter, 1963.

Harvey, David, and John Wilkins, eds.. *The Rivals of Aristophanes: Studies in Ancient Athenian Old Comedy.* London: Duckworth and the Classical Press of Wales, 2000.

Hegel, G. W. F. *Phänomenologie des Geistes.* Hamburg: Felix Meiner, 1952.

———. *Reason in History.* Trans. Robert Hartman. New York: Bobbs-Merrill, 1953.

———. *Lectures on the History of Philosophy,* vol. 1. Trans. E. S. Haldane. New York: Humanities Press, 1963.

———. *Sämtliche Werke.* Hotho edn. Stuttgart: F. Frommann, 1964.

———. *Aesthetics: Lectures on Fine Arts,* vols. 1–2. Trans. T. M. Knox. Oxford: Clarendon Press, 1973, 1975.

Heidegger, Martin. *Sein und Zeit.* Tübingen: Max Niemeyer, 1927.

———. *An Introduction to Metaphysics.* Trans. Ralph Manheim. Garden City: Anchor, 1961.

Henderson, Jeffrey. *The Maculate Muse.* New Haven and London: Yale University Press, 1975.

Hesiod. *Theogony.* In *The Homeric Hymns and Homerica.* Trans. Hugh Evelyn-Whyte. Cambridge, Mass.: Harvard University Press, 1974.

Hölderlin, Friedrich. *Werke und Briefe,* vol. 1. Frankfurt am Main: Insel, 1969.

Hornblower, Simon, and Anthony Spawforth, eds. *The Oxford Classical Dictionary.* Oxford: Oxford University Press, 1996.

Hubbard, Thomas K. *The Mask of Comedy.* Ithaca and London: Cornell University Press, 1991.

———. "Utopianism and the Sophistic City." In Gregory Dobrov, ed. *The City as Comedy: Society and Representation in Athenian Drama.* Chapel Hill: University of North Carolina Press, 1997.

Hume, David. *An Inquiry Concerning the Principles of Morality.* Indianapolis: Library of Liberal Arts, 1957.

Kant, Immanuel. *Critique of Judgment.* Trans. J. H. Bernard. New York: Haffner, 1951.

Konstan, David. *Greek Comedy and Ideology.* New York: Oxford University Press, 1995.

Landfester, Manfred. *Handlungsverlauf und Komik in den frühen Komödien des Aristophanes.* Berlin: Walter de Gruyter, 1977.

Liddell, Henry, and Robert Scott. *A Greek-English Lexicon.* Oxford: Clarendon Press, 1989.

Lord, Louis E. *Aristophanes: His Plays and His Influence.* New York: Cooper Square, 1963.

Moulton, Carroll. *Aristophanic Poetry.* Göttingen: Vandenhoeck & Ruprecht, 1981.

Murray, Gilbert. *Aristophanes.* New York: Russell & Russell, 1964.

Neukam, P., ed. *Klassische Sprachen und Literaturen,* vol. 27: *Motiv und Motivation.* Munich: P. Neukam, 1993.

Newiger, Hans-Joachim. "Metapher und Allegorie: Studien zu Aristophanes." *Monographien zur klassischen Altertumswissenschaft*, no. 16. Munich: Beck, 1957.

———, ed. *Aristophanes und die alte Komödie.* Darmstadt: Wissenschaftliche Buchgesellschaft, 1975.

Nietzsche, Friedrich. *The Birth of Tragedy and The Case of Wagner.* Trans. Walter Kaufmann. New York: Vintage, 1967.

———. *Nietzsche Werke: kritische Gesamtausgabe,* vols. 5, 8. Ed. Giorgio Colli and Mazzino Montinari. Berlin and New York: Walter de Gruyter, 1967–.

———. *Jenseits von Gut und Böse und Zur Genealogie der Moral.* Munich, 1999.

Norwood, Gilbert. *Greek Comedy.* London: Methuen & Co., 1931.

O'Regan, Daphne. *Rhetoric, Comedy and the Violence of Language.* Oxford: Oxford University Press, 1992.

Parker, L. P. E. *The Songs of Aristophanes.* Oxford: Clarendon Press, 1997.

Plato. *Platonis Opera,* vols. 1–3. Ed. John Burnet. Oxford: Clarendon Press, 1967–1968.

———. *Protagoras.* Trans. Benjamin Jowett, extensively rev. Martin Ostwald. Ed. Gregory Vlastos. New York: Bobbs-Merrill, 1956.

———. *Republic.* Trans. Allan Bloom. New York: Basic, 1968.

———. *Plato's Sophist: The Professor of Wisdom.* Trans. Eva Brann, Peter Kalkavage, and Eric Salem. Newburyport, Mass.: Focus / R. Pullins, 1996.

———. *Complete Works.* Ed. John Cooper. Indianapolis: Hackett, 1997.

———. *Phaedo.* Trans. Eva Brann, Peter Kalkavage, and Eric Salem. Newburyport, Mass.: Focus / R. Pullins, 1998.

Riu, Xavier. *Dionysism and Comedy.* London: Rowman & Littlefield, 1999.

Rosen, Ralph M. "Cratinus' *Pytine* and the Construction of the Comic Self." In David Harvey and John Wilkins, eds. *The Rivals of Aristophanes.* London: Duckworth and the Classical Press of Wales, 2000.

Russo, Carlo Fernando. *Aristophanes: An Author for the Stage.* Trans. Kevin Wren. London: Routledge, 1994.

Sallis, John. *Being and Logos: Reading the Platonic Dialogues.* Bloomington and Indianapolis: Indiana University Press, 1996.

———. *Platonic Legacies.* Albany: State University of New York Press, 2004.

Sallis, John, and Kenneth Maly, eds. *Heraclitean Fragments: A Companion Volume to the Heidegger/Fink Seminar on Heraclitus.* University: University of Alabama Press, 1980.

Sallis, John, and John E. Russon. *Retracing the Platonic Text.* Evanston, Ill.: Northwestern University Press, 2000.

Schiller, Friedrich. *Gedanken über den Gebrauch des Gemeinen und Niedrigen in der Kunst.* In *Sämtliche Werke,* vol. 5. Munich: Carl Hanser, 1960.

———. *Naive and Sentimental Poetry and On the Sublime.* Trans. Julius A. Elias. New York: Frederick Ungar, 1966.

Schmidt, Dennis J. *On Germans and Other Greeks: Tragedy and Ethical Life.* Bloomington and Indianapolis: Indiana University Press, 2001.

Slater, Niall W. *Spectator Politics: Metatheater and Performance in Aristophanes.* Philadelphia: University of Pennsylvania Press, 2002.

Solomos, Alexēs. *The Living Aristophanes.* Trans. Alexēs Solomos and Marvin Felheim. Ann Arbor: University of Michigan Press, 1974.

Sophocles. *Antigone, The Women of Trachis, Philoctetes, Oedipus at Colonus.* Trans. Hugh Lloyd-Jones. Cambridge, Mass.: Harvard University Press, 1994.

Spatz, Lois. *Aristophanes.* Boston: Twayne, 1978.

Strauss, Leo. *Socrates and Aristophanes.* New York: Basic, 1966.

Van Steen, Gonda A. H. *Venom in Verse: Aristophanes in Modern Greece.* Princeton: Princeton University Press, 2000.

Vlastos, Gregory. *Socrates: Ironist and Philosopher.* Ithaca: Cornell University Press, 1991.

Watkins, Mel, ed. *African-American Humor: The Best Black Comedy from Slavery to Today.* Chicago: Lawrence Hill, 2002.

Weil, Simone. *The Iliad or The Poem of Force.* Trans. Mary McCarthy. Wallingford, Penn.: Pendle Hill, 1976.

Whitman, Cedric. *Aristophanes and the Comic Hero.* Cambridge, Mass.: Harvard University Press, 1984.

Wilamowitz-Moellendorff, U. v., and Bruno Snell. *Platon: sein Leben und seine Werke.* Berlin: Weidmann, 1948.

Xenophon. *Anabasis IV–VII, Symposium, and Apology.* Trans. O. J. Todd. Cambridge, Mass.: Harvard University Press, 1961.

Index

Bernard Freydberg is Research Professor of Philosophy at Koç University, Istanbul. He previously held the position of Professor of Philosophy at Slippery Rock University. He is the author of *Imagination in Kant's* Critique of Practical Reason (Indiana University Press, 2005).